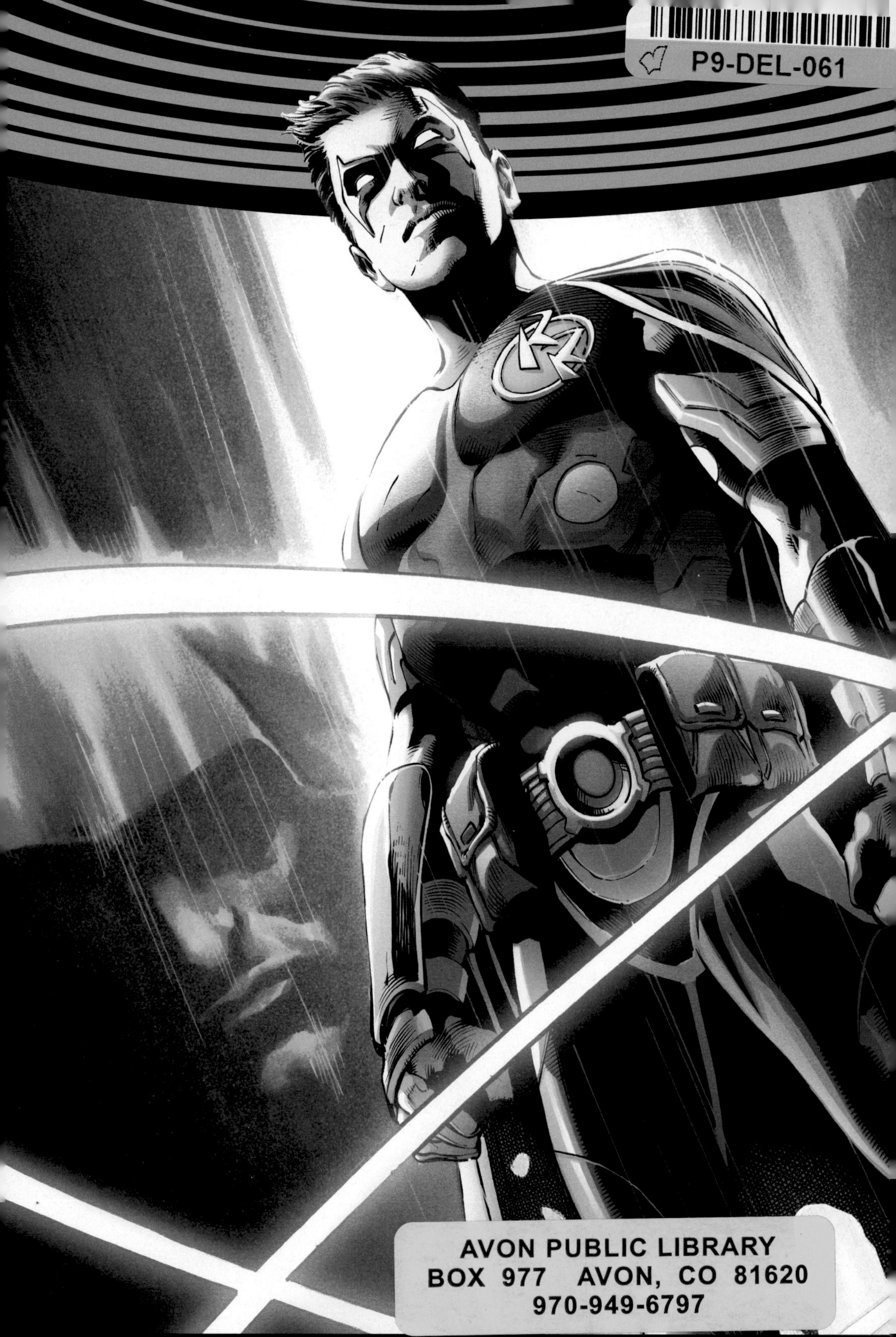

BATMAN: DETECTIVE COMICS

VOL. 5 A LONELY PLACE OF LIVING

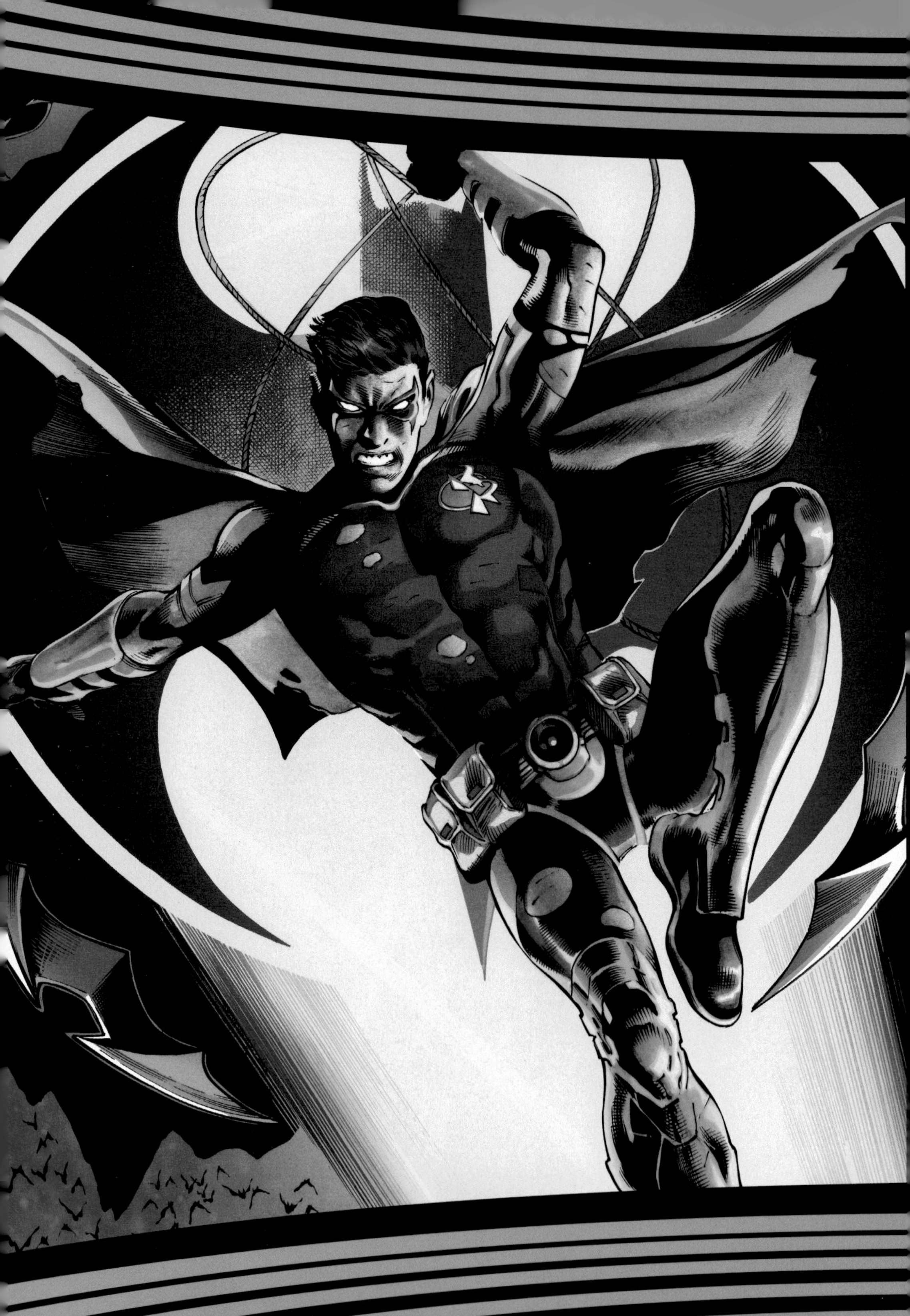

BATMAN: DETECTIVE COMICS
VOL.5 A LONELY PLACE OF LIVING

JAMES TYNION IV
CHRISTOPHER SEBELA
writers

EDDY BARROWS * **ALVARO MARTINEZ** * **CARMEN CARNERO**
pencillers

EBER FERREIRA * **RAUL FERNANDEZ** * **CARMEN CARNERO**
inkers

ADRIANO LUCAS * **TOMEU MOREY** * **ULISES ARREOLA**
KELLY FITZPATRICK * **JEAN-FRANCOIS BEAULIEU**
colorists

SAL CIPRIANO
letterer

EDDY BARROWS, EBER FERREIRA and **ADRIANO LUCAS**
collection cover artists

BATMAN created by **BOB KANE** with **BILL FINGER**
SUPERMAN created by **JERRY SIEGEL** and **JOE SHUSTER**
By special arrangement with the Jerry Siegel family
ANARKY created by **ALAN GRANT** and **NORM BREYFOGLE**

CHRIS CONROY Editor - Original Series * **ANDREW MARINO** Assistant Editor - Original Series
JEB WOODARD Group Editor - Collected Editions * **ROBIN WILDMAN** Editor - Collected Edition
STEVE COOK Design Director - Books * **MONIQUE NARBONETA** Publication Design

BOB HARRAS Senior VP - Editor-in-Chief, DC Comics
PAT McCALLUM Executive Editor, DC Comics

DIANE NELSON President * **DAN DiDIO** Publisher * **JIM LEE** Publisher * **GEOFF JOHNS** President & Chief Creative Officer
AMIT DESAI Executive VP - Business & Marketing Strategy, Direct to Consumer & Global Franchise Management
SAM ADES Senior VP & General Manager, Digital Services * **BOBBIE CHASE** VP & Executive Editor, Young Reader & Talent Development
MARK CHIARELLO Senior VP - Art, Design & Collected Editions * **JOHN CUNNINGHAM** Senior VP - Sales & Trade Marketing
ANNE DePIES Senior VP - Business Strategy, Finance & Administration * **DON FALLETTI** VP - Manufacturing Operations
LAWRENCE GANEM VP - Editorial Administration & Talent Relations * **ALISON GILL** Senior VP - Manufacturing & Operations
HANK KANALZ Senior VP - Editorial Strategy & Administration * **JAY KOGAN** VP - Legal Affairs * **JACK MAHAN** VP - Business Affairs
NICK J. NAPOLITANO VP - Manufacturing Administration * **EDDIE SCANNELL** VP - Consumer Marketing
COURTNEY SIMMONS Senior VP - Publicity & Communications * **JIM (SKI) SOKOLOWSKI** VP - Comic Book Specialty Sales & Trade Marketing
NANCY SPEARS VP - Mass, Book, Digital Sales & Trade Marketing * **MICHELE R. WELLS** VP - Content Strategy

BATMAN: DETECTIVE COMICS VOL. 5 – A LONELY PLACE OF LIVING

Published by DC Comics. Compilation and all new material Copyright © 2018 DC Comics. All Rights Reserved.
Originally published in single magazine form in DETECTIVE COMICS 963-968. Copyright © 2017 DC Comics.
All Rights Reserved. All characters, their distinctive likenesses and related elements featured in this publication are trademarks of DC Comics.
The stories, characters and incidents featured in this publication are entirely fictional.
DC Comics does not read or accept unsolicited ideas, stories or artwork.

DC Comics, 2900 West Alameda Ave., Burbank, CA 91505
Printed by LSC Communications, Kendallville, IN, USA. 3/2/18. First Printing.
ISBN: 978-1-4012-7822-9

Library of Congress Cataloging-in-Publication Data is available.

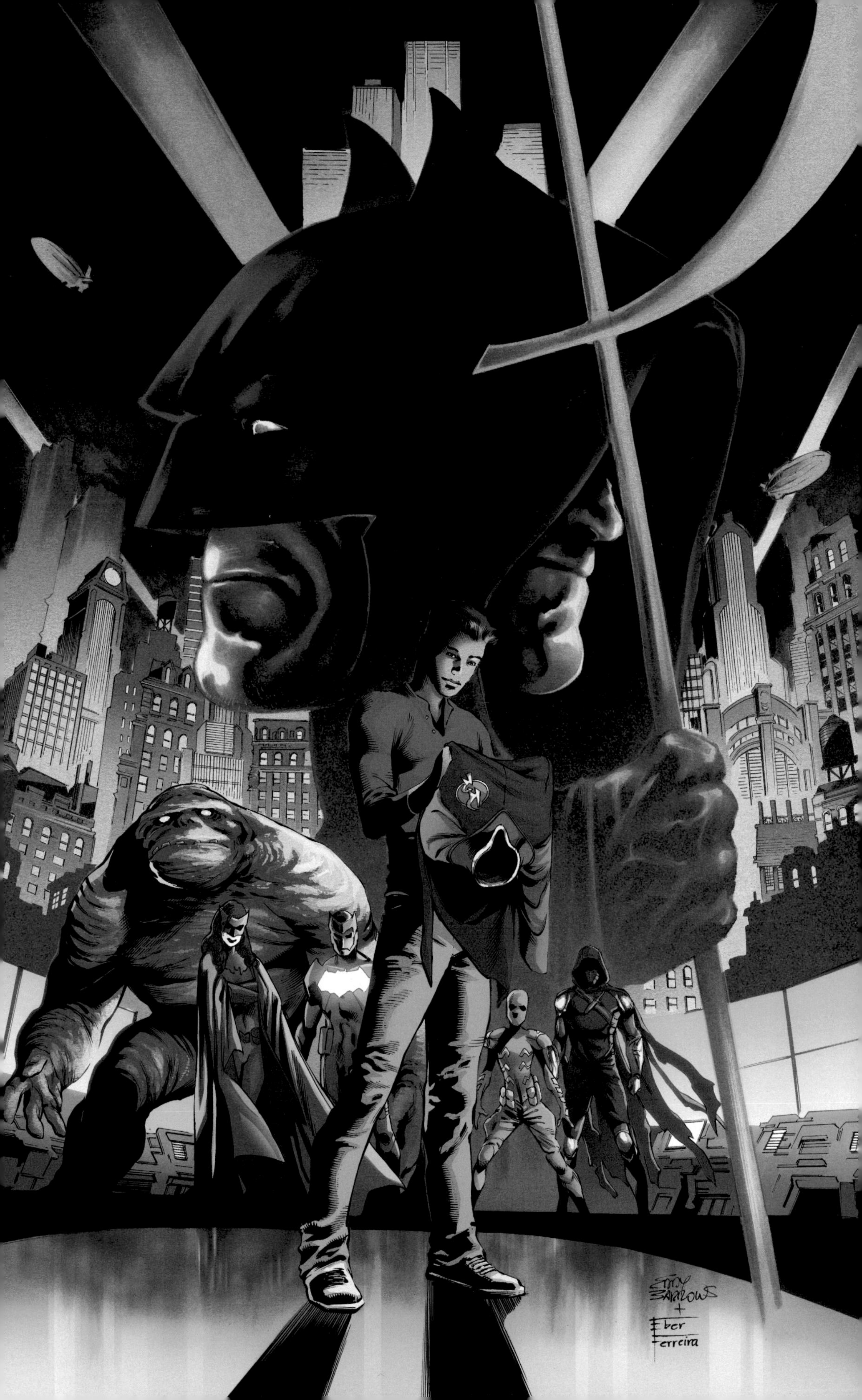
STEVE BARROWS
+
Eber
Ferreira

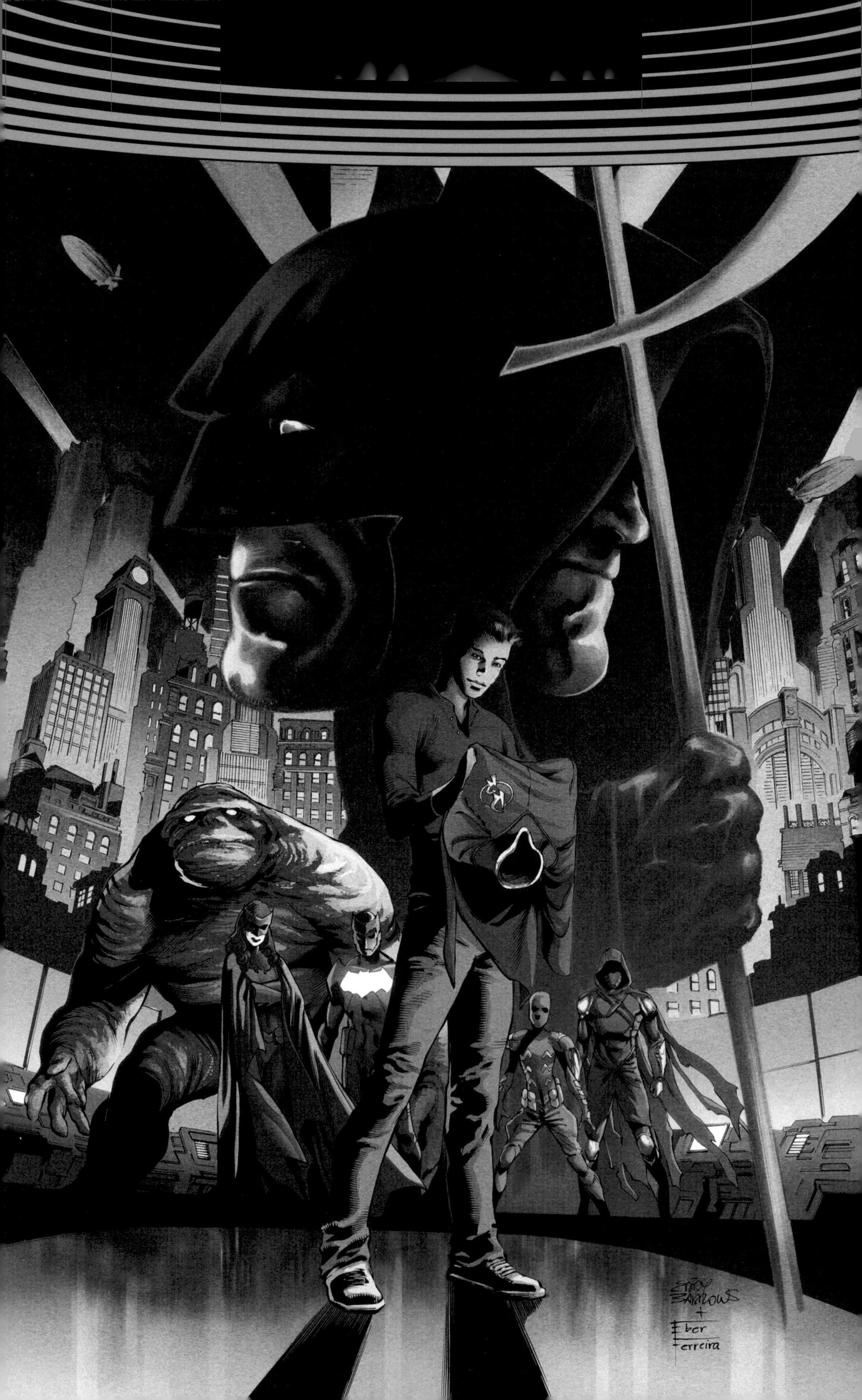
BARROWS
+
Eber
Ferreira

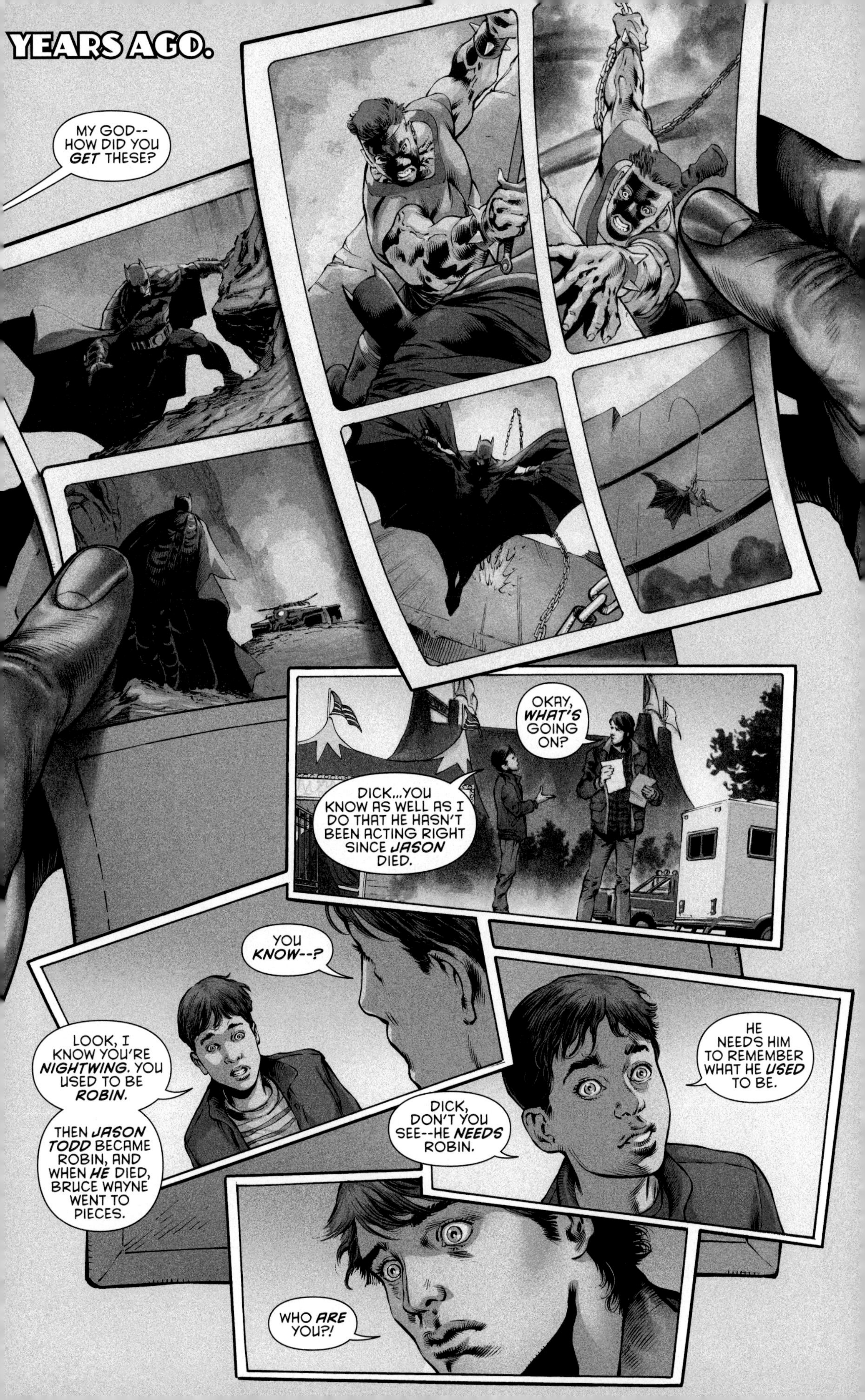
YEARS AGO.
MY GOD-- HOW DID YOU GET THESE?
OKAY, WHAT'S GOING ON?
DICK...YOU KNOW AS WELL AS I DO THAT HE HASN'T BEEN ACTING RIGHT SINCE JASON DIED.
YOU KNOW--?
LOOK, I KNOW YOU'RE NIGHTWING. YOU USED TO BE ROBIN.
THEN JASON TODD BECAME ROBIN, AND WHEN HE DIED, BRUCE WAYNE WENT TO PIECES.
DICK, DON'T YOU SEE--HE NEEDS ROBIN.
HE NEEDS HIM TO REMEMBER WHAT HE USED TO BE.
WHO ARE YOU?!

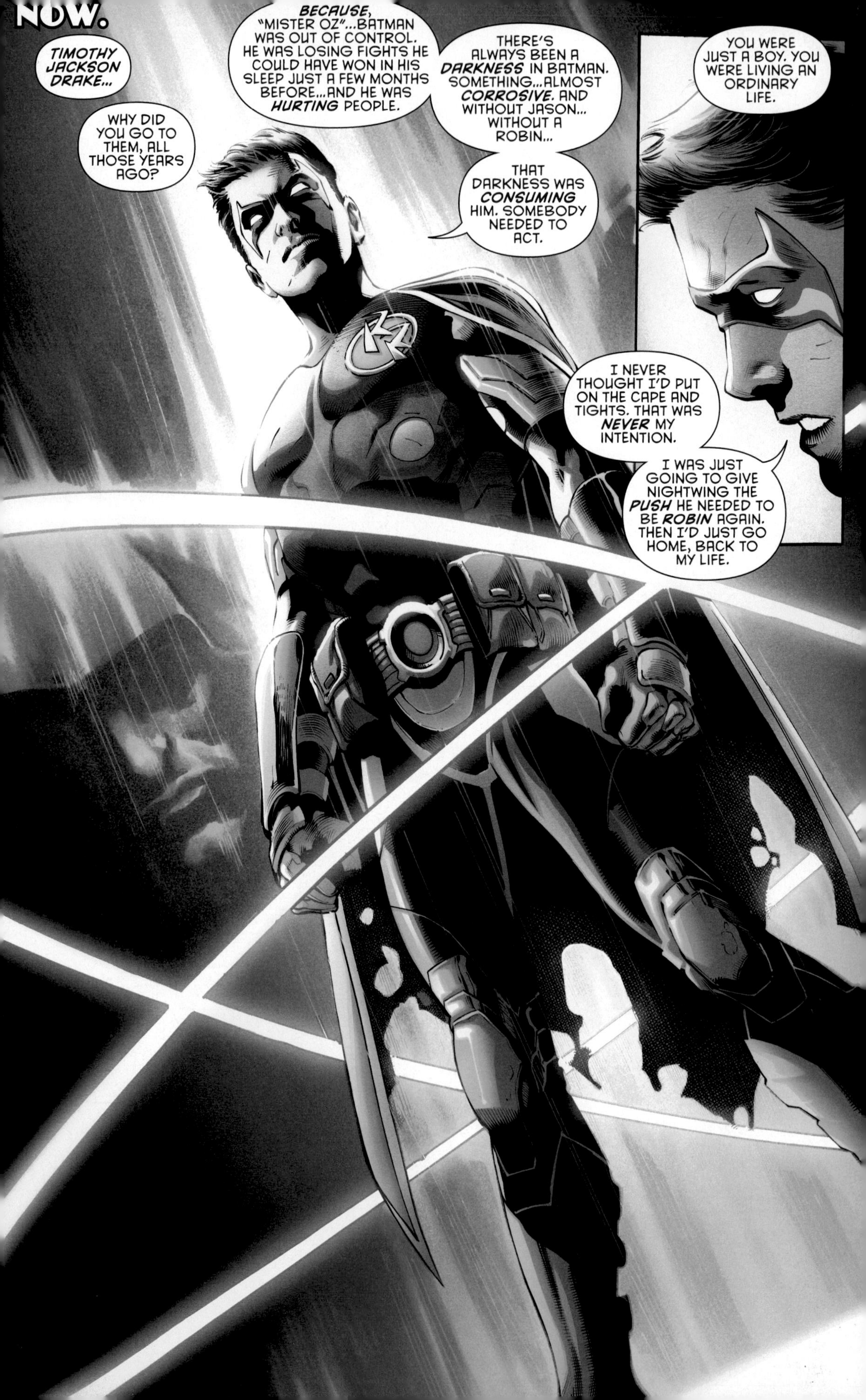
NOW.
TIMOTHY JACKSON DRAKE...
WHY DID YOU GO TO THEM, ALL THOSE YEARS AGO?
BECAUSE, "MISTER OZ"...BATMAN WAS OUT OF CONTROL. HE WAS LOSING FIGHTS HE COULD HAVE WON IN HIS SLEEP JUST A FEW MONTHS BEFORE...AND HE WAS HURTING PEOPLE.
THERE'S ALWAYS BEEN A DARKNESS IN BATMAN. SOMETHING...ALMOST CORROSIVE. AND WITHOUT JASON... WITHOUT A ROBIN...
THAT DARKNESS WAS CONSUMING HIM. SOMEBODY NEEDED TO ACT.
YOU WERE JUST A BOY. YOU WERE LIVING AN ORDINARY LIFE.
I NEVER THOUGHT I'D PUT ON THE CAPE AND TIGHTS. THAT WAS NEVER MY INTENTION.
I WAS JUST GOING TO GIVE NIGHTWING THE PUSH HE NEEDED TO BE ROBIN AGAIN. THEN I'D JUST GO HOME, BACK TO MY LIFE.

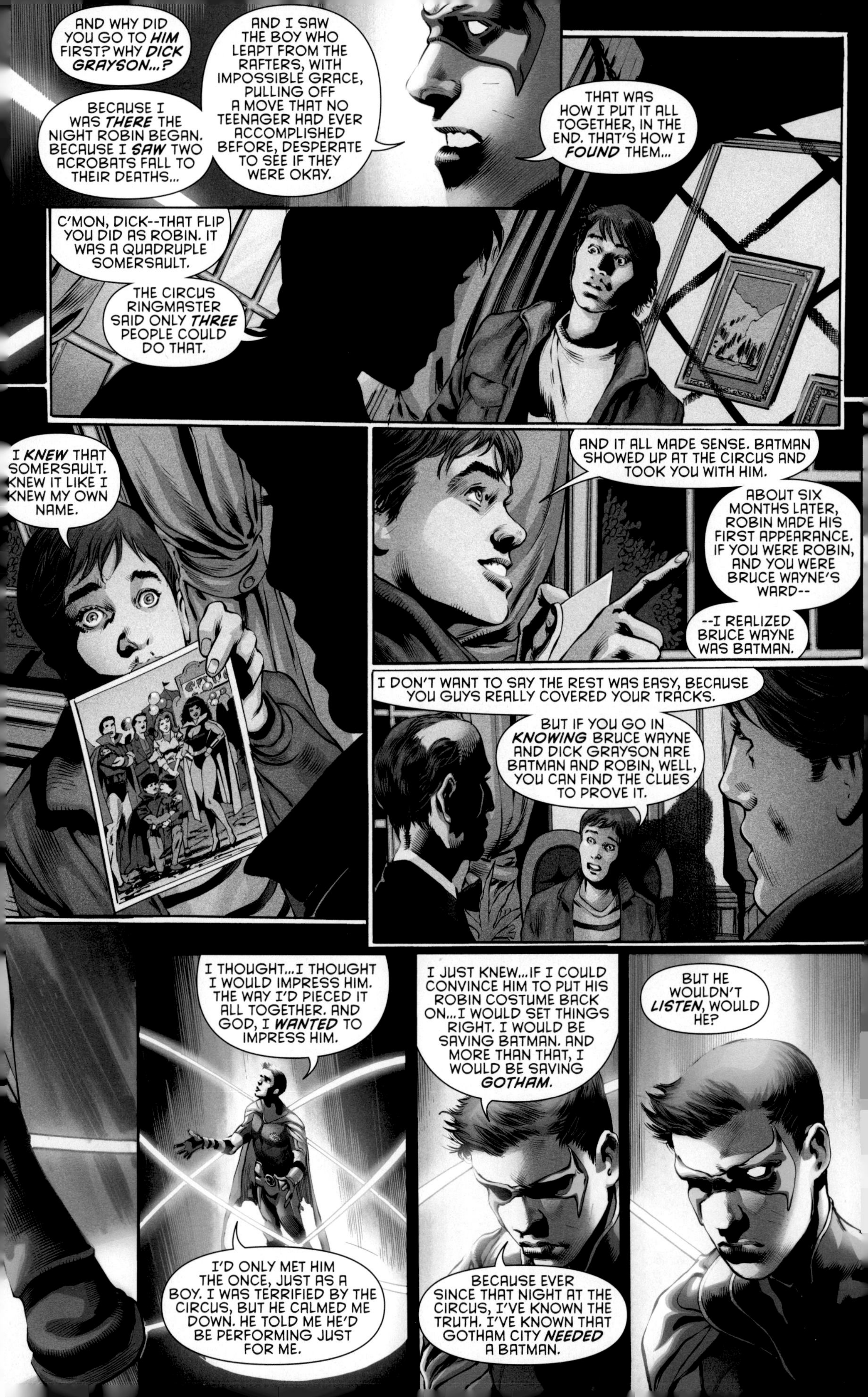
AND WHY DID YOU GO TO HIM FIRST? WHY DICK GRAYSON...?
BECAUSE I WAS THERE THE NIGHT ROBIN BEGAN. BECAUSE I SAW TWO ACROBATS FALL TO THEIR DEATHS...
AND I SAW THE BOY WHO LEAPT FROM THE RAFTERS, WITH IMPOSSIBLE GRACE, PULLING OFF A MOVE THAT NO TEENAGER HAD EVER ACCOMPLISHED BEFORE, DESPERATE TO SEE IF THEY WERE OKAY.
THAT WAS HOW I PUT IT ALL TOGETHER, IN THE END. THAT'S HOW I FOUND THEM...
C'MON, DICK--THAT FLIP YOU DID AS ROBIN. IT WAS A QUADRUPLE SOMERSAULT.
THE CIRCUS RINGMASTER SAID ONLY THREE PEOPLE COULD DO THAT.
I KNEW THAT SOMERSAULT. KNEW IT LIKE I KNEW MY OWN NAME.
AND IT ALL MADE SENSE. BATMAN SHOWED UP AT THE CIRCUS AND TOOK YOU WITH HIM.
ABOUT SIX MONTHS LATER, ROBIN MADE HIS FIRST APPEARANCE. IF YOU WERE ROBIN, AND YOU WERE BRUCE WAYNE'S WARD--
--I REALIZED BRUCE WAYNE WAS BATMAN.
I DON'T WANT TO SAY THE REST WAS EASY, BECAUSE YOU GUYS REALLY COVERED YOUR TRACKS.
BUT IF YOU GO IN KNOWING BRUCE WAYNE AND DICK GRAYSON ARE BATMAN AND ROBIN, WELL, YOU CAN FIND THE CLUES TO PROVE IT.
I THOUGHT...I THOUGHT I WOULD IMPRESS HIM. THE WAY I'D PIECED IT ALL TOGETHER. AND GOD, I WANTED TO IMPRESS HIM.
I'D ONLY MET HIM THE ONCE, JUST AS A BOY. I WAS TERRIFIED BY THE CIRCUS, BUT HE CALMED ME DOWN. HE TOLD ME HE'D BE PERFORMING JUST FOR ME.
I JUST KNEW...IF I COULD CONVINCE HIM TO PUT HIS ROBIN COSTUME BACK ON...I WOULD SET THINGS RIGHT. I WOULD BE SAVING BATMAN. AND MORE THAN THAT, I WOULD BE SAVING GOTHAM.
BECAUSE EVER SINCE THAT NIGHT AT THE CIRCUS, I'VE KNOWN THE TRUTH. I'VE KNOWN THAT GOTHAM CITY NEEDED A BATMAN.
BUT HE WOULDN'T LISTEN, WOULD HE?

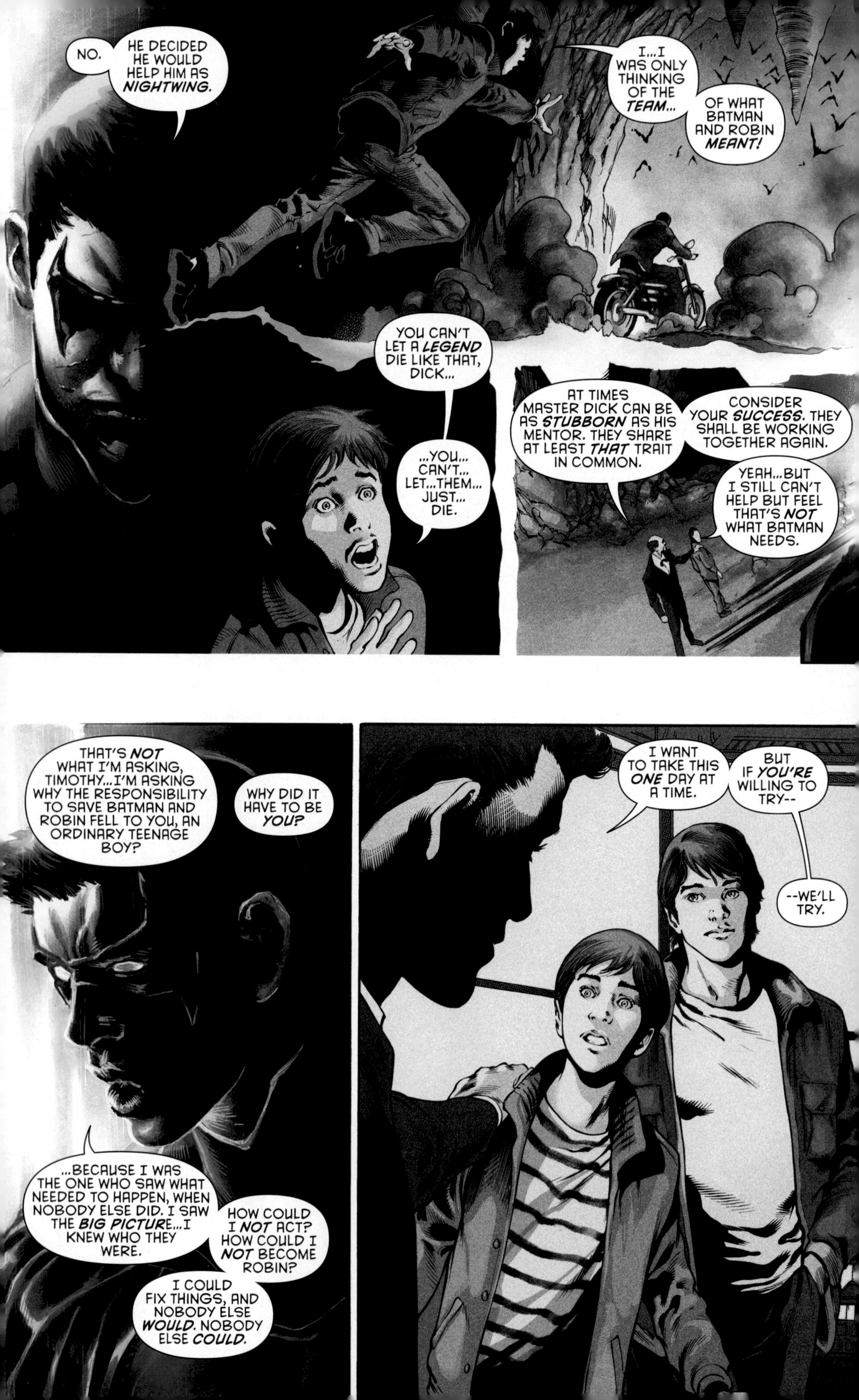
NO.
HE DECIDED HE WOULD HELP HIM AS NIGHTWING.
I...I WAS ONLY THINKING OF THE TEAM...
OF WHAT BATMAN AND ROBIN MEANT!
YOU CAN'T LET A LEGEND DIE LIKE THAT, DICK...
...YOU... CAN'T... LET...THEM... JUST... DIE.
AT TIMES MASTER DICK CAN BE AS STUBBORN AS HIS MENTOR. THEY SHARE AT LEAST THAT TRAIT IN COMMON.
CONSIDER YOUR SUCCESS. THEY SHALL BE WORKING TOGETHER AGAIN.
YEAH...BUT I STILL CAN'T HELP BUT FEEL THAT'S NOT WHAT BATMAN NEEDS.
THAT'S NOT WHAT I'M ASKING, TIMOTHY...I'M ASKING WHY THE RESPONSIBILITY TO SAVE BATMAN AND ROBIN FELL TO YOU, AN ORDINARY TEENAGE BOY?
WHY DID IT HAVE TO BE YOU?
...BECAUSE I WAS THE ONE WHO SAW WHAT NEEDED TO HAPPEN, WHEN NOBODY ELSE DID. I SAW THE BIG PICTURE...I KNEW WHO THEY WERE.
HOW COULD I NOT ACT? HOW COULD I NOT BECOME ROBIN?
I COULD FIX THINGS, AND NOBODY ELSE WOULD. NOBODY ELSE COULD.
I WANT TO TAKE THIS ONE DAY AT A TIME.
BUT IF YOU'RE WILLING TO TRY--
--WE'LL TRY.

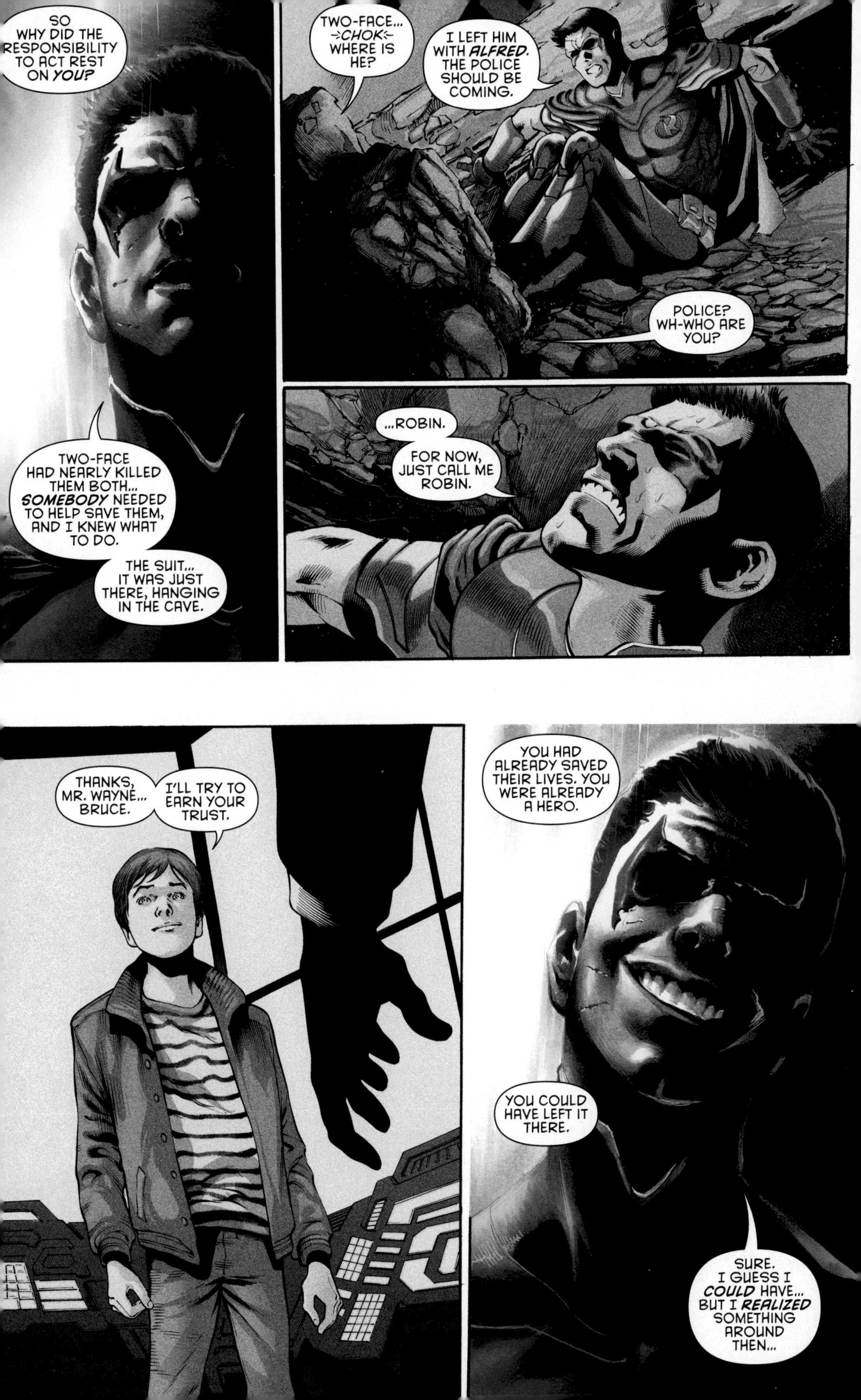
SO WHY DID THE RESPONSIBILITY TO ACT REST ON *YOU*?
TWO-FACE... ⇾*CHOK*⇽ WHERE IS HE?
I LEFT HIM WITH ***ALFRED***. THE POLICE SHOULD BE COMING.
POLICE? WH-WHO ARE YOU?
TWO-FACE HAD NEARLY KILLED THEM BOTH... ***SOMEBODY*** NEEDED TO HELP SAVE THEM, AND I KNEW WHAT TO DO.
THE SUIT... IT WAS JUST THERE, HANGING IN THE CAVE.
...ROBIN.
FOR NOW, JUST CALL ME ROBIN.
THANKS, MR. WAYNE... BRUCE.
I'LL TRY TO EARN YOUR TRUST.
YOU HAD ALREADY SAVED THEIR LIVES. YOU WERE ALREADY A HERO.
YOU COULD HAVE LEFT IT THERE.
SURE. I GUESS I ***COULD*** HAVE... BUT I ***REALIZED*** SOMETHING AROUND THEN...

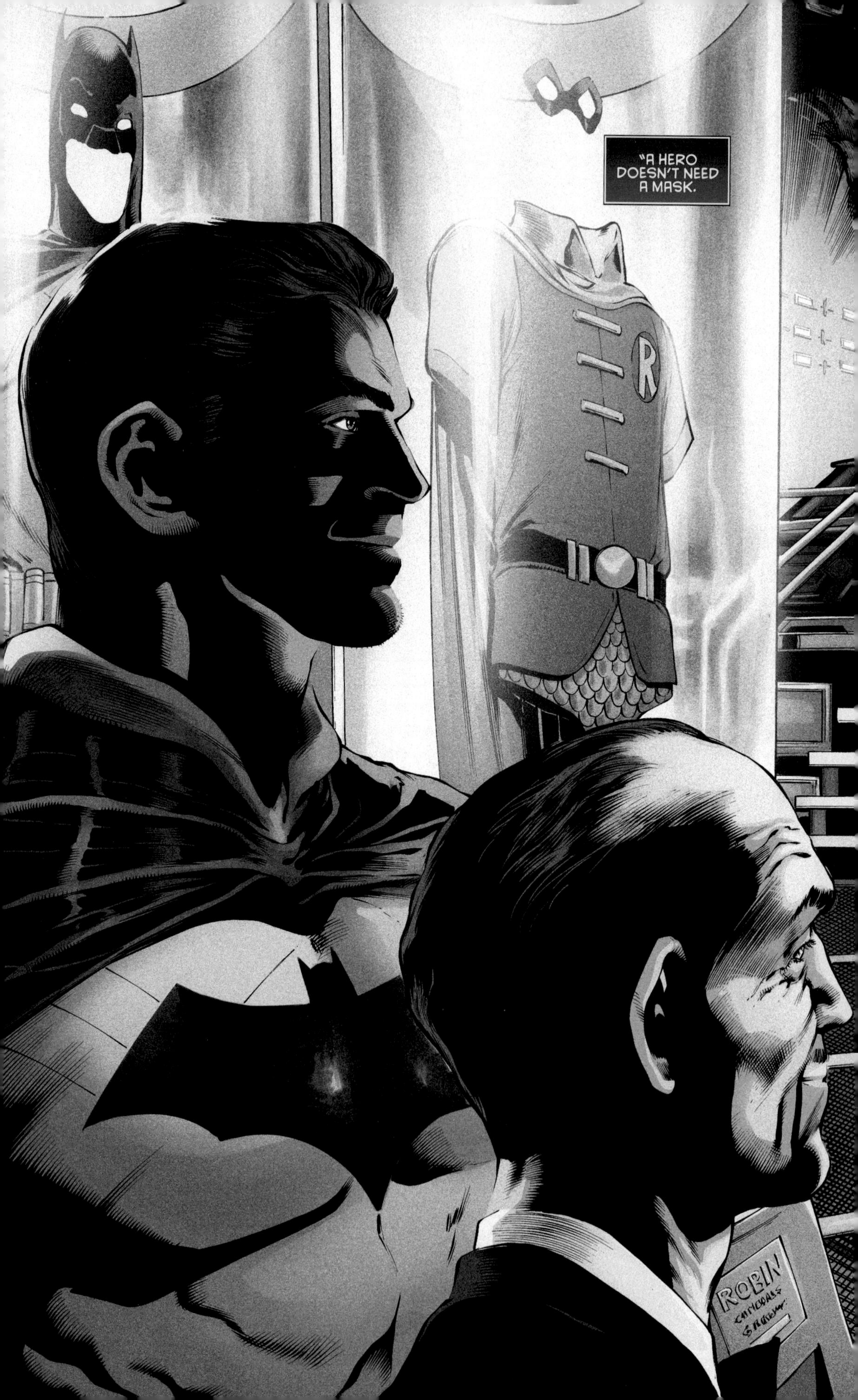
"A HERO DOESN'T NEED A MASK.
ROBIN

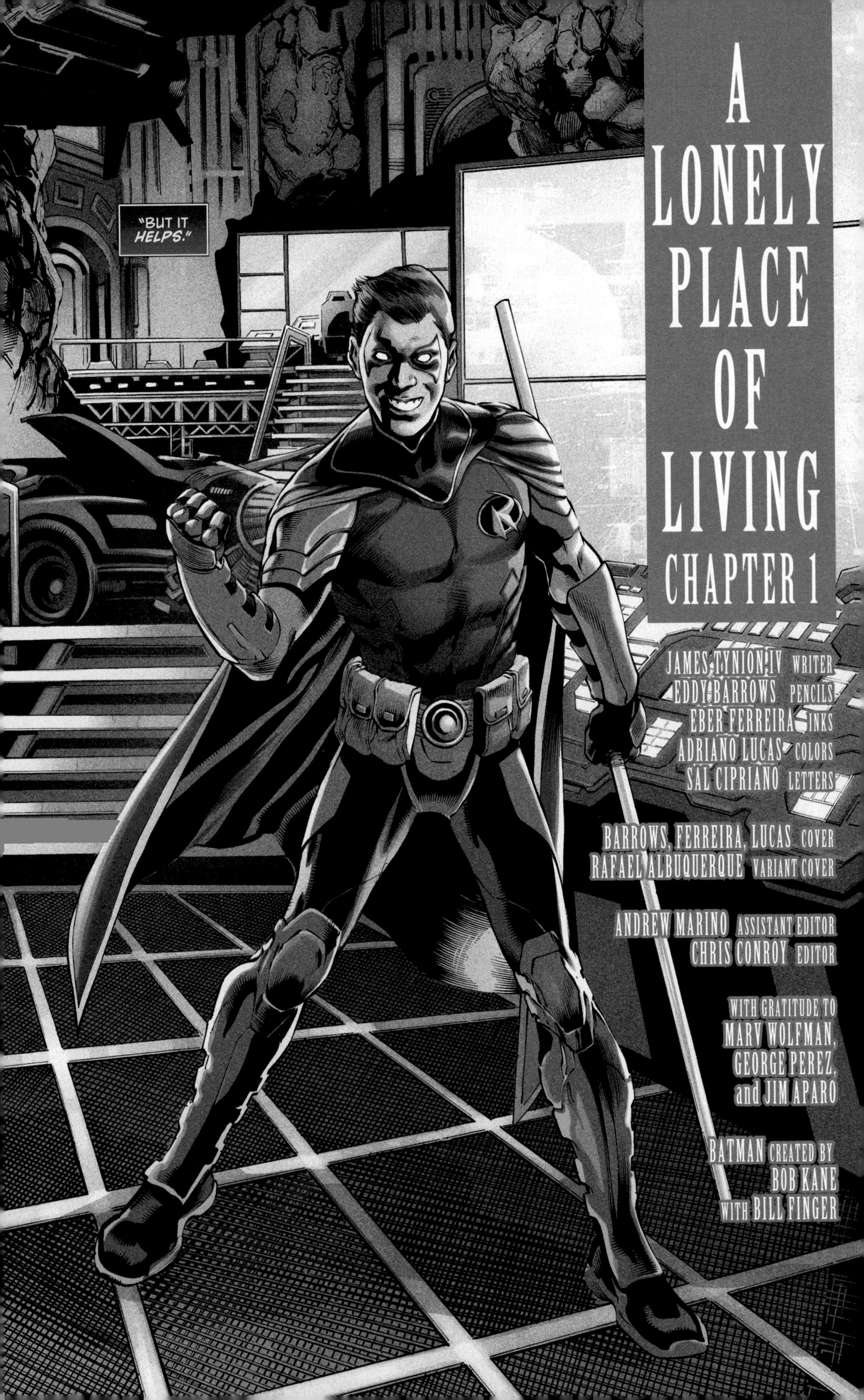

"BUT IT HELPS."
A LONELY PLACE OF LIVING
CHAPTER 1
JAMES TYNION IV WRITER
EDDY BARROWS PENCILS
EBER FERREIRA INKS
ADRIANO LUCAS COLORS
SAL CIPRIANO LETTERS
BARROWS, FERREIRA, LUCAS COVER
RAFAEL ALBUQUERQUE VARIANT COVER
ANDREW MARINO ASSISTANT EDITOR
CHRIS CONROY EDITOR
WITH GRATITUDE TO MARV WOLFMAN, GEORGE PEREZ, and JIM APARO
BATMAN CREATED BY BOB KANE WITH BILL FINGER

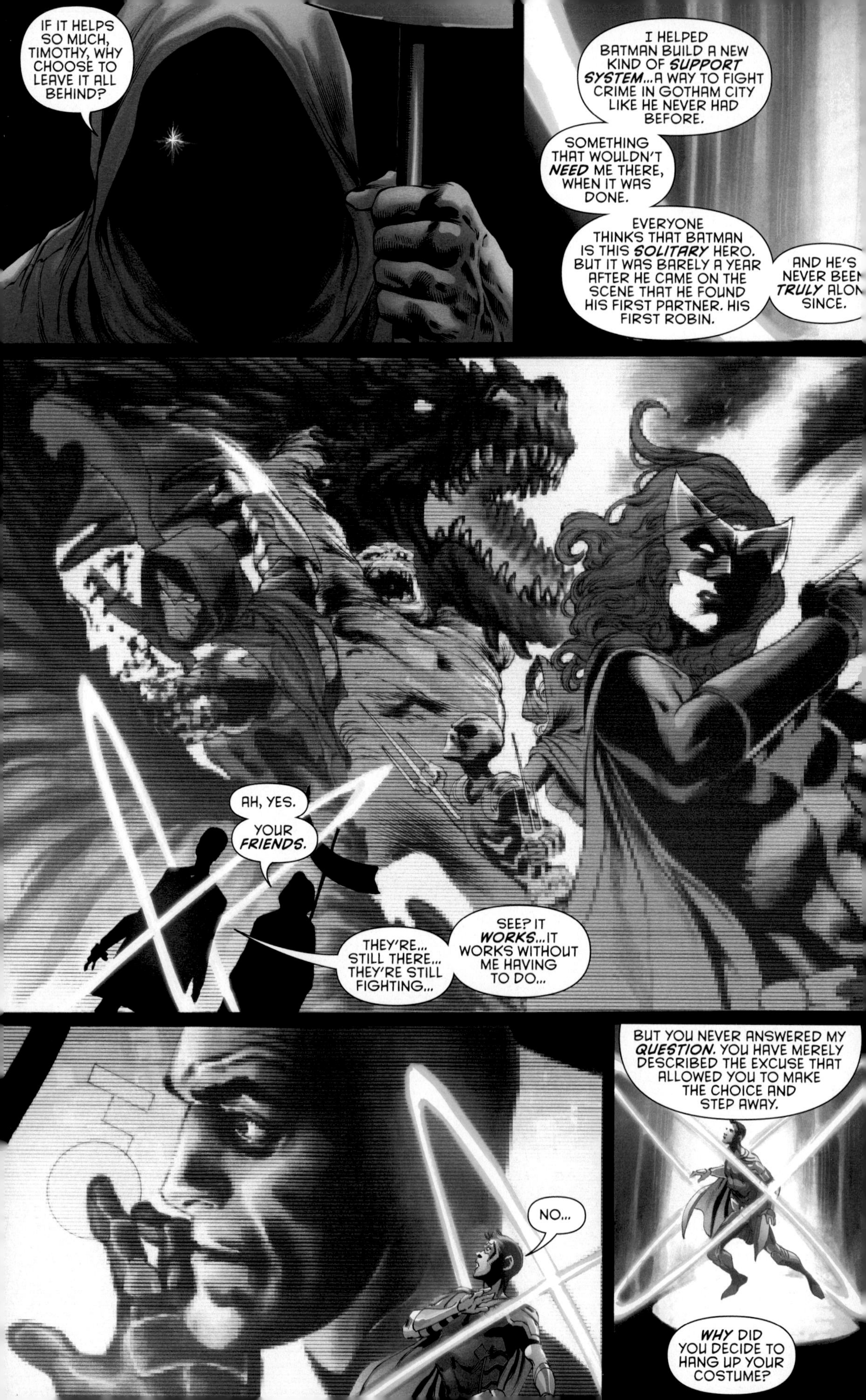
IF IT HELPS SO MUCH, TIMOTHY, WHY CHOOSE TO LEAVE IT ALL BEHIND?
I HELPED BATMAN BUILD A NEW KIND OF SUPPORT SYSTEM...A WAY TO FIGHT CRIME IN GOTHAM CITY LIKE HE NEVER HAD BEFORE.
SOMETHING THAT WOULDN'T NEED ME THERE, WHEN IT WAS DONE.
EVERYONE THINKS THAT BATMAN IS THIS SOLITARY HERO. BUT IT WAS BARELY A YEAR AFTER HE CAME ON THE SCENE THAT HE FOUND HIS FIRST PARTNER. HIS FIRST ROBIN.
AND HE'S NEVER BEEN TRULY ALON SINCE.
AH, YES.
YOUR FRIENDS.
THEY'RE... STILL THERE... THEY'RE STILL FIGHTING...
SEE? IT WORKS...IT WORKS WITHOUT ME HAVING TO DO...
NO...
BUT YOU NEVER ANSWERED MY QUESTION. YOU HAVE MERELY DESCRIBED THE EXCUSE THAT ALLOWED YOU TO MAKE THE CHOICE AND STEP AWAY.
WHY DID YOU DECIDE TO HANG UP YOUR COSTUME?

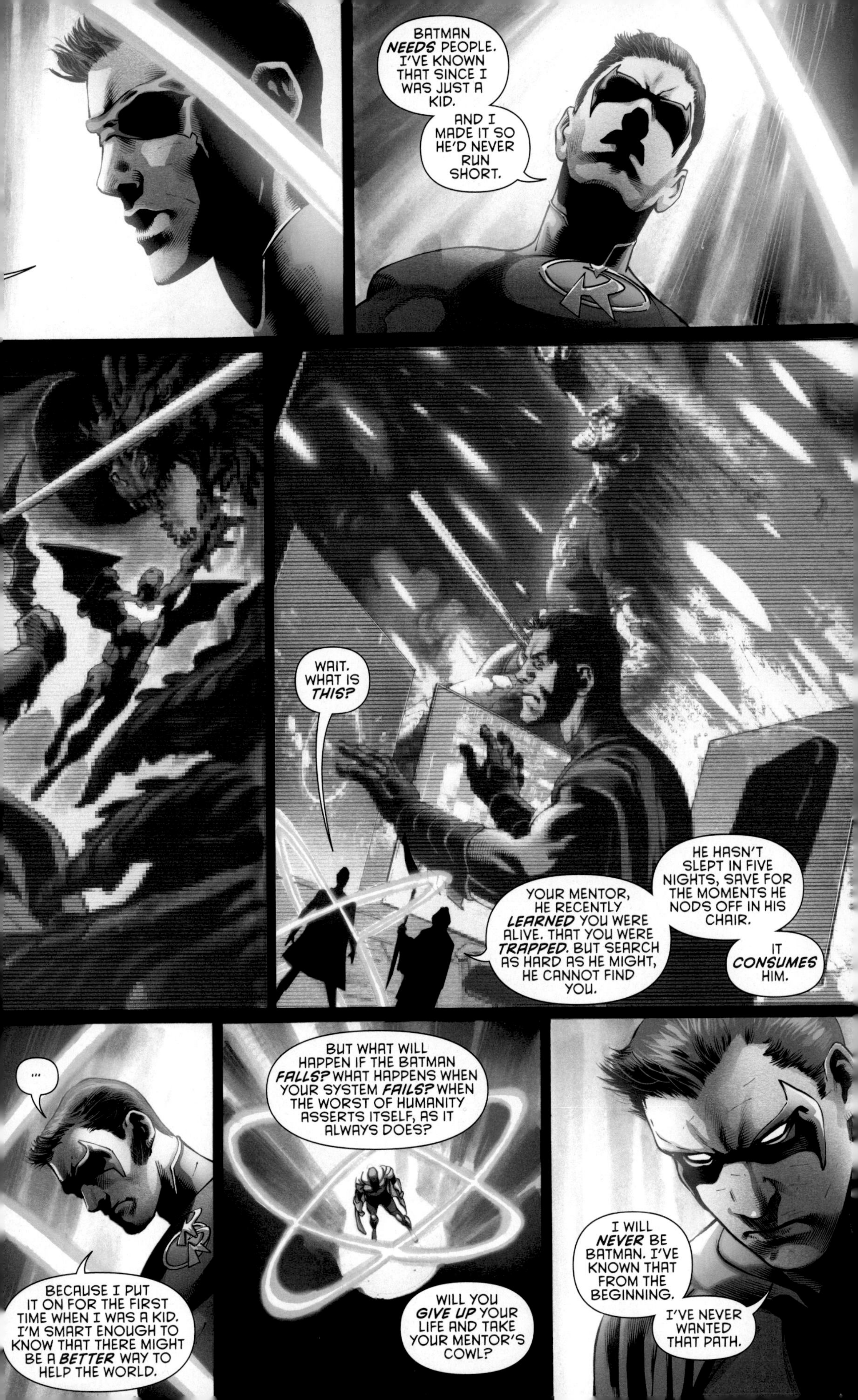
BATMAN NEEDS PEOPLE. I'VE KNOWN THAT SINCE I WAS JUST A KID.
AND I MADE IT SO HE'D NEVER RUN SHORT.
WAIT. WHAT IS THIS?
YOUR MENTOR, HE RECENTLY LEARNED YOU WERE ALIVE. THAT YOU WERE TRAPPED. BUT SEARCH AS HARD AS HE MIGHT, HE CANNOT FIND YOU.
HE HASN'T SLEPT IN FIVE NIGHTS, SAVE FOR THE MOMENTS HE NODS OFF IN HIS CHAIR.
IT CONSUMES HIM.
...
BUT WHAT WILL HAPPEN IF THE BATMAN FALLS? WHAT HAPPENS WHEN YOUR SYSTEM FAILS? WHEN THE WORST OF HUMANITY ASSERTS ITSELF, AS IT ALWAYS DOES?
WILL YOU GIVE UP YOUR LIFE AND TAKE YOUR MENTOR'S COWL?
I WILL NEVER BE BATMAN. I'VE KNOWN THAT FROM THE BEGINNING.
I'VE NEVER WANTED THAT PATH.
BECAUSE I PUT IT ON FOR THE FIRST TIME WHEN I WAS A KID. I'M SMART ENOUGH TO KNOW THAT THERE MIGHT BE A BETTER WAY TO HELP THE WORLD.

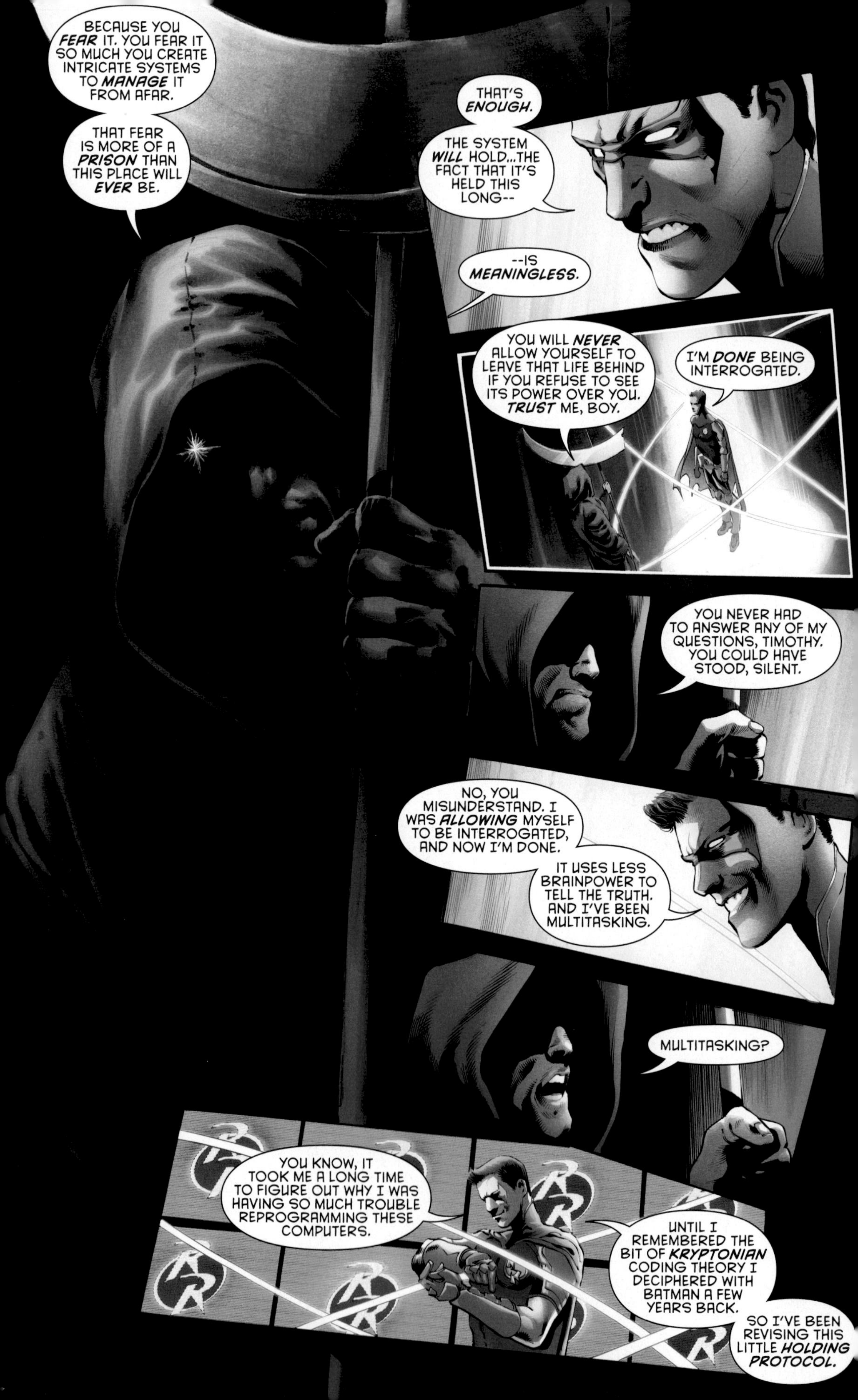

BECAUSE YOU FEAR IT. YOU FEAR IT SO MUCH YOU CREATE INTRICATE SYSTEMS TO MANAGE IT FROM AFAR.
THAT FEAR IS MORE OF A PRISON THAN THIS PLACE WILL EVER BE.
THAT'S ENOUGH.
THE SYSTEM WILL HOLD...THE FACT THAT IT'S HELD THIS LONG--
--IS MEANINGLESS.
YOU WILL NEVER ALLOW YOURSELF TO LEAVE THAT LIFE BEHIND IF YOU REFUSE TO SEE ITS POWER OVER YOU. TRUST ME, BOY.
I'M DONE BEING INTERROGATED.
YOU NEVER HAD TO ANSWER ANY OF MY QUESTIONS, TIMOTHY. YOU COULD HAVE STOOD, SILENT.
NO, YOU MISUNDERSTAND. I WAS ALLOWING MYSELF TO BE INTERROGATED, AND NOW I'M DONE.
IT USES LESS BRAINPOWER TO TELL THE TRUTH. AND I'VE BEEN MULTITASKING.
MULTITASKING?
YOU KNOW, IT TOOK ME A LONG TIME TO FIGURE OUT WHY I WAS HAVING SO MUCH TROUBLE REPROGRAMMING THESE COMPUTERS.
UNTIL I REMEMBERED THE BIT OF KRYPTONIAN CODING THEORY I DECIPHERED WITH BATMAN A FEW YEARS BACK.
SO I'VE BEEN REVISING THIS LITTLE HOLDING PROTOCOL.

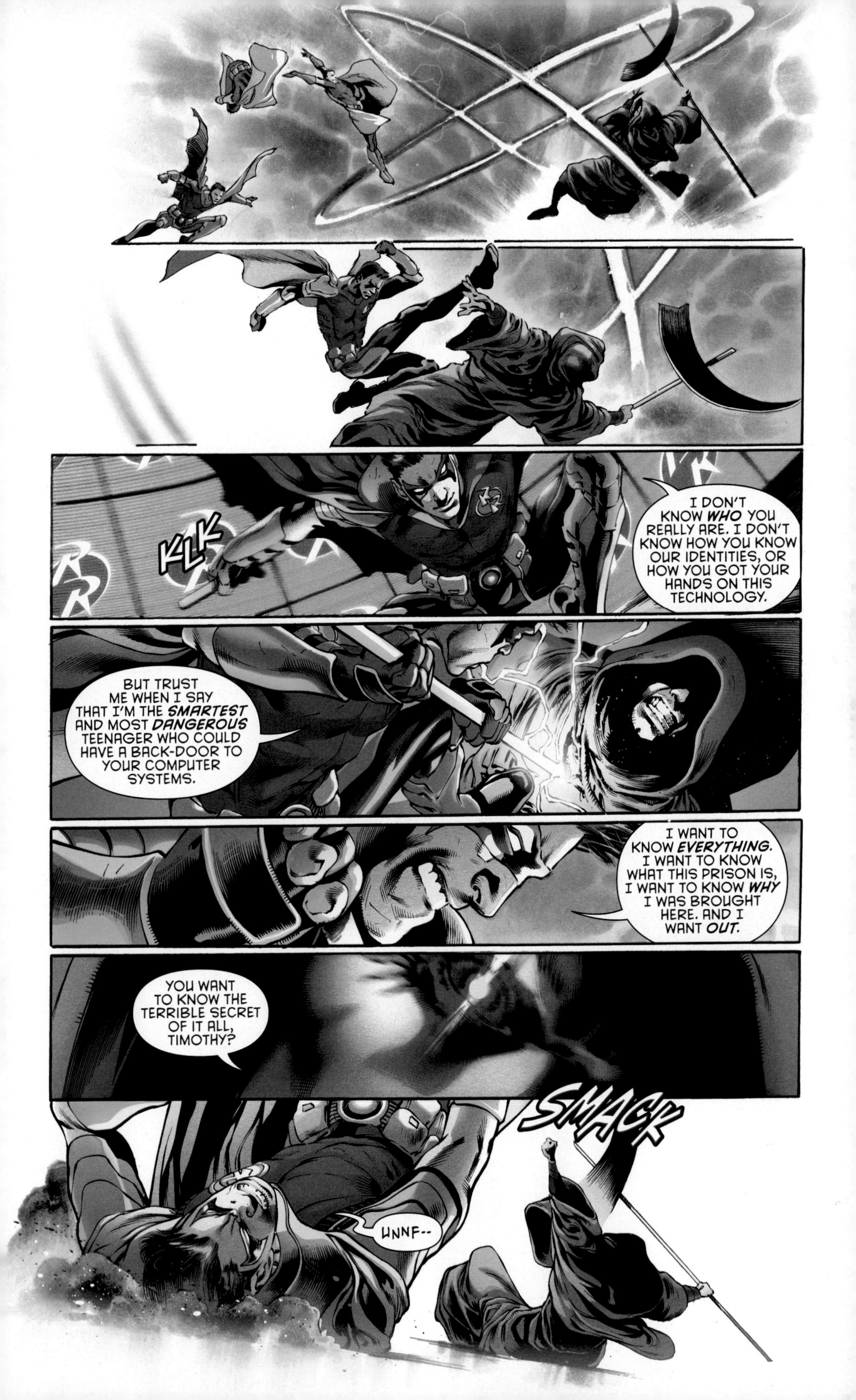
KLK
I DON'T KNOW WHO YOU REALLY ARE. I DON'T KNOW HOW YOU KNOW OUR IDENTITIES, OR HOW YOU GOT YOUR HANDS ON THIS TECHNOLOGY.
BUT TRUST ME WHEN I SAY THAT I'M THE SMARTEST AND MOST DANGEROUS TEENAGER WHO COULD HAVE A BACK-DOOR TO YOUR COMPUTER SYSTEMS.
I WANT TO KNOW EVERYTHING. I WANT TO KNOW WHAT THIS PRISON IS, I WANT TO KNOW WHY I WAS BROUGHT HERE. AND I WANT OUT.
YOU WANT TO KNOW THE TERRIBLE SECRET OF IT ALL, TIMOTHY?
SMACK
UNNF--

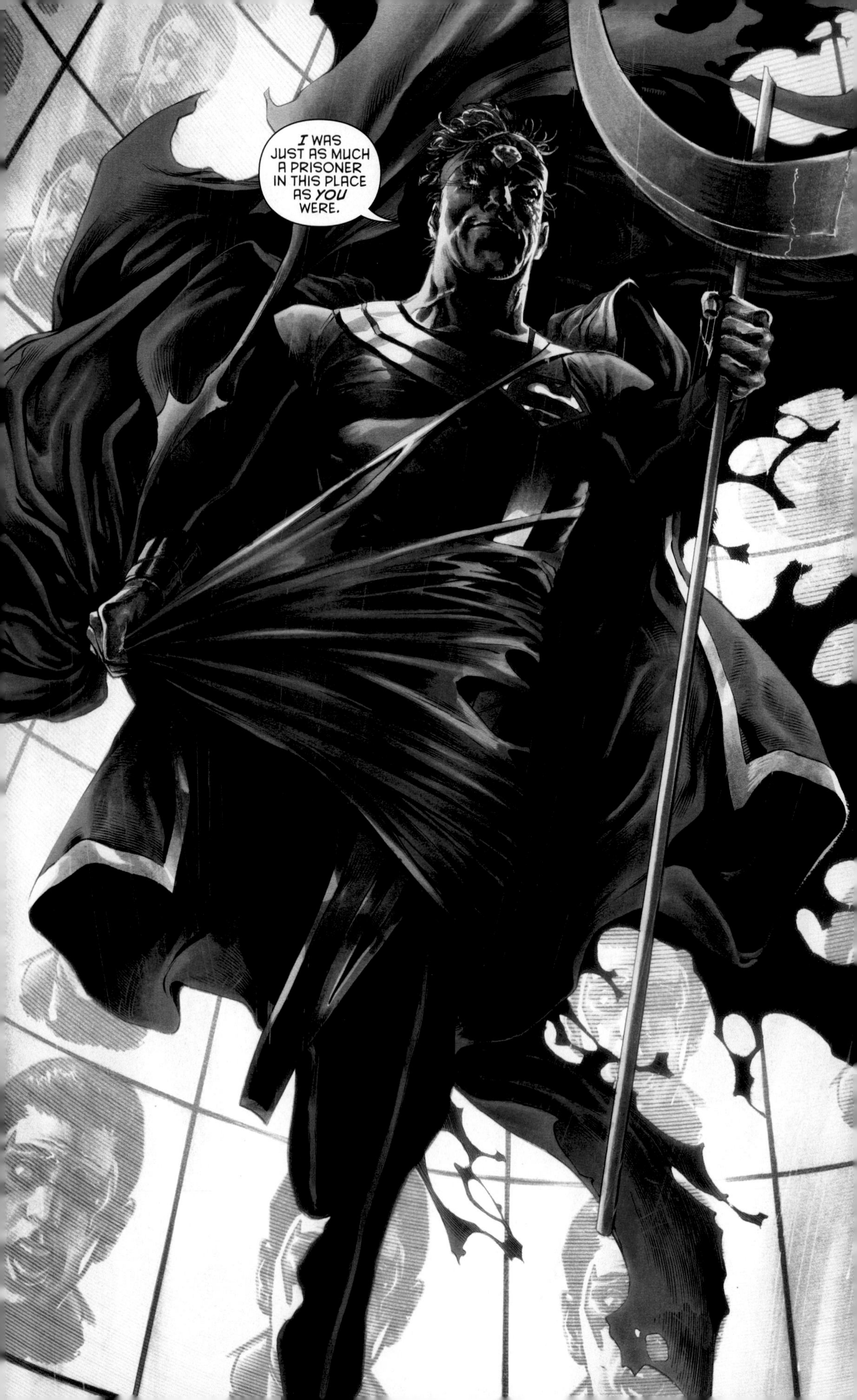
I WAS JUST AS MUCH A PRISONER IN THIS PLACE AS YOU WERE.

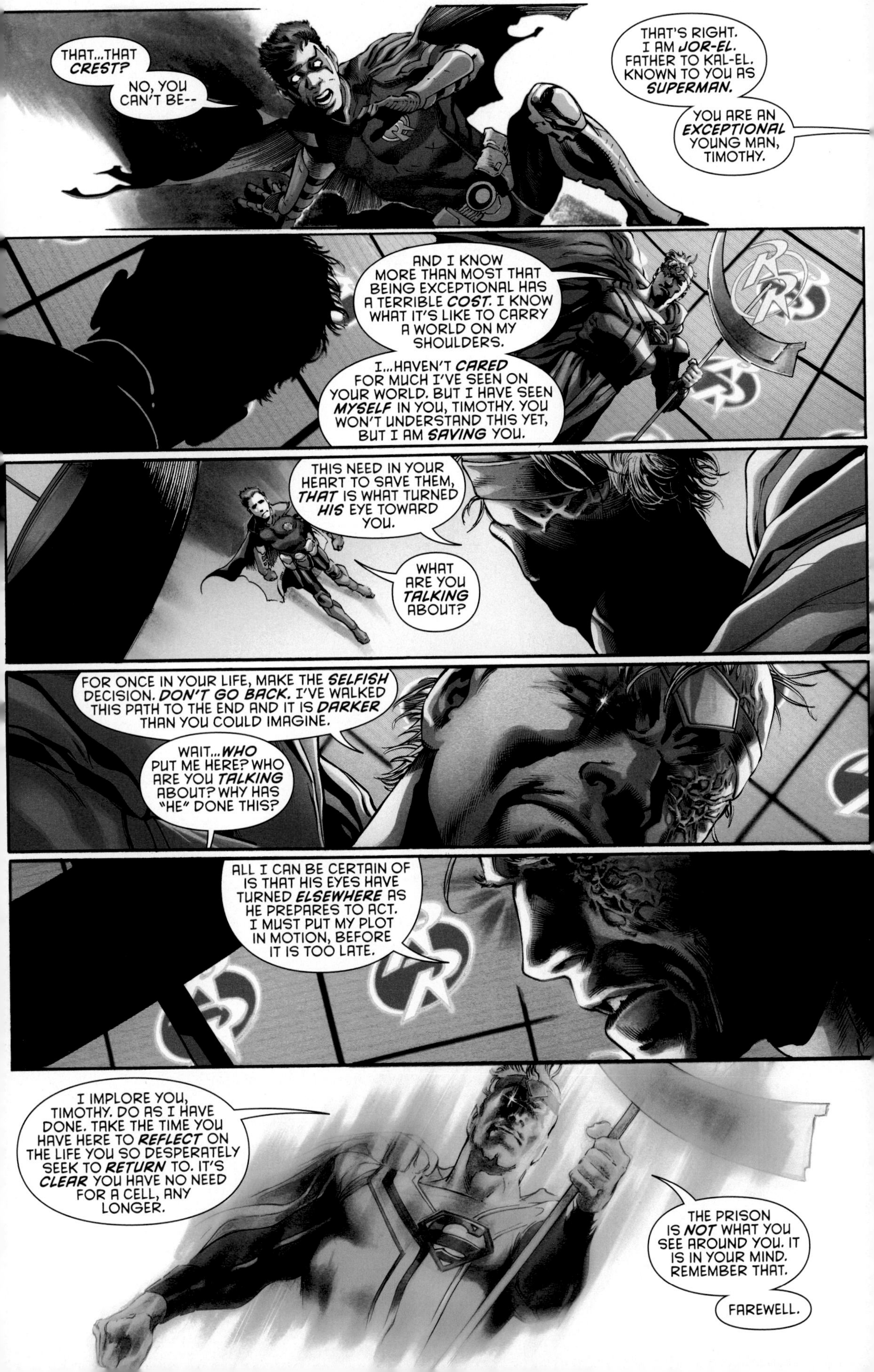
THAT...THAT CREST?
NO, YOU CAN'T BE--
THAT'S RIGHT. I AM JOR-EL. FATHER TO KAL-EL. KNOWN TO YOU AS SUPERMAN.
YOU ARE AN EXCEPTIONAL YOUNG MAN, TIMOTHY.
AND I KNOW MORE THAN MOST THAT BEING EXCEPTIONAL HAS A TERRIBLE COST. I KNOW WHAT IT'S LIKE TO CARRY A WORLD ON MY SHOULDERS.
I...HAVEN'T CARED FOR MUCH I'VE SEEN ON YOUR WORLD. BUT I HAVE SEEN MYSELF IN YOU, TIMOTHY. YOU WON'T UNDERSTAND THIS YET, BUT I AM SAVING YOU.
THIS NEED IN YOUR HEART TO SAVE THEM, THAT IS WHAT TURNED HIS EYE TOWARD YOU.
WHAT ARE YOU TALKING ABOUT?
FOR ONCE IN YOUR LIFE, MAKE THE SELFISH DECISION. DON'T GO BACK. I'VE WALKED THIS PATH TO THE END AND IT IS DARKER THAN YOU COULD IMAGINE.
WAIT...WHO PUT ME HERE? WHO ARE YOU TALKING ABOUT? WHY HAS "HE" DONE THIS?
ALL I CAN BE CERTAIN OF IS THAT HIS EYES HAVE TURNED ELSEWHERE AS HE PREPARES TO ACT. I MUST PUT MY PLOT IN MOTION, BEFORE IT IS TOO LATE.
I IMPLORE YOU, TIMOTHY. DO AS I HAVE DONE. TAKE THE TIME YOU HAVE HERE TO REFLECT ON THE LIFE YOU SO DESPERATELY SEEK TO RETURN TO. IT'S CLEAR YOU HAVE NO NEED FOR A CELL, ANY LONGER.
THE PRISON IS NOT WHAT YOU SEE AROUND YOU. IT IS IN YOUR MIND. REMEMBER THAT.
FAREWELL.

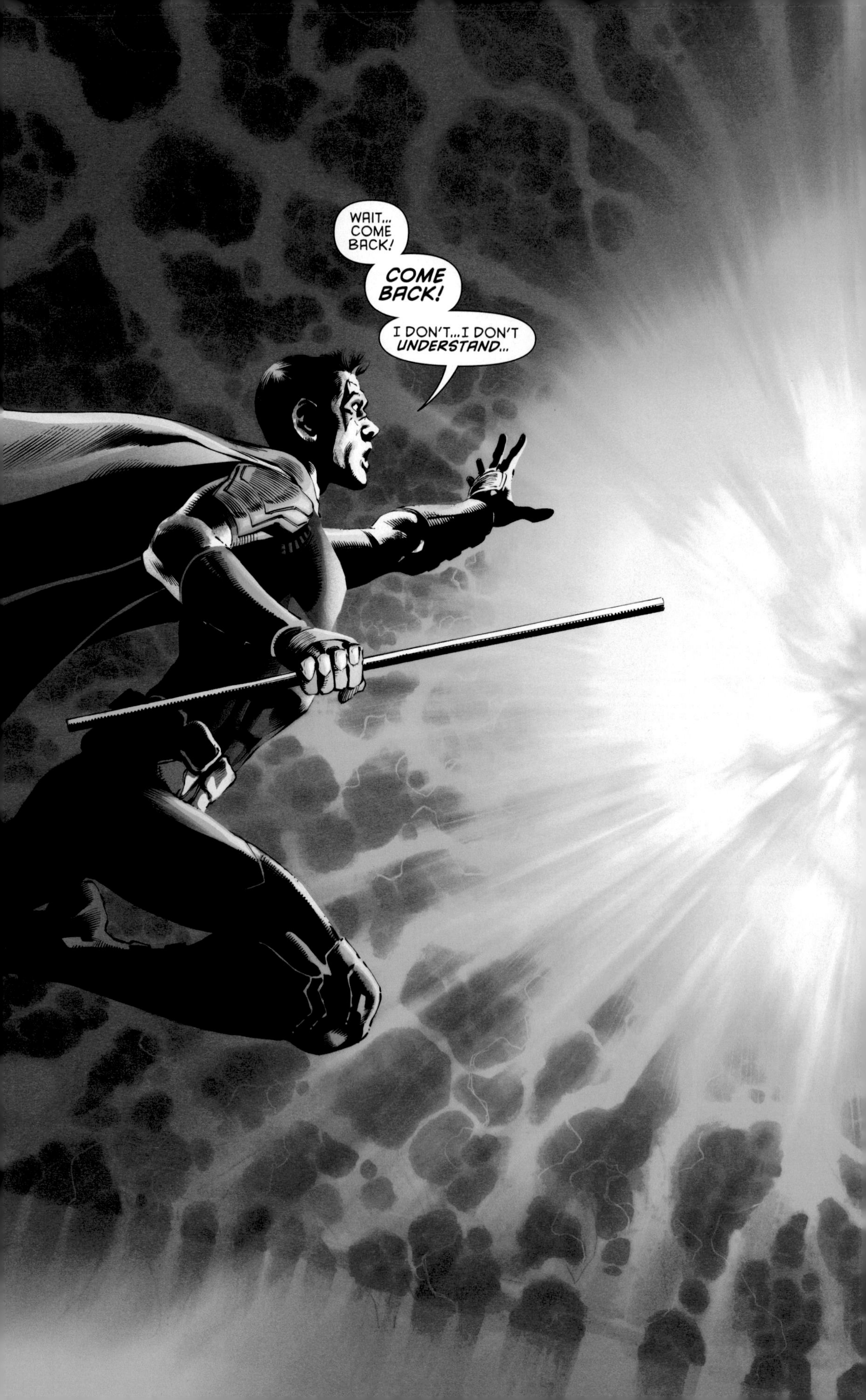
WAIT... COME BACK!
COME BACK!
I DON'T...I DON'T UNDERSTAND...

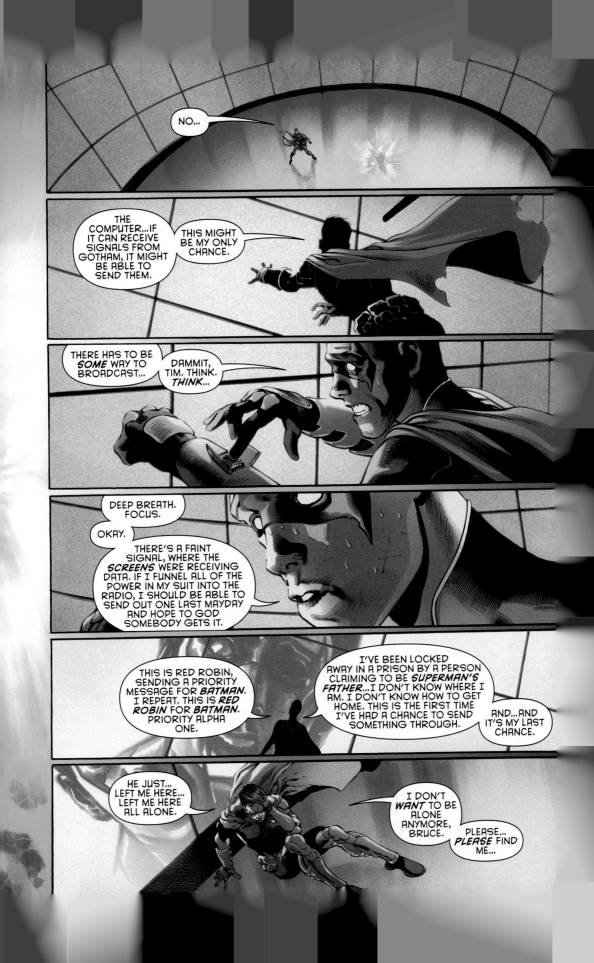

NO...

THE COMPUTER...IF IT CAN RECEIVE SIGNALS FROM GOTHAM, IT MIGHT BE ABLE TO SEND THEM.

THIS MIGHT BE MY ONLY CHANCE.

THERE HAS TO BE *SOME* WAY TO BROADCAST...

DAMMIT, TIM. THINK. *THINK*...

DEEP BREATH. FOCUS.

OKAY.

THERE'S A FAINT SIGNAL, WHERE THE *SCREENS* WERE RECEIVING DATA. IF I FUNNEL ALL OF THE POWER IN MY SUIT INTO THE RADIO, I SHOULD BE ABLE TO SEND OUT ONE LAST MAYDAY AND HOPE TO GOD SOMEBODY GETS IT.

THIS IS RED ROBIN, SENDING A PRIORITY MESSAGE FOR *BATMAN*. I REPEAT. THIS IS *RED ROBIN* FOR *BATMAN*. PRIORITY ALPHA ONE.

I'VE BEEN LOCKED AWAY IN A PRISON BY A PERSON CLAIMING TO BE *SUPERMAN'S FATHER*...I DON'T KNOW WHERE I AM. I DON'T KNOW HOW TO GET HOME. THIS IS THE FIRST TIME I'VE HAD A CHANCE TO SEND SOMETHING THROUGH.

AND...AND IT'S MY LAST CHANCE.

HE JUST... LEFT ME HERE... LEFT ME HERE ALL ALONE.

I DON'T *WANT* TO BE ALONE ANYMORE, BRUCE.

PLEASE... *PLEASE* FIND ME...

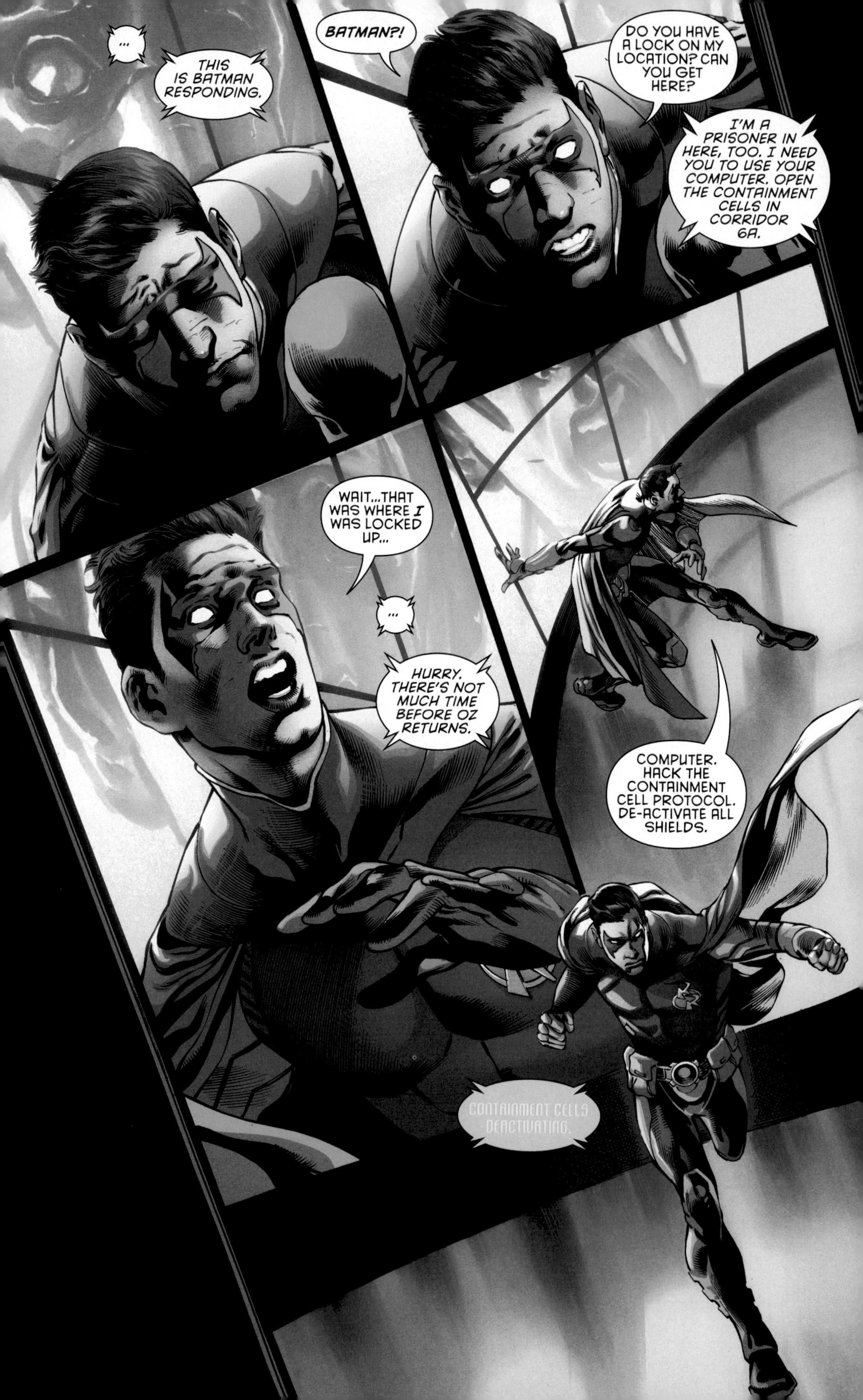
...
THIS IS BATMAN RESPONDING.
BATMAN?!
DO YOU HAVE A LOCK ON MY LOCATION? CAN YOU GET HERE?
I'M A PRISONER IN HERE, TOO. I NEED YOU TO USE YOUR COMPUTER. OPEN THE CONTAINMENT CELLS IN CORRIDOR 6A.
WAIT...THAT WAS WHERE I WAS LOCKED UP...
...
HURRY. THERE'S NOT MUCH TIME BEFORE OZ RETURNS.
COMPUTER. HACK THE CONTAINMENT CELL PROTOCOL. DE-ACTIVATE ALL SHIELDS.
CONTAINMENT CELLS DEACTIVATING.

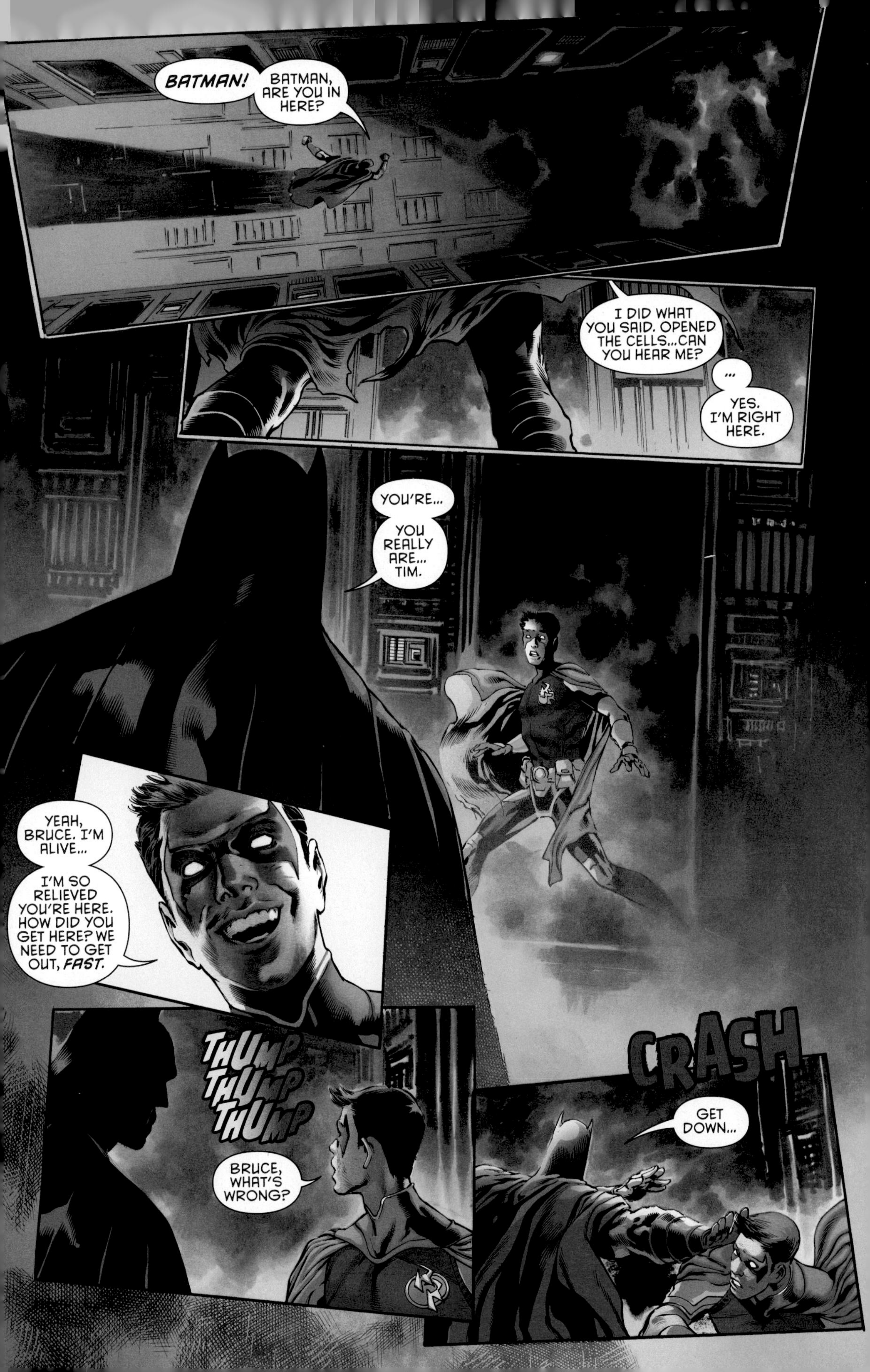
BATMAN!
BATMAN, ARE YOU IN HERE?
I DID WHAT YOU SAID. OPENED THE CELLS...CAN YOU HEAR ME?
...
YES. I'M RIGHT HERE.
YOU'RE...
YOU REALLY ARE... TIM.
YEAH, BRUCE. I'M ALIVE...
I'M SO RELIEVED YOU'RE HERE. HOW DID YOU GET HERE? WE NEED TO GET OUT, FAST.
THUMP THUMP THUMP
BRUCE, WHAT'S WRONG?
CRASH
GET DOWN...

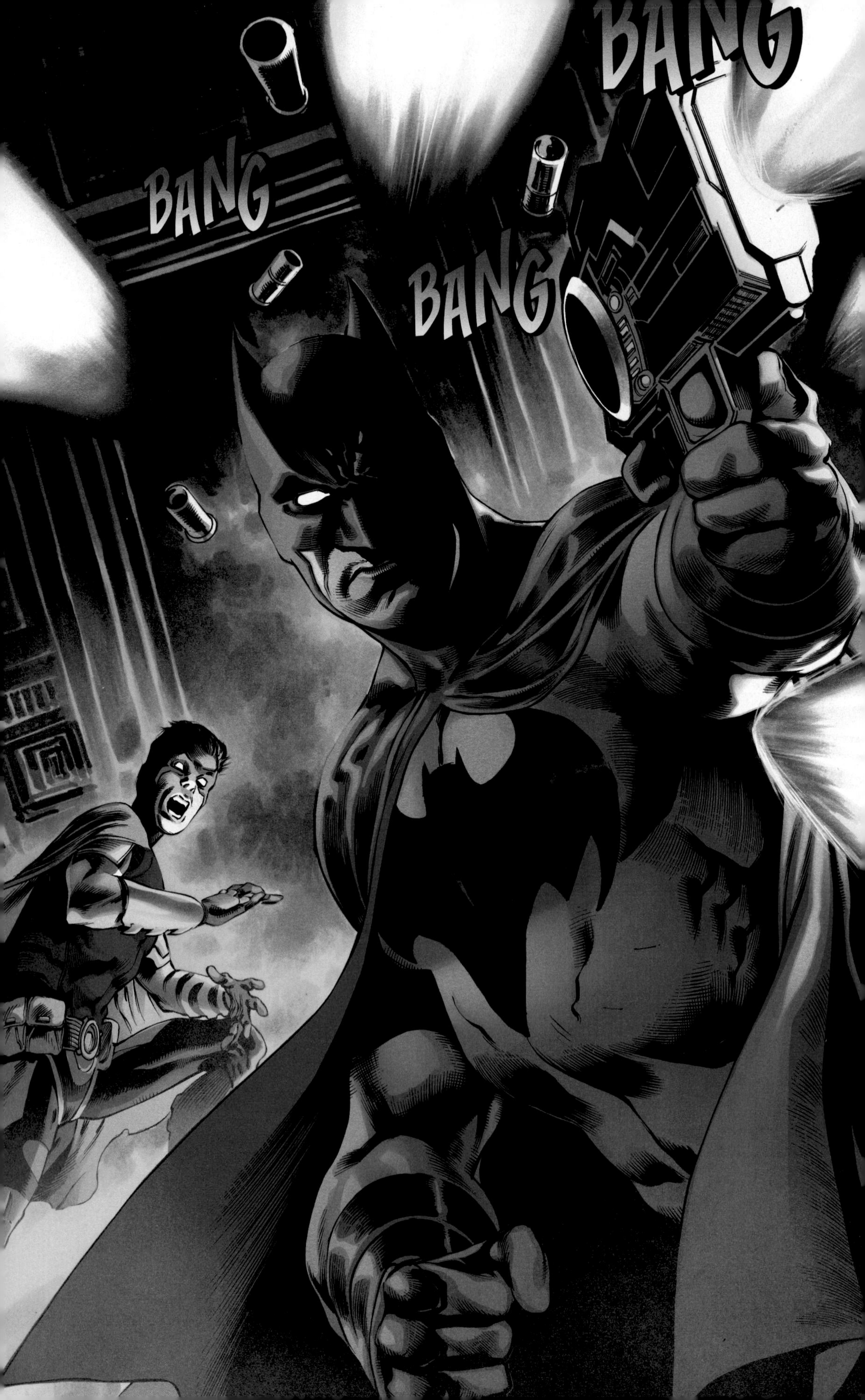
BANG
BANG
BANG

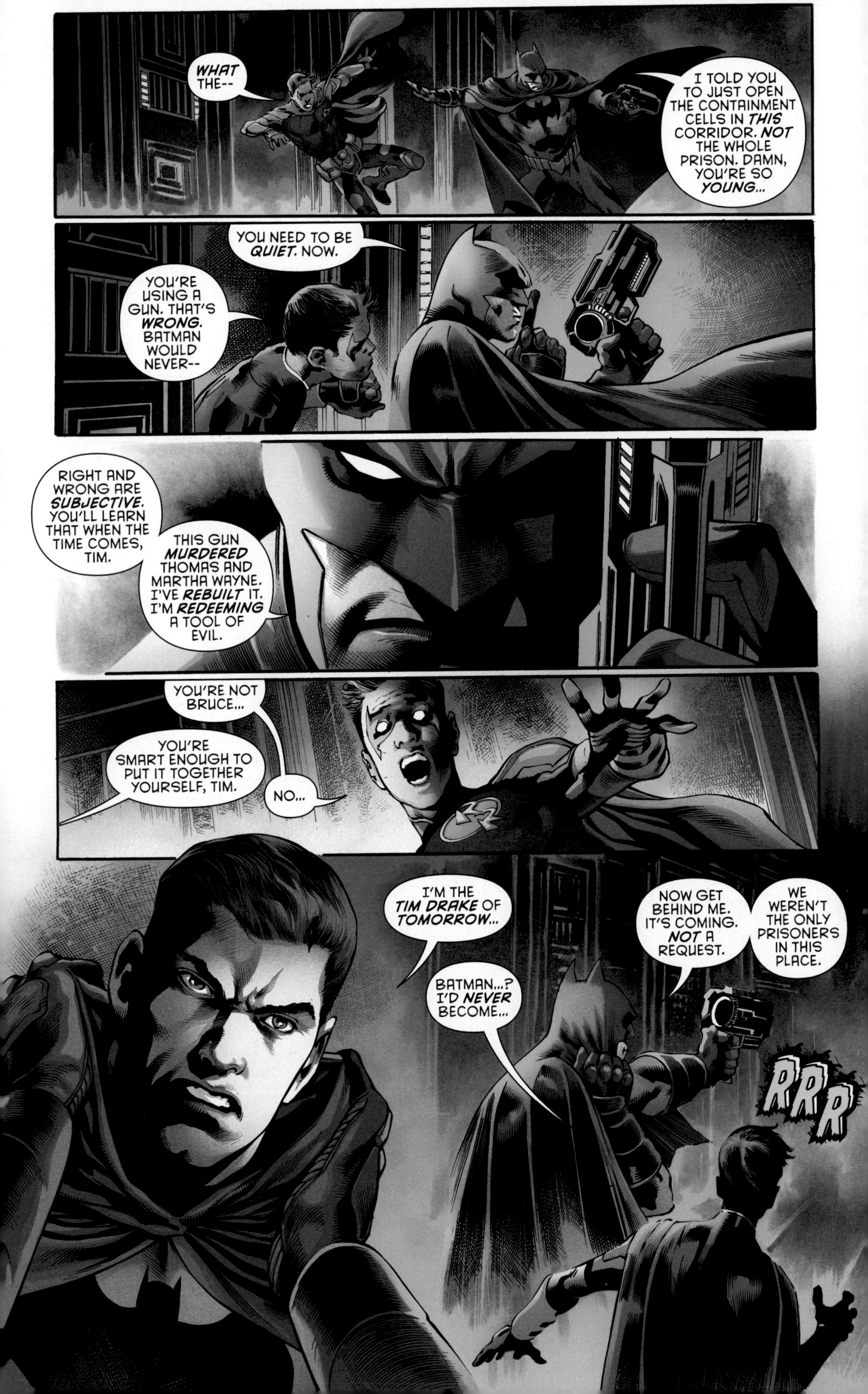
WHAT THE--
I TOLD YOU TO JUST OPEN THE CONTAINMENT CELLS IN THIS CORRIDOR. NOT THE WHOLE PRISON. DAMN, YOU'RE SO YOUNG...
YOU NEED TO BE QUIET. NOW.
YOU'RE USING A GUN. THAT'S WRONG. BATMAN WOULD NEVER--
RIGHT AND WRONG ARE SUBJECTIVE. YOU'LL LEARN THAT WHEN THE TIME COMES, TIM.
THIS GUN MURDERED THOMAS AND MARTHA WAYNE. I'VE REBUILT IT. I'M REDEEMING A TOOL OF EVIL.
YOU'RE NOT BRUCE...
YOU'RE SMART ENOUGH TO PUT IT TOGETHER YOURSELF, TIM.
NO...
I'M THE TIM DRAKE OF TOMORROW...
BATMAN...? I'D NEVER BECOME...
NOW GET BEHIND ME. IT'S COMING. NOT A REQUEST.
WE WEREN'T THE ONLY PRISONERS IN THIS PLACE.
RRR

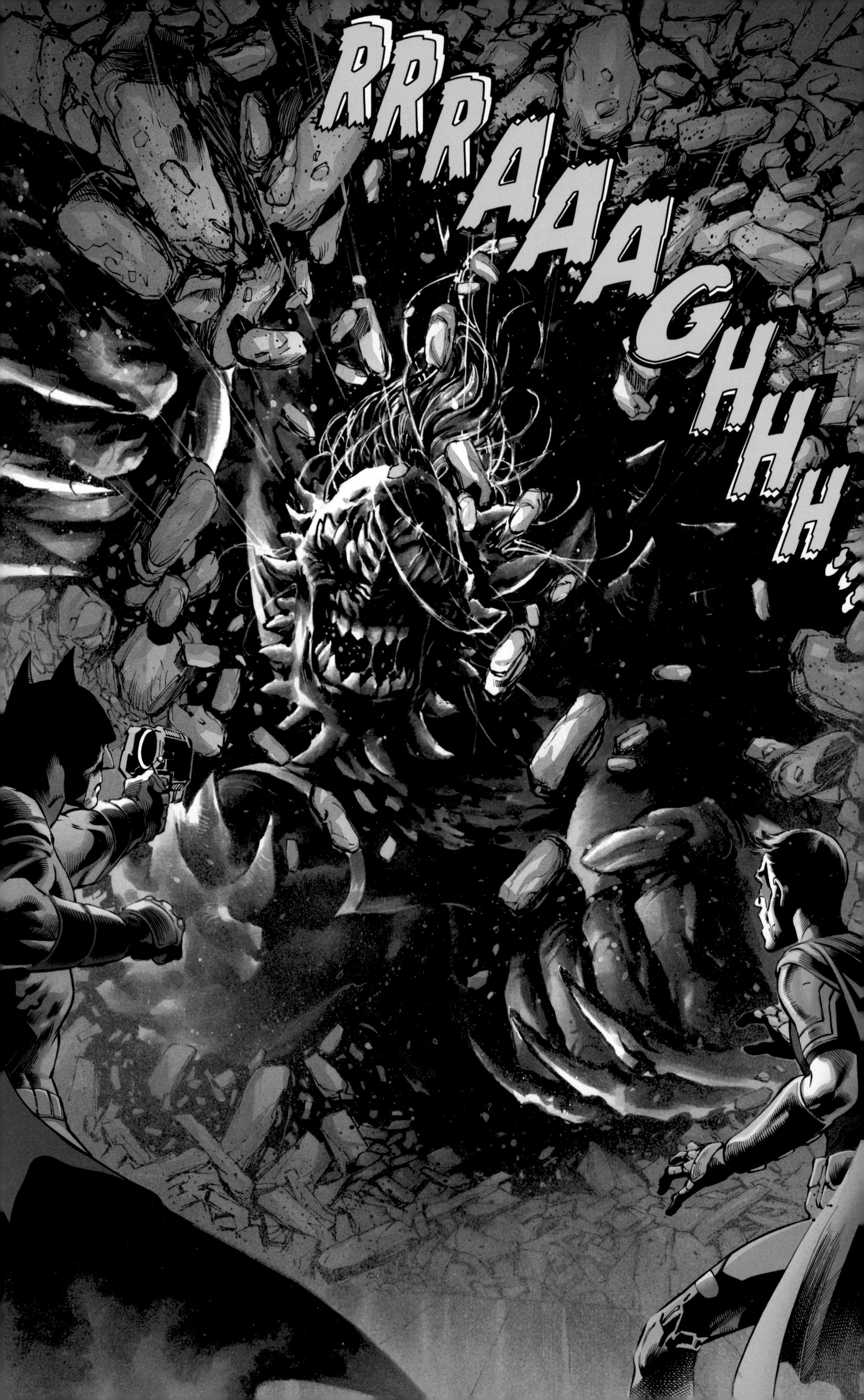
RRRAAAAGHHHH...

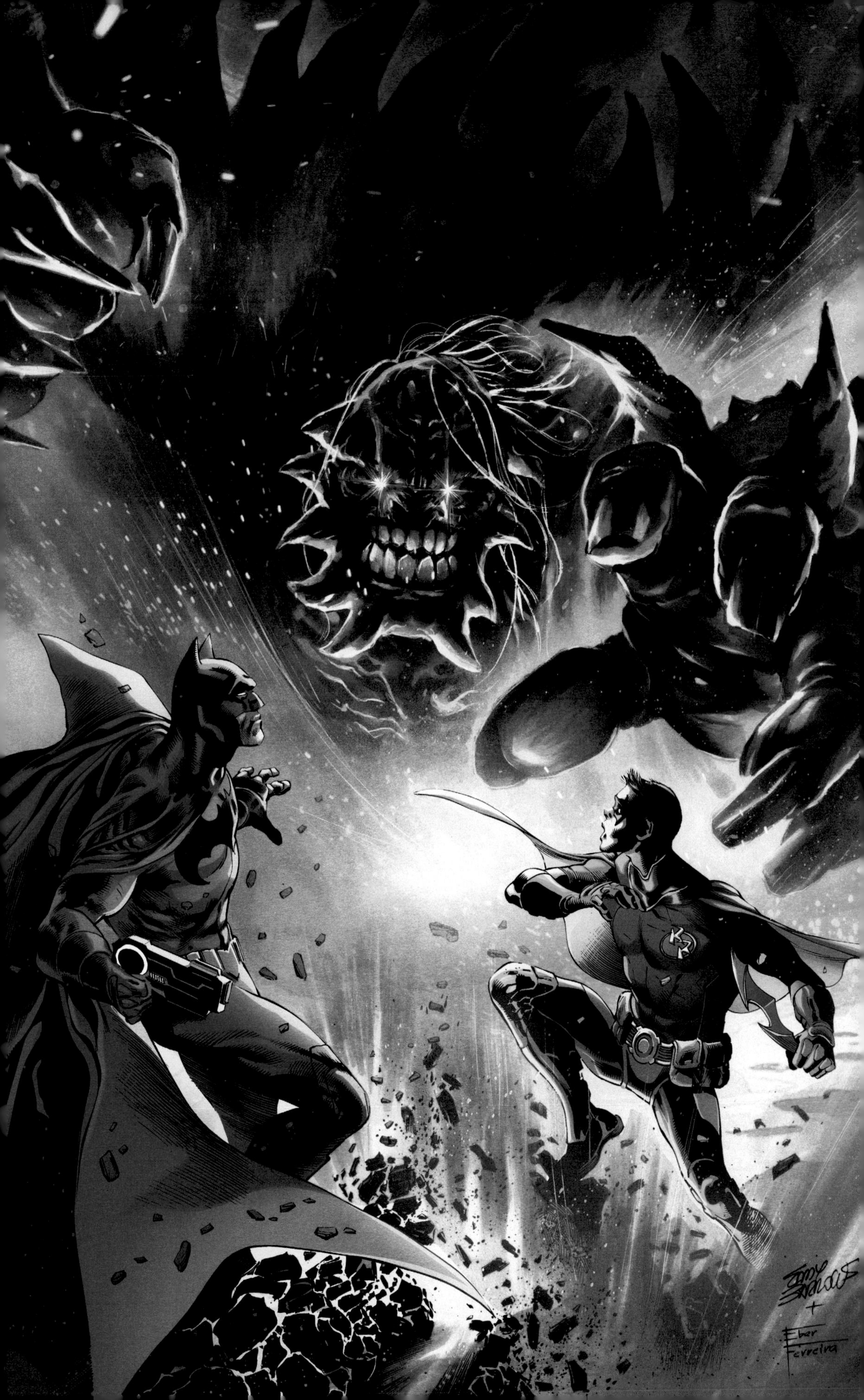

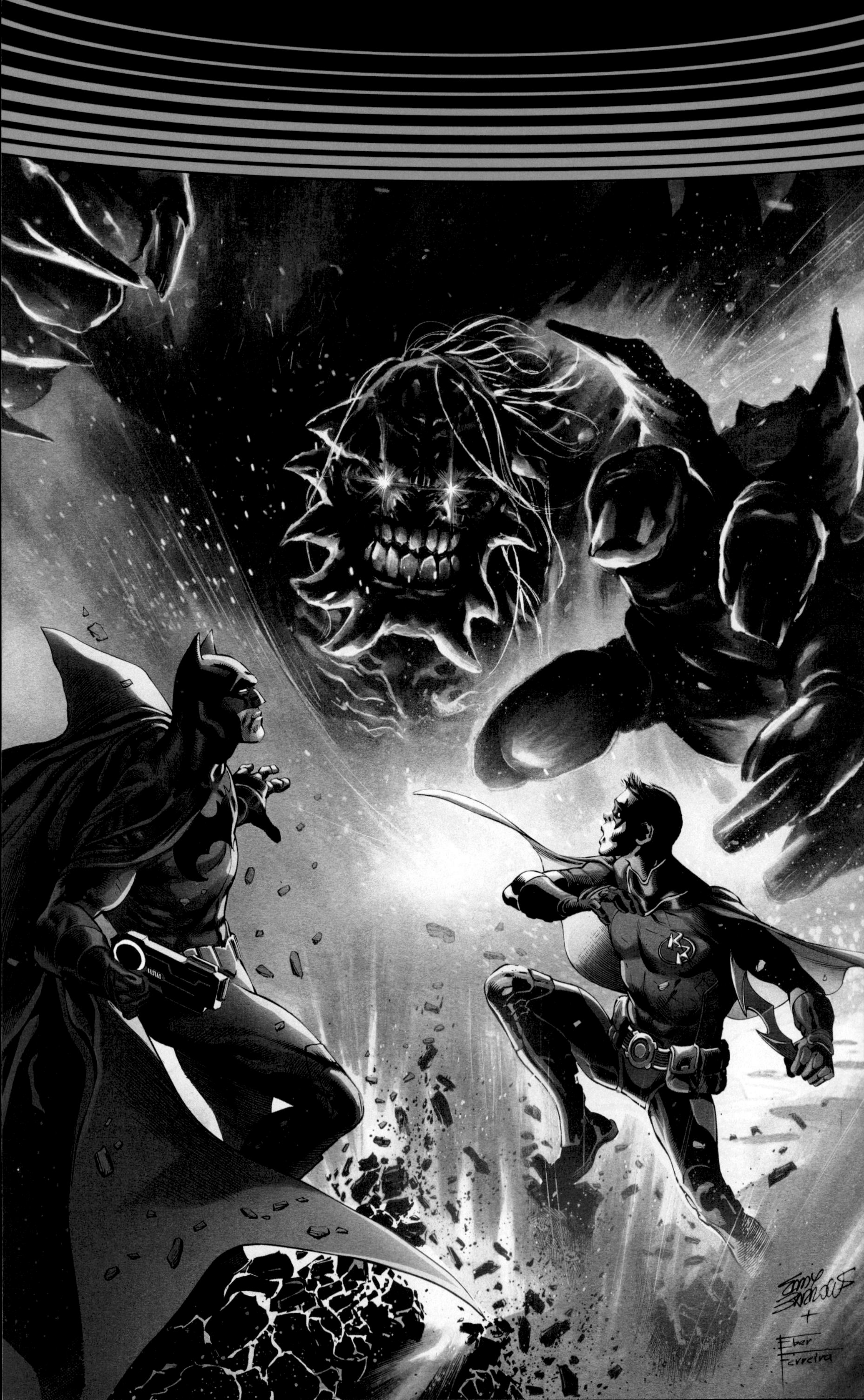

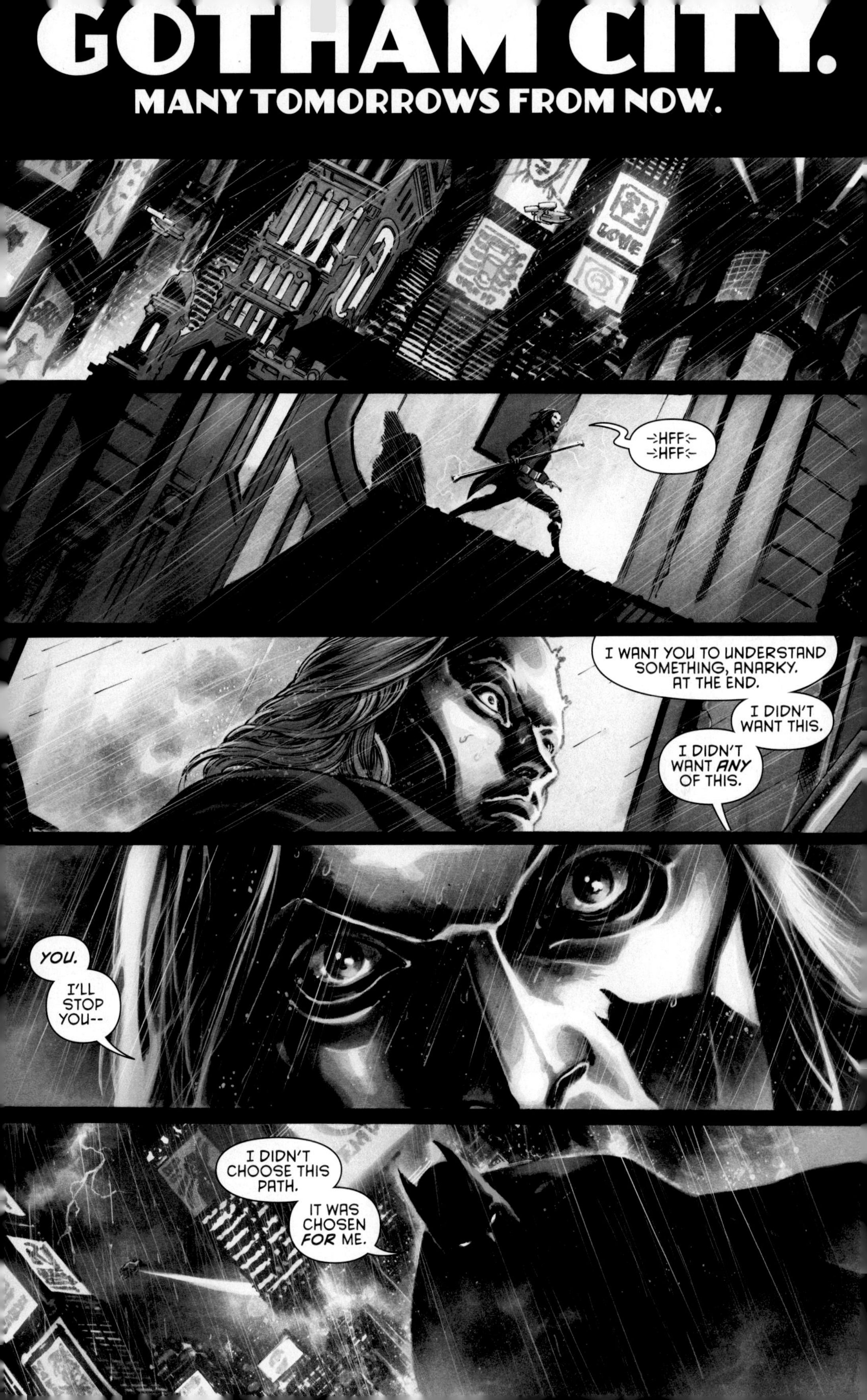
GOTHAM CITY.
MANY TOMORROWS FROM NOW.
HFF HFF
I WANT YOU TO UNDERSTAND SOMETHING, ANARKY. AT THE END.
I DIDN'T WANT THIS.
I DIDN'T WANT *ANY* OF THIS.
YOU.
I'LL STOP YOU--
I DIDN'T CHOOSE THIS PATH.
IT WAS CHOSEN *FOR* ME.

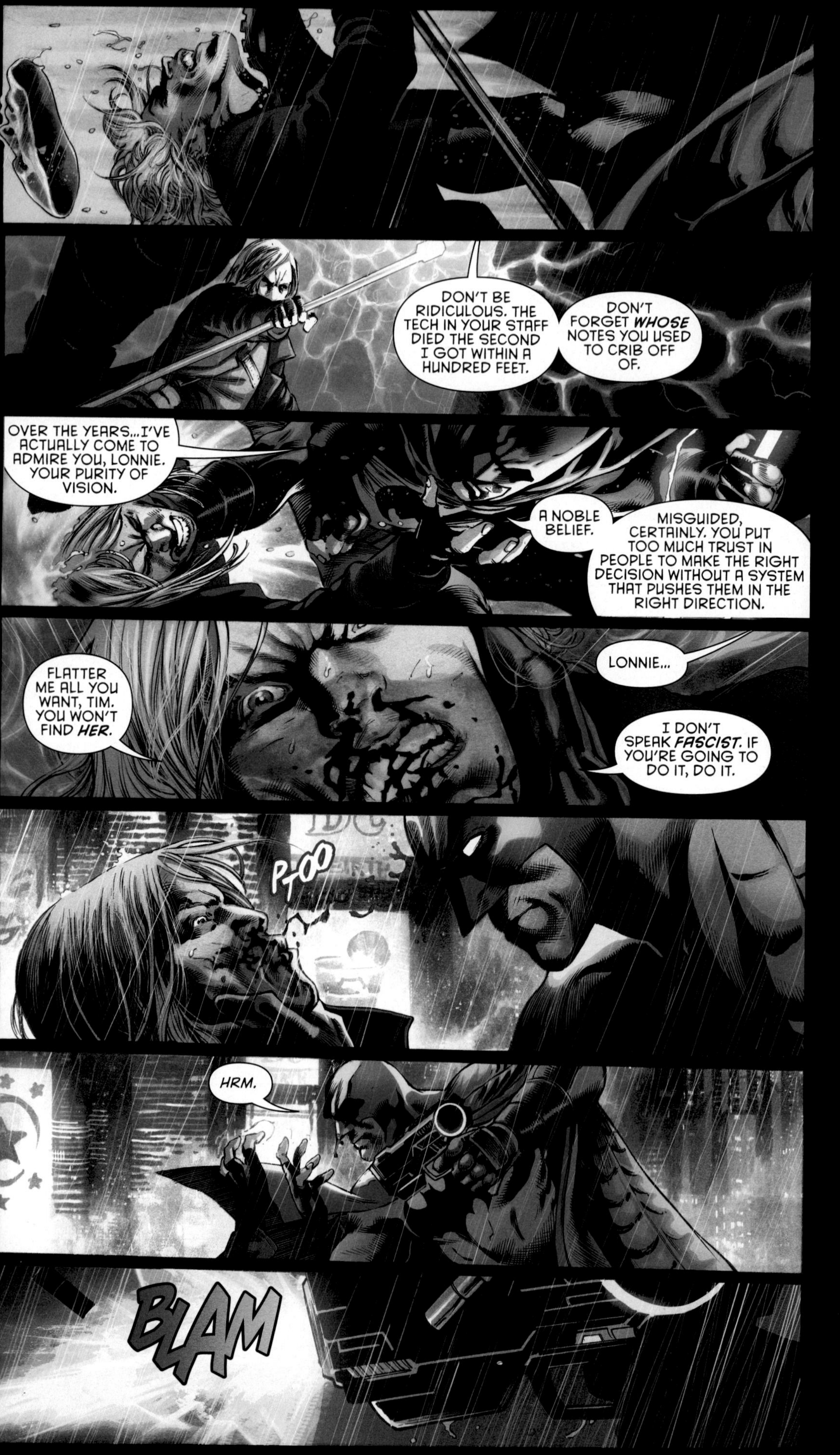
DON'T BE RIDICULOUS. THE TECH IN YOUR STAFF DIED THE SECOND I GOT WITHIN A HUNDRED FEET.
DON'T FORGET *WHOSE* NOTES YOU USED TO CRIB OFF OF.
OVER THE YEARS...I'VE ACTUALLY COME TO ADMIRE YOU, LONNIE. YOUR PURITY OF VISION.
A NOBLE BELIEF.
MISGUIDED, CERTAINLY. YOU PUT TOO MUCH TRUST IN PEOPLE TO MAKE THE RIGHT DECISION WITHOUT A SYSTEM THAT PUSHES THEM IN THE RIGHT DIRECTION.
FLATTER ME ALL YOU WANT, TIM. YOU WON'T FIND *HER*.
LONNIE...
I DON'T SPEAK *FASCIST*. IF YOU'RE GOING TO DO IT, DO IT.
PTOO
HRM.
BLAM

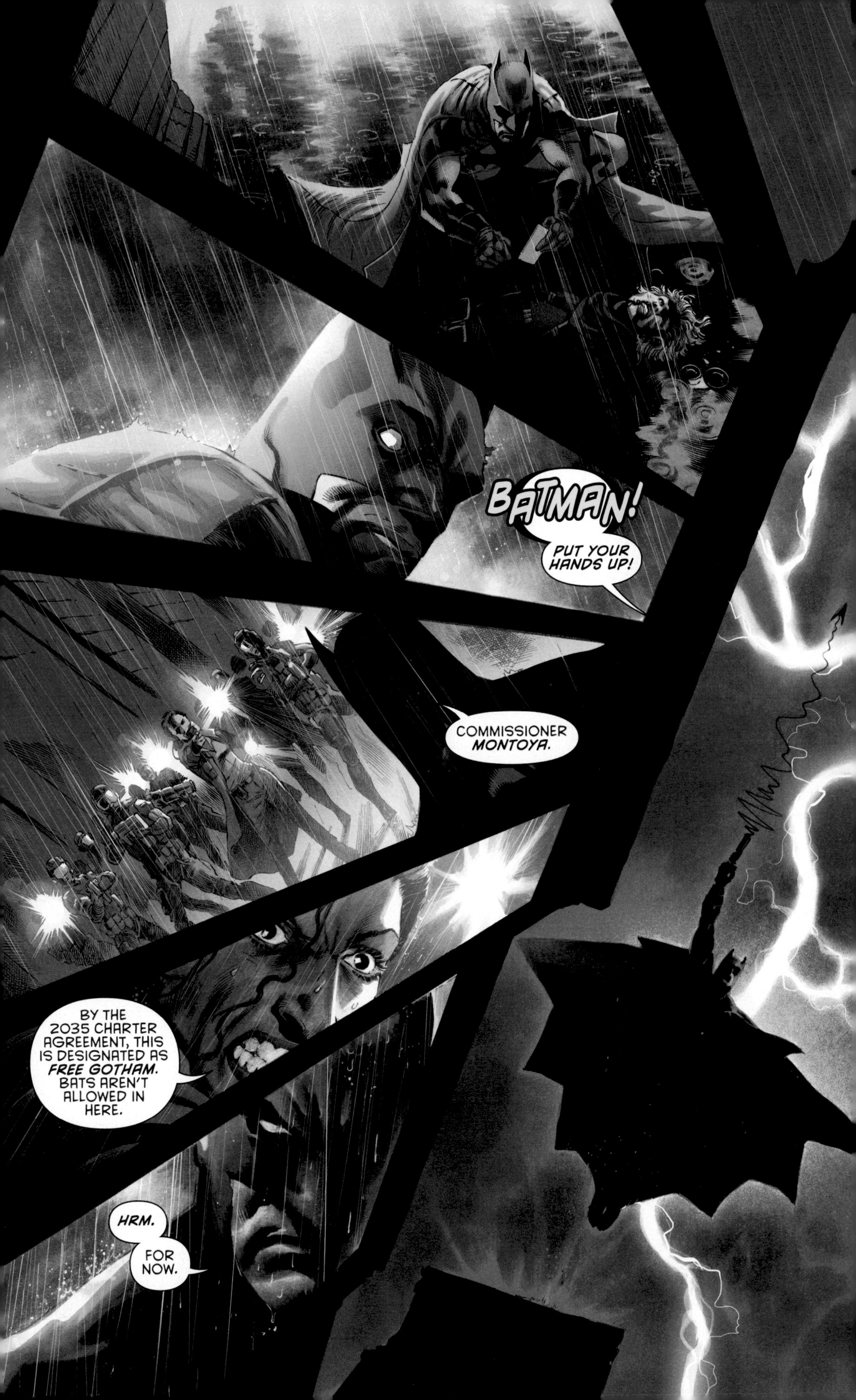
BATMAN!
PUT YOUR HANDS UP!
COMMISSIONER MONTOYA.
BY THE 2035 CHARTER AGREEMENT, THIS IS DESIGNATED AS FREE GOTHAM. BATS AREN'T ALLOWED IN HERE.
HRM.
FOR NOW.

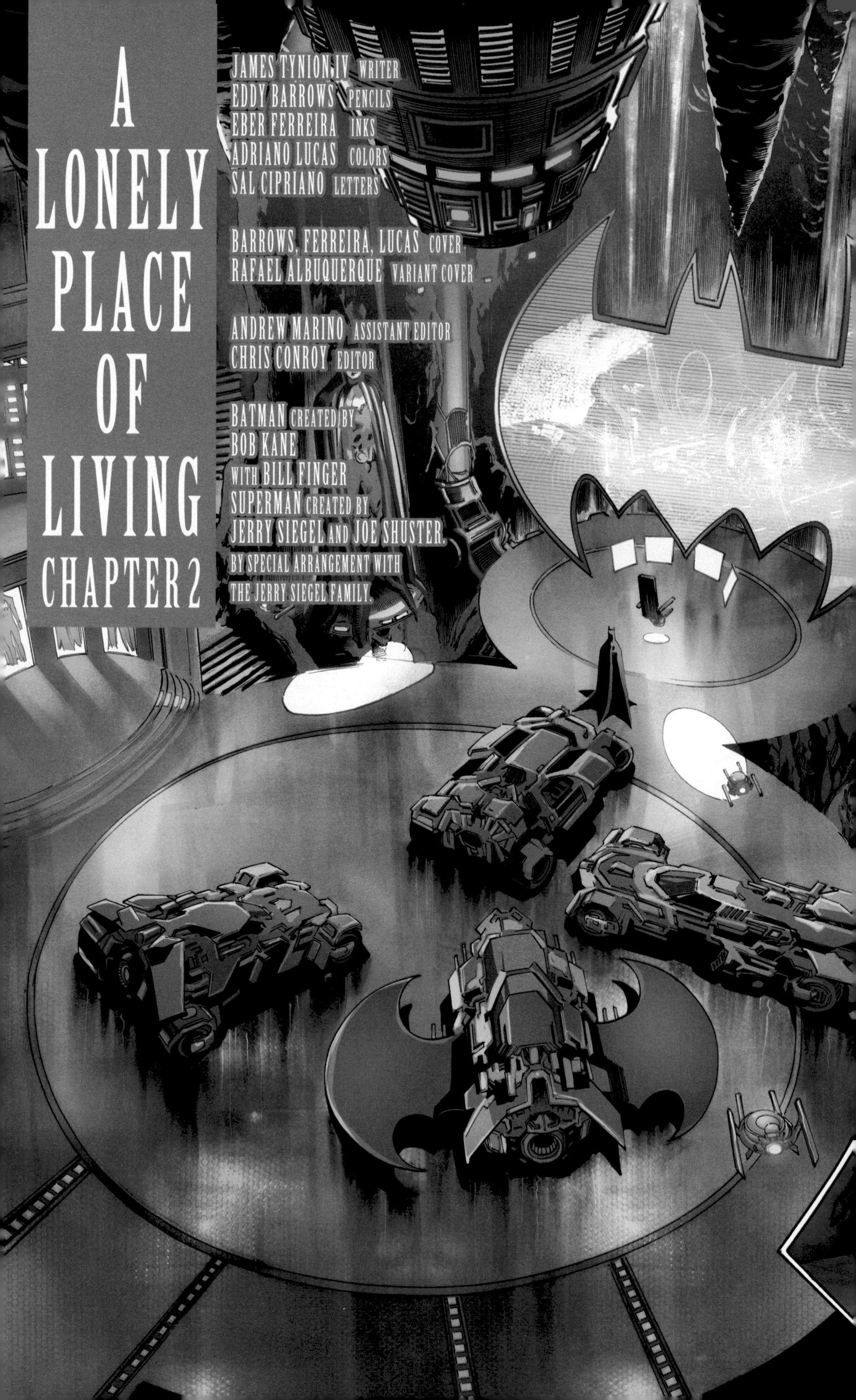
A LONELY PLACE OF LIVING
CHAPTER 2
JAMES TYNION IV WRITER
EDDY BARROWS PENCILS
EBER FERREIRA INKS
ADRIANO LUCAS COLORS
SAL CIPRIANO LETTERS
BARROWS, FERREIRA, LUCAS COVER
RAFAEL ALBUQUERQUE VARIANT COVER
ANDREW MARINO ASSISTANT EDITOR
CHRIS CONROY EDITOR
BATMAN CREATED BY
BOB KANE
WITH BILL FINGER
SUPERMAN CREATED BY
JERRY SIEGEL AND JOE SHUSTER.
BY SPECIAL ARRANGEMENT WITH
THE JERRY SIEGEL FAMILY.

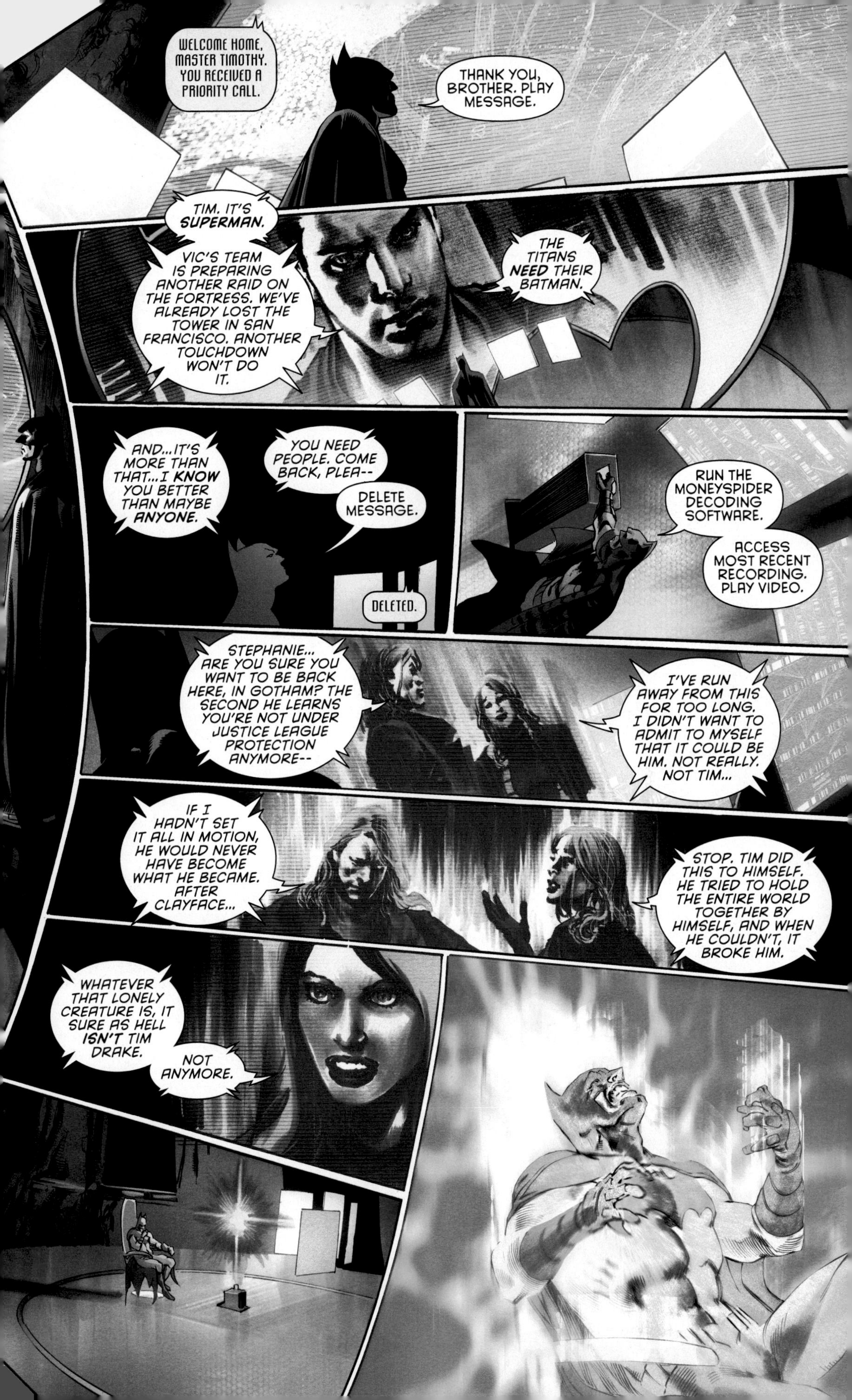
WELCOME HOME, MASTER TIMOTHY. YOU RECEIVED A PRIORITY CALL.
THANK YOU, BROTHER. PLAY MESSAGE.
TIM. IT'S SUPERMAN.
VIC'S TEAM IS PREPARING ANOTHER RAID ON THE FORTRESS. WE'VE ALREADY LOST THE TOWER IN SAN FRANCISCO. ANOTHER TOUCHDOWN WON'T DO IT.
THE TITANS NEED THEIR BATMAN.
AND...IT'S MORE THAN THAT...I KNOW YOU BETTER THAN MAYBE ANYONE.
YOU NEED PEOPLE. COME BACK, PLEA--
DELETE MESSAGE.
DELETED.
RUN THE MONEYSPIDER DECODING SOFTWARE.
ACCESS MOST RECENT RECORDING. PLAY VIDEO.
STEPHANIE... ARE YOU SURE YOU WANT TO BE BACK HERE, IN GOTHAM? THE SECOND HE LEARNS YOU'RE NOT UNDER JUSTICE LEAGUE PROTECTION ANYMORE--
I'VE RUN AWAY FROM THIS FOR TOO LONG. I DIDN'T WANT TO ADMIT TO MYSELF THAT IT COULD BE HIM. NOT REALLY. NOT TIM...
IF I HADN'T SET IT ALL IN MOTION, HE WOULD NEVER HAVE BECOME WHAT HE BECAME. AFTER CLAYFACE...
STOP. TIM DID THIS TO HIMSELF. HE TRIED TO HOLD THE ENTIRE WORLD TOGETHER BY HIMSELF, AND WHEN HE COULDN'T, IT BROKE HIM.
WHATEVER THAT LONELY CREATURE IS, IT SURE AS HELL ISN'T TIM DRAKE.
NOT ANYMORE.

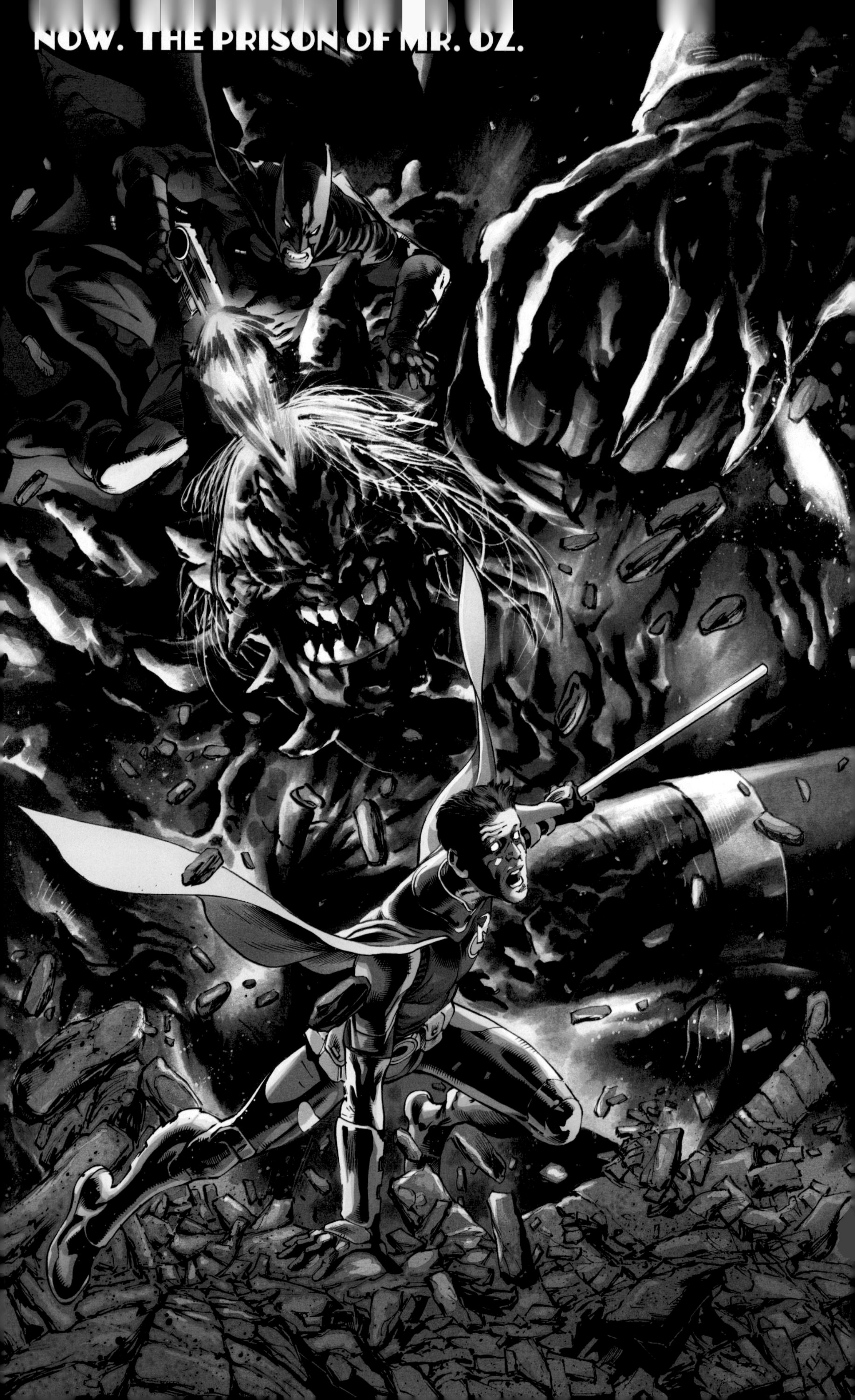
NOW. THE PRISON OF MR. OZ.

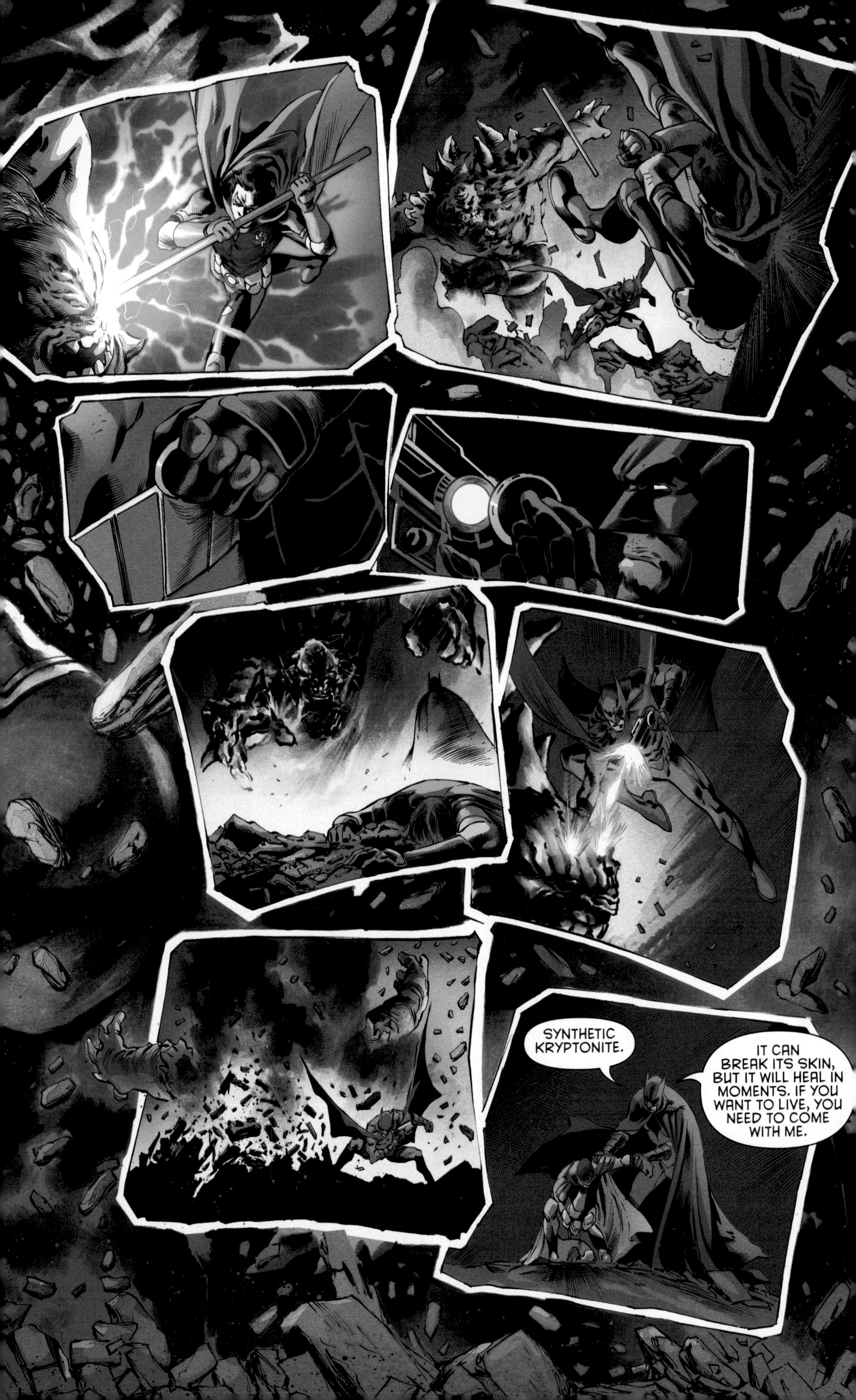
SYNTHETIC KRYPTONITE.
IT CAN BREAK ITS SKIN, BUT IT WILL HEAL IN MOMENTS. IF YOU WANT TO LIVE, YOU NEED TO COME WITH ME.

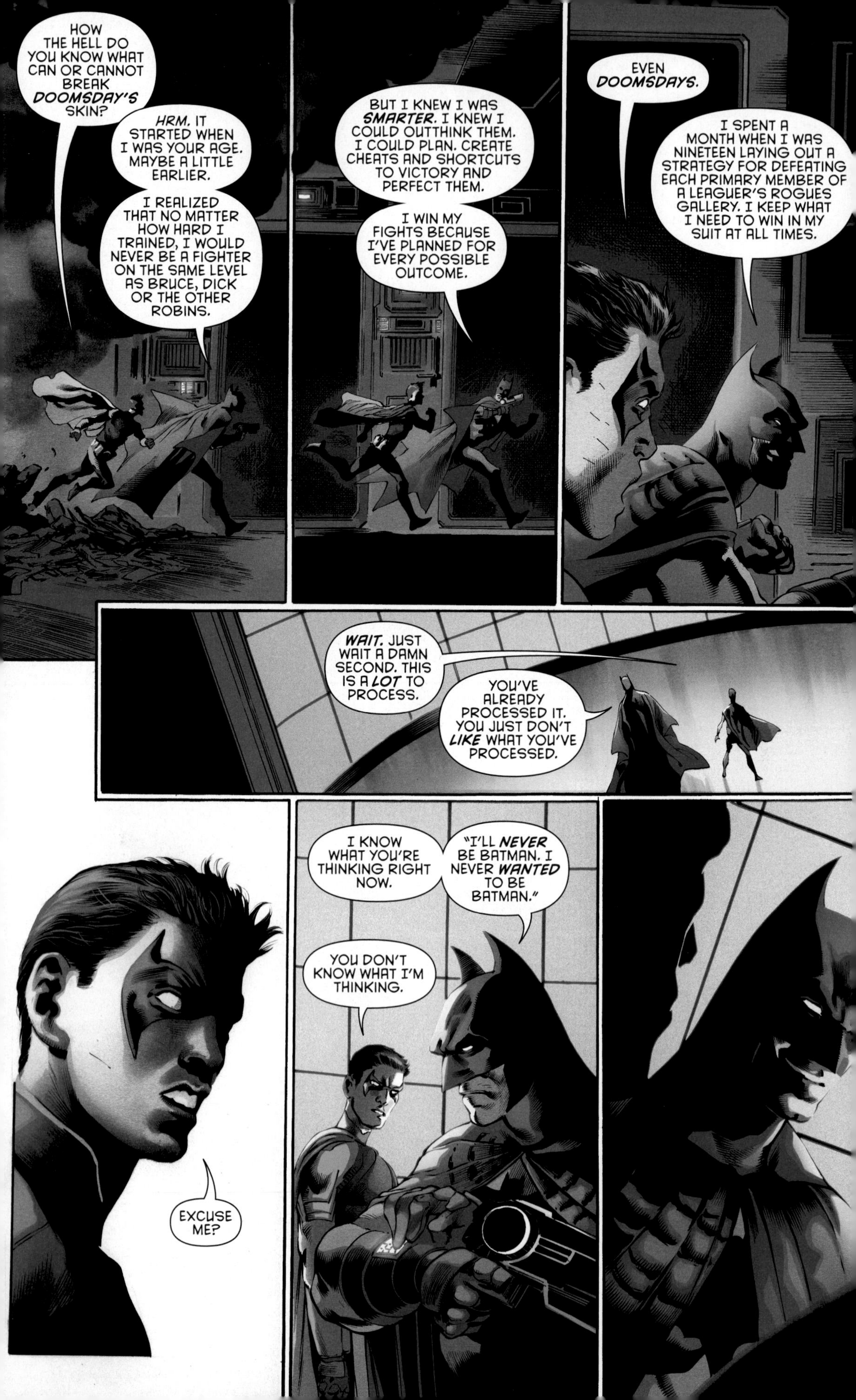
HOW THE HELL DO YOU KNOW WHAT CAN OR CANNOT BREAK DOOMSDAY'S SKIN?
HRM. IT STARTED WHEN I WAS YOUR AGE. MAYBE A LITTLE EARLIER.
I REALIZED THAT NO MATTER HOW HARD I TRAINED, I WOULD NEVER BE A FIGHTER ON THE SAME LEVEL AS BRUCE, DICK OR THE OTHER ROBINS.
BUT I KNEW I WAS SMARTER. I KNEW I COULD OUTTHINK THEM. I COULD PLAN. CREATE CHEATS AND SHORTCUTS TO VICTORY AND PERFECT THEM.
I WIN MY FIGHTS BECAUSE I'VE PLANNED FOR EVERY POSSIBLE OUTCOME.
EVEN DOOMSDAYS.
I SPENT A MONTH WHEN I WAS NINETEEN LAYING OUT A STRATEGY FOR DEFEATING EACH PRIMARY MEMBER OF A LEAGUER'S ROGUES GALLERY. I KEEP WHAT I NEED TO WIN IN MY SUIT AT ALL TIMES.
WAIT. JUST WAIT A DAMN SECOND. THIS IS A LOT TO PROCESS.
YOU'VE ALREADY PROCESSED IT. YOU JUST DON'T LIKE WHAT YOU'VE PROCESSED.
EXCUSE ME?
I KNOW WHAT YOU'RE THINKING RIGHT NOW.
"I'LL NEVER BE BATMAN. I NEVER WANTED TO BE BATMAN."
YOU DON'T KNOW WHAT I'M THINKING.

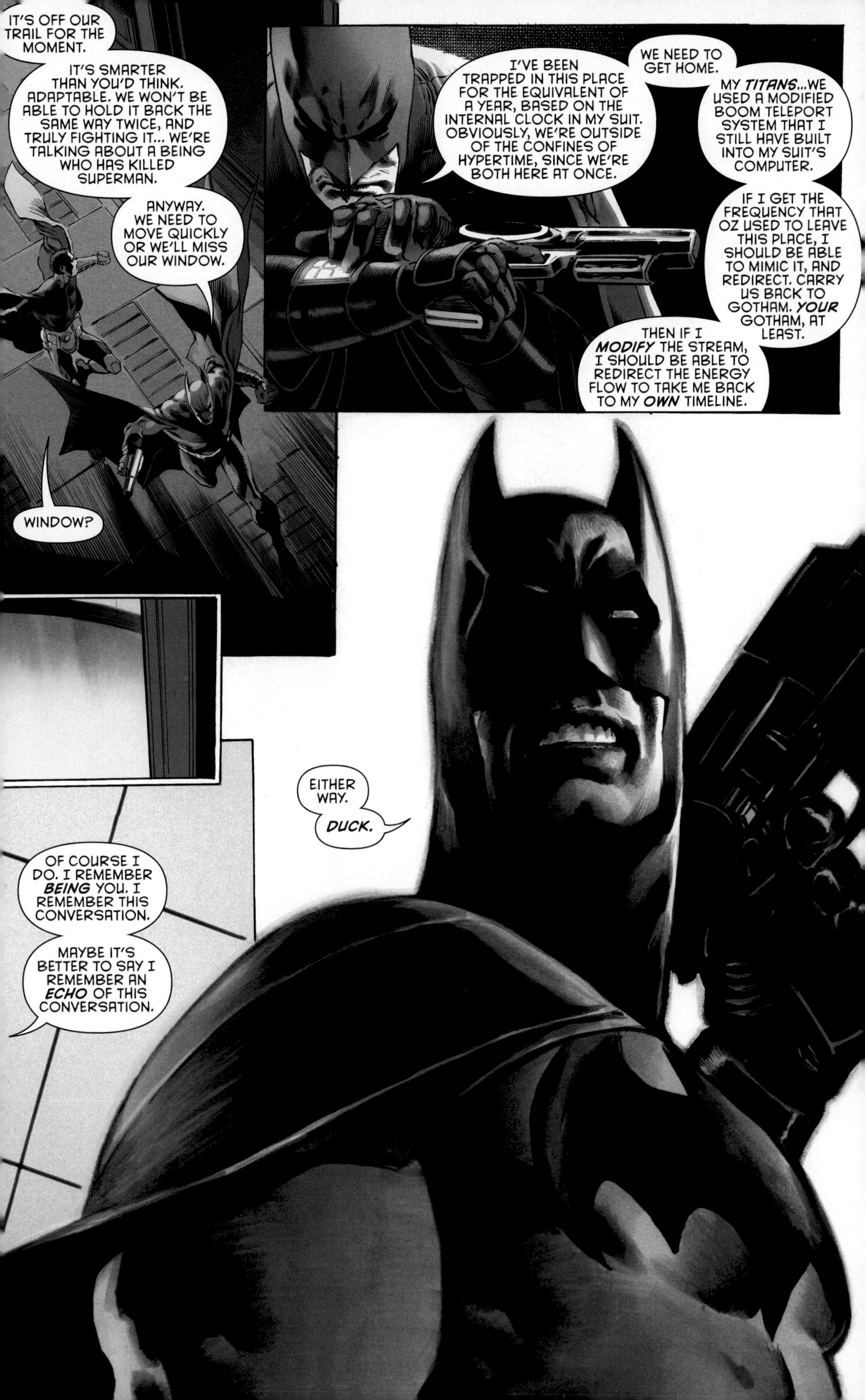
IT'S OFF OUR TRAIL FOR THE MOMENT.
IT'S SMARTER THAN YOU'D THINK. ADAPTABLE. WE WON'T BE ABLE TO HOLD IT BACK THE SAME WAY TWICE, AND TRULY FIGHTING IT... WE'RE TALKING ABOUT A BEING WHO HAS KILLED SUPERMAN.
ANYWAY. WE NEED TO MOVE QUICKLY OR WE'LL MISS OUR WINDOW.
WINDOW?
I'VE BEEN TRAPPED IN THIS PLACE FOR THE EQUIVALENT OF A YEAR, BASED ON THE INTERNAL CLOCK IN MY SUIT. OBVIOUSLY, WE'RE OUTSIDE OF THE CONFINES OF HYPERTIME, SINCE WE'RE BOTH HERE AT ONCE.
WE NEED TO GET HOME.
MY *TITANS*...WE USED A MODIFIED BOOM TELEPORT SYSTEM THAT I STILL HAVE BUILT INTO MY SUIT'S COMPUTER.
IF I GET THE FREQUENCY THAT OZ USED TO LEAVE THIS PLACE, I SHOULD BE ABLE TO MIMIC IT, AND REDIRECT. CARRY US BACK TO GOTHAM. *YOUR* GOTHAM, AT LEAST.
THEN IF I *MODIFY* THE STREAM, I SHOULD BE ABLE TO REDIRECT THE ENERGY FLOW TO TAKE ME BACK TO MY *OWN* TIMELINE.
OF COURSE I DO. I REMEMBER *BEING* YOU. I REMEMBER THIS CONVERSATION.
MAYBE IT'S BETTER TO SAY I REMEMBER AN *ECHO* OF THIS CONVERSATION.
EITHER WAY.
DUCK.

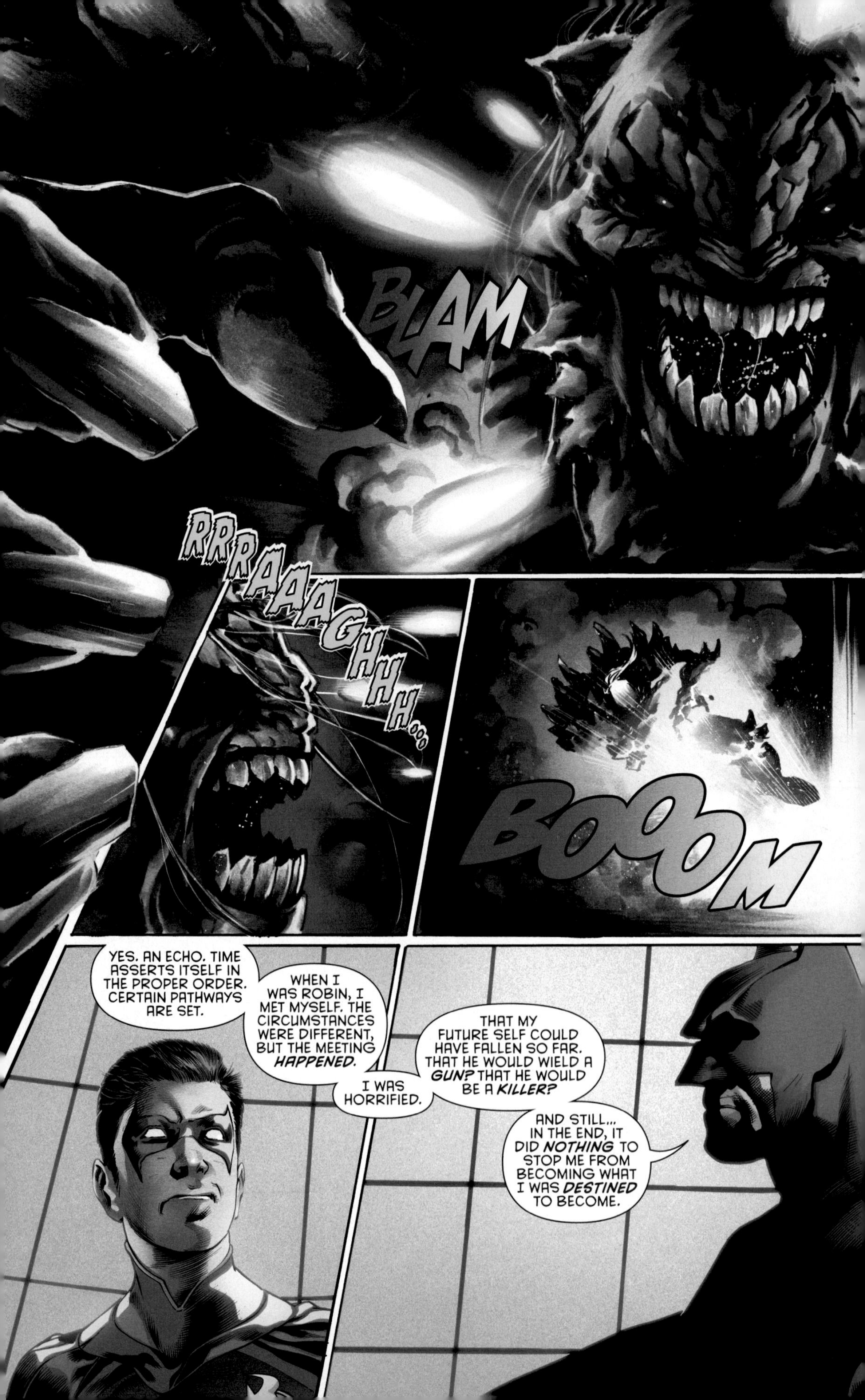
BLAM
RRRAAAAGHHH...
BOOOOM
YES. AN ECHO. TIME ASSERTS ITSELF IN THE PROPER ORDER. CERTAIN PATHWAYS ARE SET.
WHEN I WAS ROBIN, I MET MYSELF. THE CIRCUMSTANCES WERE DIFFERENT, BUT THE MEETING HAPPENED.
I WAS HORRIFIED.
THAT MY FUTURE SELF COULD HAVE FALLEN SO FAR. THAT HE WOULD WIELD A GUN? THAT HE WOULD BE A KILLER?
AND STILL... IN THE END, IT DID NOTHING TO STOP ME FROM BECOMING WHAT I WAS DESTINED TO BECOME.

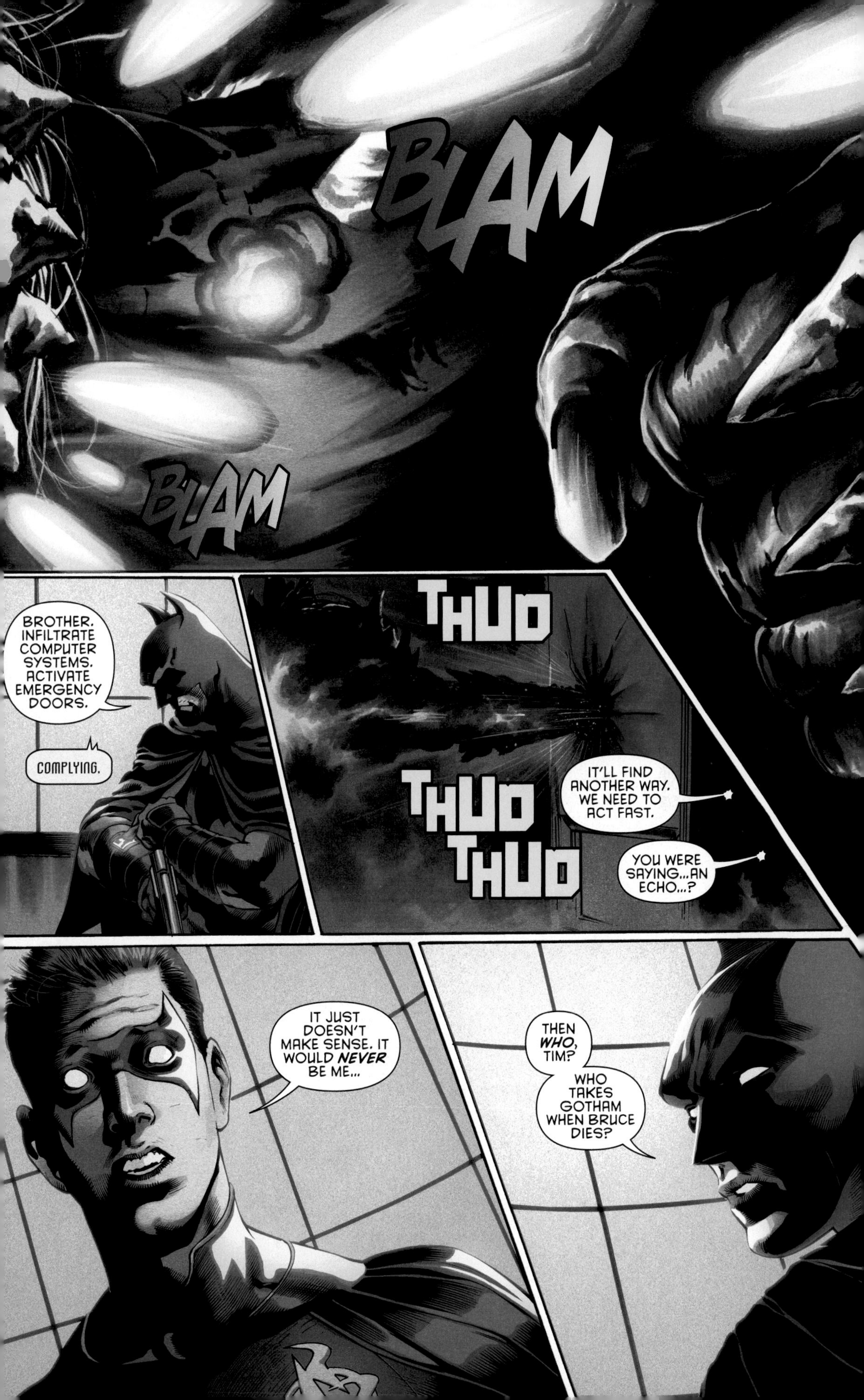
BLAM
BLAM
BROTHER. INFILTRATE COMPUTER SYSTEMS. ACTIVATE EMERGENCY DOORS.
COMPLYING.
THUD
THUD
THUD
THUD
IT'LL FIND ANOTHER WAY. WE NEED TO ACT FAST.
YOU WERE SAYING...AN ECHO...?
IT JUST DOESN'T MAKE SENSE. IT WOULD *NEVER* BE ME...
THEN *WHO*, TIM?
WHO TAKES GOTHAM WHEN BRUCE DIES?

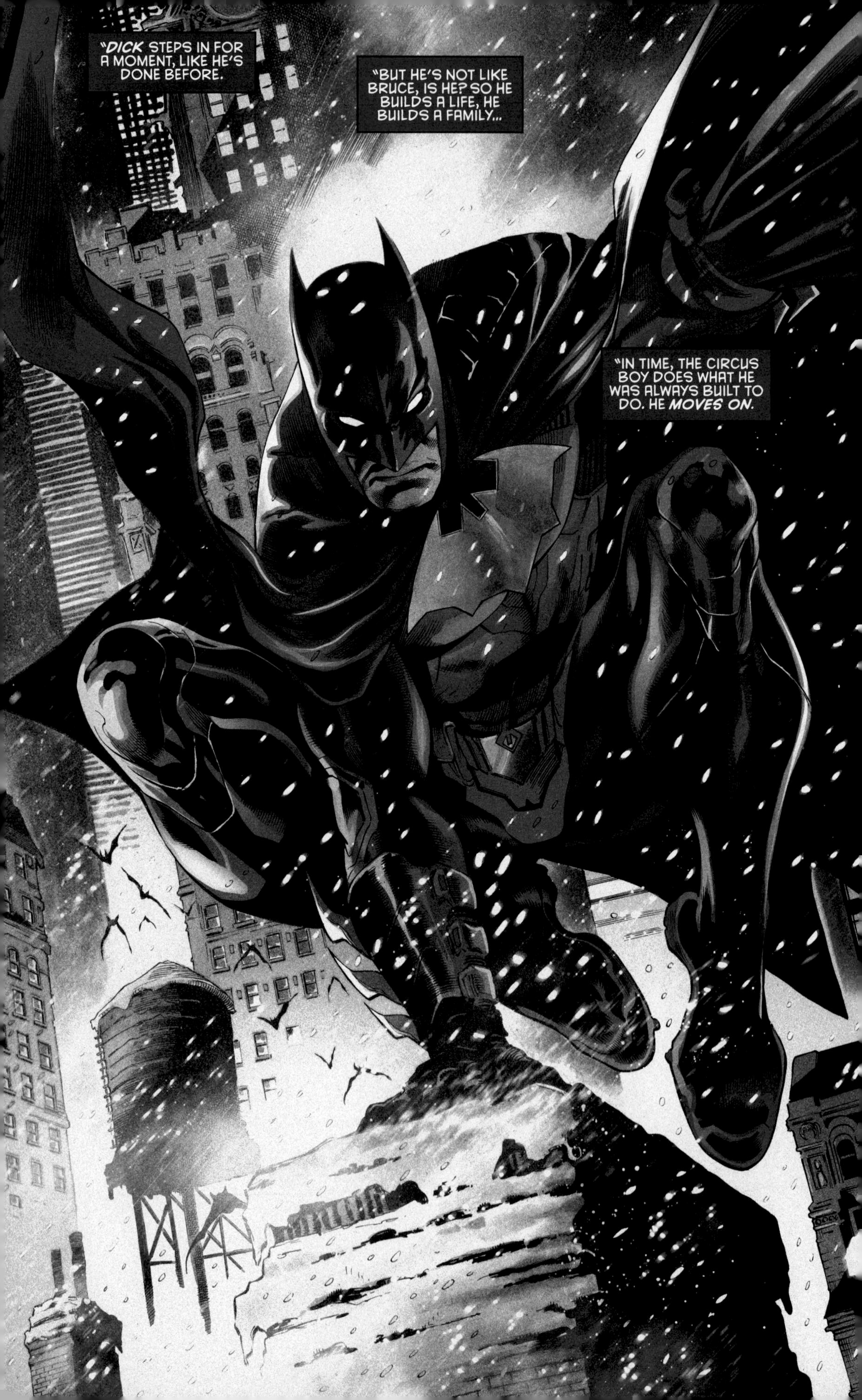
"DICK STEPS IN FOR A MOMENT, LIKE HE'S DONE BEFORE.
"BUT HE'S NOT LIKE BRUCE, IS HE? SO HE BUILDS A LIFE, HE BUILDS A FAMILY...
"IN TIME, THE CIRCUS BOY DOES WHAT HE WAS ALWAYS BUILT TO DO. HE MOVES ON.

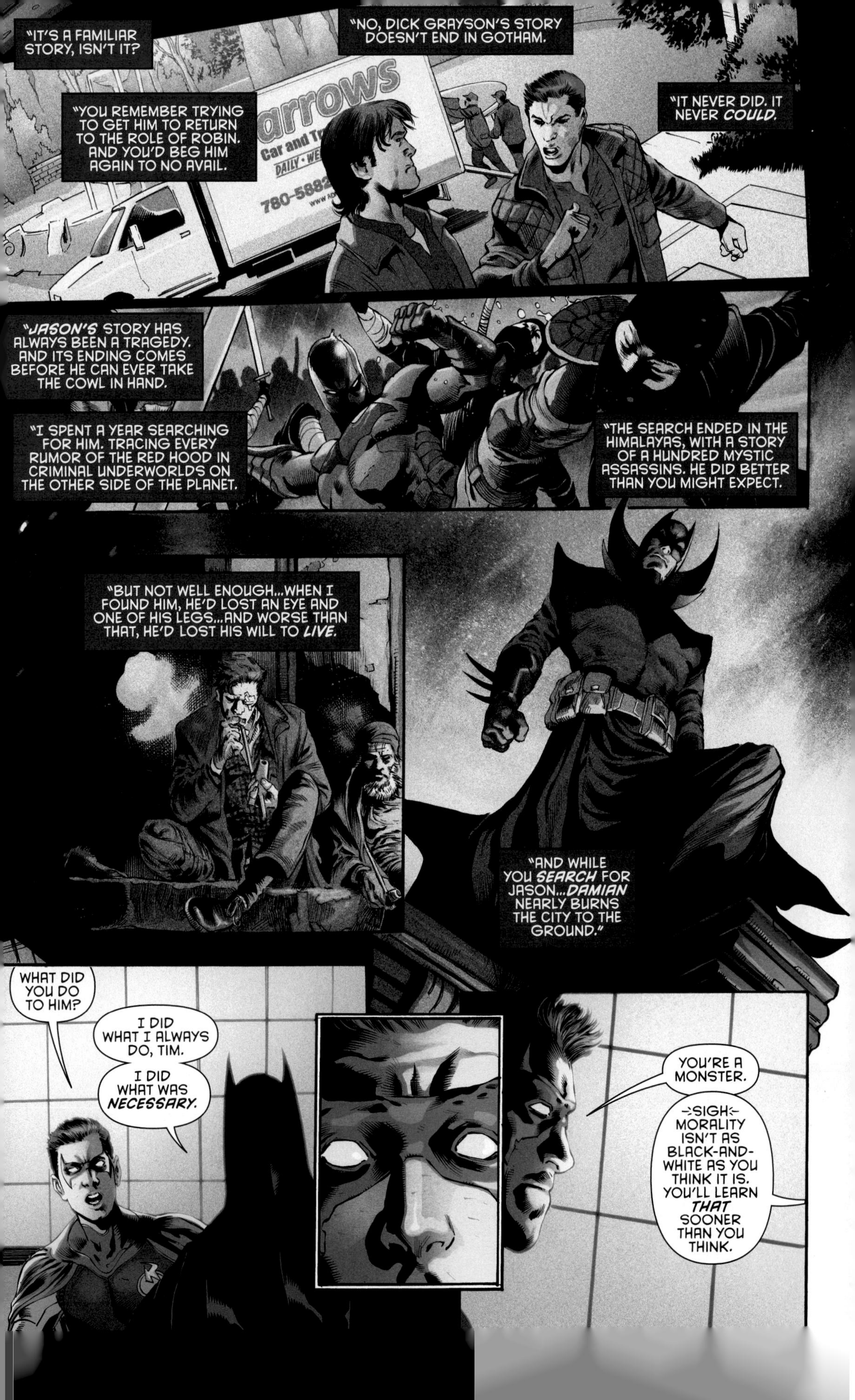

"IT'S A FAMILIAR STORY, ISN'T IT?
"NO, DICK GRAYSON'S STORY DOESN'T END IN GOTHAM.
"YOU REMEMBER TRYING TO GET HIM TO RETURN TO THE ROLE OF ROBIN. AND YOU'D BEG HIM AGAIN TO NO AVAIL.
"IT NEVER DID. IT NEVER COULD.
"JASON'S STORY HAS ALWAYS BEEN A TRAGEDY. AND ITS ENDING COMES BEFORE HE CAN EVER TAKE THE COWL IN HAND.
"I SPENT A YEAR SEARCHING FOR HIM. TRACING EVERY RUMOR OF THE RED HOOD IN CRIMINAL UNDERWORLDS ON THE OTHER SIDE OF THE PLANET.
"THE SEARCH ENDED IN THE HIMALAYAS, WITH A STORY OF A HUNDRED MYSTIC ASSASSINS. HE DID BETTER THAN YOU MIGHT EXPECT.
"BUT NOT WELL ENOUGH...WHEN I FOUND HIM, HE'D LOST AN EYE AND ONE OF HIS LEGS...AND WORSE THAN THAT, HE'D LOST HIS WILL TO LIVE.
"AND WHILE YOU SEARCH FOR JASON...DAMIAN NEARLY BURNS THE CITY TO THE GROUND."
WHAT DID YOU DO TO HIM?
I DID WHAT I ALWAYS DO, TIM.
I DID WHAT WAS NECESSARY.
YOU'RE A MONSTER.
-SIGH- MORALITY ISN'T AS BLACK-AND-WHITE AS YOU THINK IT IS. YOU'LL LEARN THAT SOONER THAN YOU THINK.

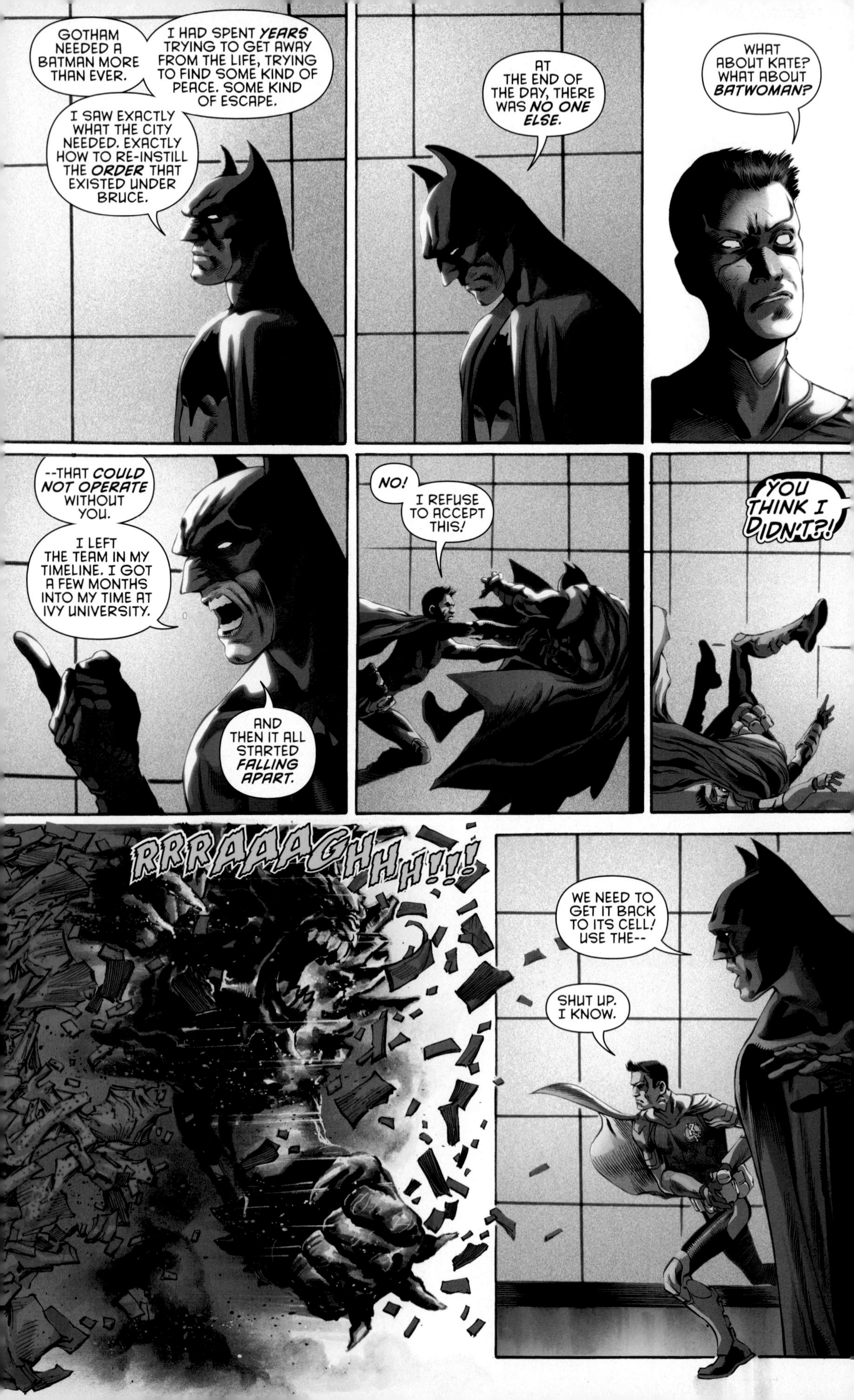
GOTHAM NEEDED A BATMAN MORE THAN EVER.
I HAD SPENT YEARS TRYING TO GET AWAY FROM THE LIFE, TRYING TO FIND SOME KIND OF PEACE. SOME KIND OF ESCAPE.
I SAW EXACTLY WHAT THE CITY NEEDED. EXACTLY HOW TO RE-INSTILL THE ORDER THAT EXISTED UNDER BRUCE.
AT THE END OF THE DAY, THERE WAS NO ONE ELSE.
WHAT ABOUT KATE? WHAT ABOUT BATWOMAN?
--THAT COULD NOT OPERATE WITHOUT YOU.
I LEFT THE TEAM IN MY TIMELINE. I GOT A FEW MONTHS INTO MY TIME AT IVY UNIVERSITY.
AND THEN IT ALL STARTED FALLING APART.
NO!
I REFUSE TO ACCEPT THIS!
YOU THINK I DIDN'T?!
RRRAAAGHHH!!!
WE NEED TO GET IT BACK TO ITS CELL! USE THE--
SHUT UP. I KNOW.

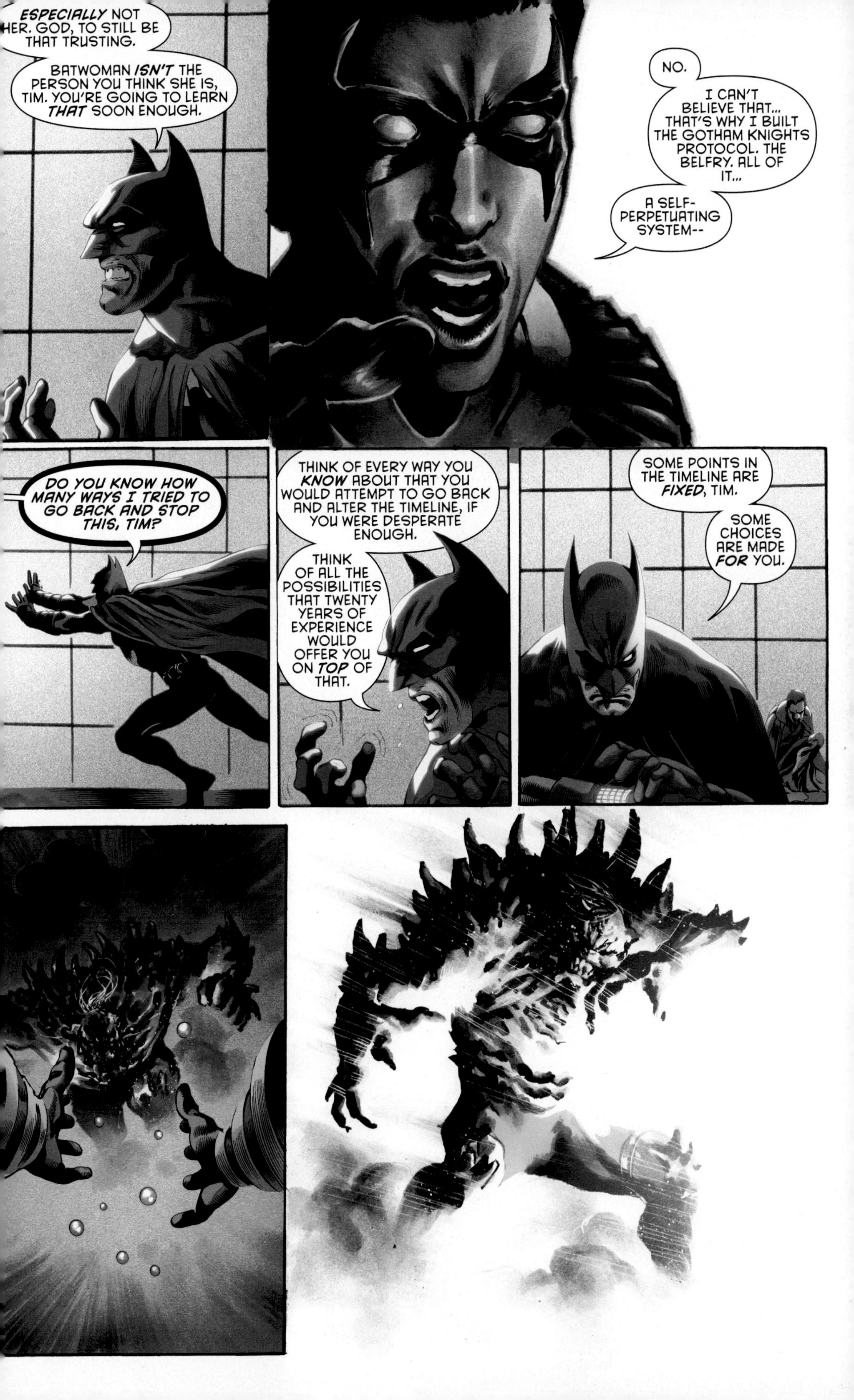

ESPECIALLY NOT HER. GOD, TO STILL BE THAT TRUSTING.
BATWOMAN ISN'T THE PERSON YOU THINK SHE IS, TIM. YOU'RE GOING TO LEARN THAT SOON ENOUGH.
NO.
I CAN'T BELIEVE THAT... THAT'S WHY I BUILT THE GOTHAM KNIGHTS PROTOCOL. THE BELFRY. ALL OF IT...
A SELF-PERPETUATING SYSTEM--
DO YOU KNOW HOW MANY WAYS I TRIED TO GO BACK AND STOP THIS, TIM?
THINK OF EVERY WAY YOU KNOW ABOUT THAT YOU WOULD ATTEMPT TO GO BACK AND ALTER THE TIMELINE, IF YOU WERE DESPERATE ENOUGH.
THINK OF ALL THE POSSIBILITIES THAT TWENTY YEARS OF EXPERIENCE WOULD OFFER YOU ON TOP OF THAT.
SOME POINTS IN THE TIMELINE ARE FIXED, TIM.
SOME CHOICES ARE MADE FOR YOU.

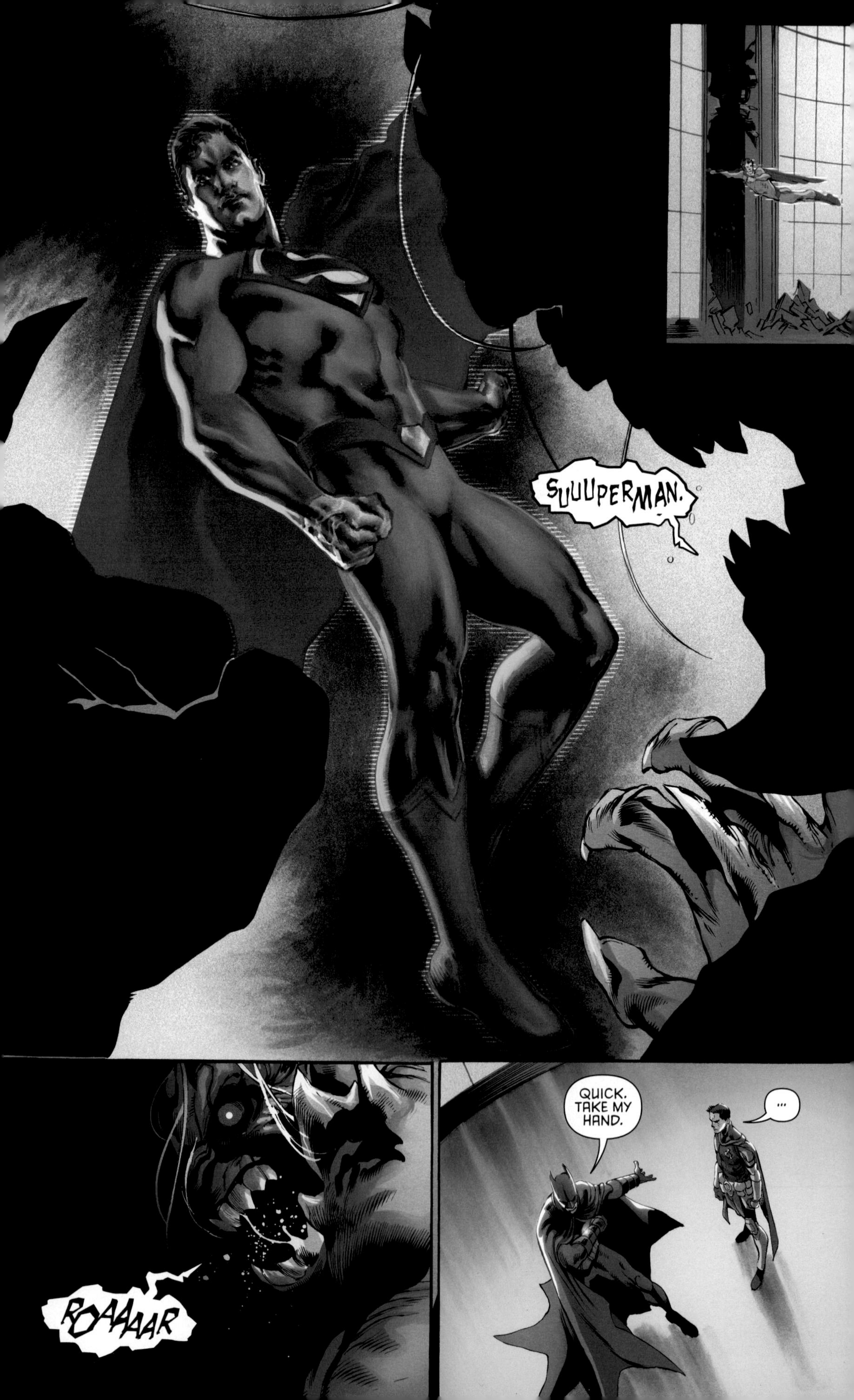
SUUUPERMAN.
ROAAAAR
QUICK. TAKE MY HAND.
...

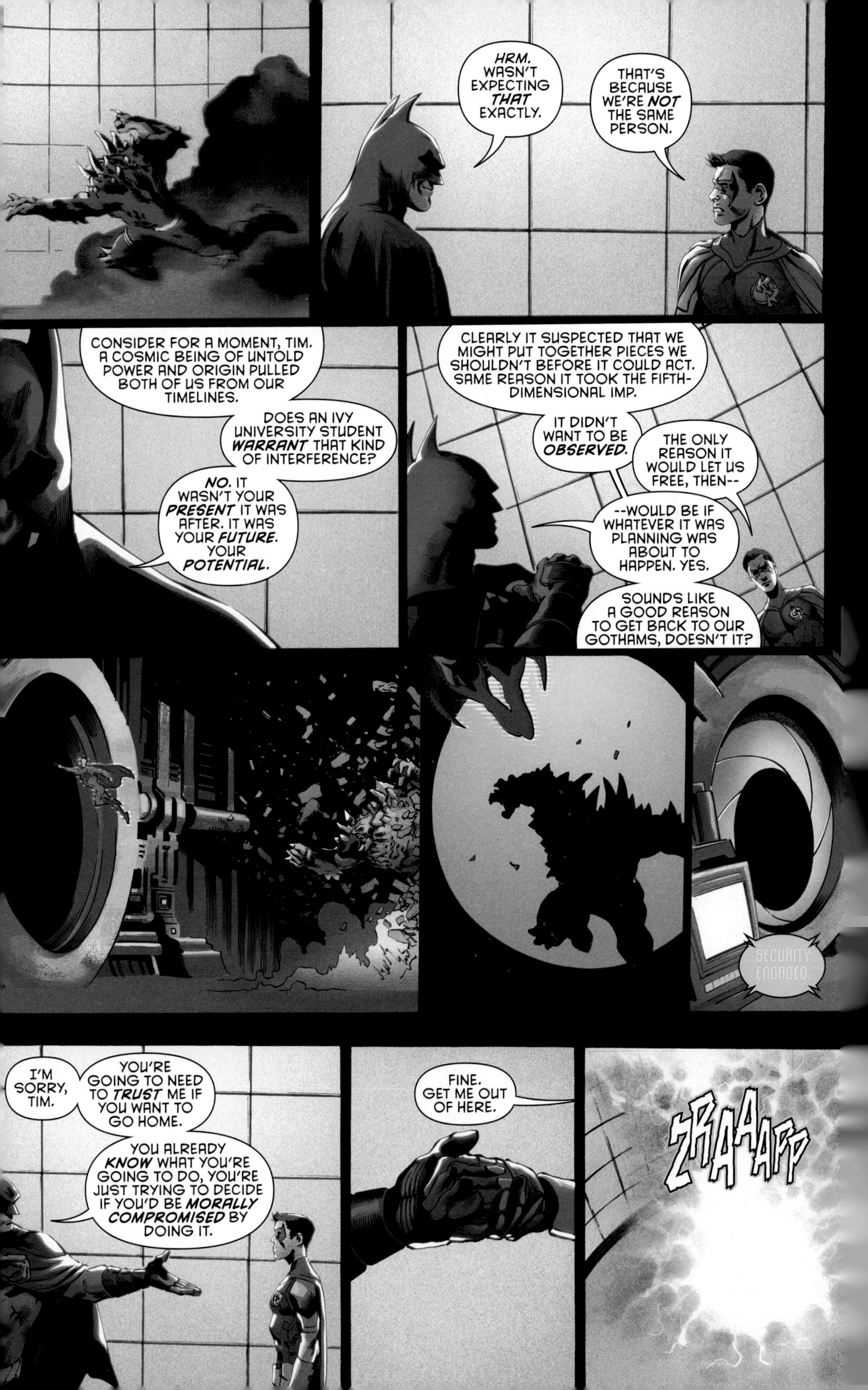
HRM. WASN'T EXPECTING THAT EXACTLY.
THAT'S BECAUSE WE'RE NOT THE SAME PERSON.
CONSIDER FOR A MOMENT, TIM. A COSMIC BEING OF UNTOLD POWER AND ORIGIN PULLED BOTH OF US FROM OUR TIMELINES.
DOES AN IVY UNIVERSITY STUDENT WARRANT THAT KIND OF INTERFERENCE?
NO. IT WASN'T YOUR PRESENT IT WAS AFTER. IT WAS YOUR FUTURE. YOUR POTENTIAL.
CLEARLY IT SUSPECTED THAT WE MIGHT PUT TOGETHER PIECES WE SHOULDN'T BEFORE IT COULD ACT. SAME REASON IT TOOK THE FIFTH-DIMENSIONAL IMP.
IT DIDN'T WANT TO BE OBSERVED.
THE ONLY REASON IT WOULD LET US FREE, THEN--
--WOULD BE IF WHATEVER IT WAS PLANNING WAS ABOUT TO HAPPEN. YES.
SOUNDS LIKE A GOOD REASON TO GET BACK TO OUR GOTHAMS, DOESN'T IT?
SECURITY ENGAGED.
I'M SORRY, TIM.
YOU'RE GOING TO NEED TO TRUST ME IF YOU WANT TO GO HOME.
YOU ALREADY KNOW WHAT YOU'RE GOING TO DO, YOU'RE JUST TRYING TO DECIDE IF YOU'D BE MORALLY COMPROMISED BY DOING IT.
FINE. GET ME OUT OF HERE.
ZRAAAPP

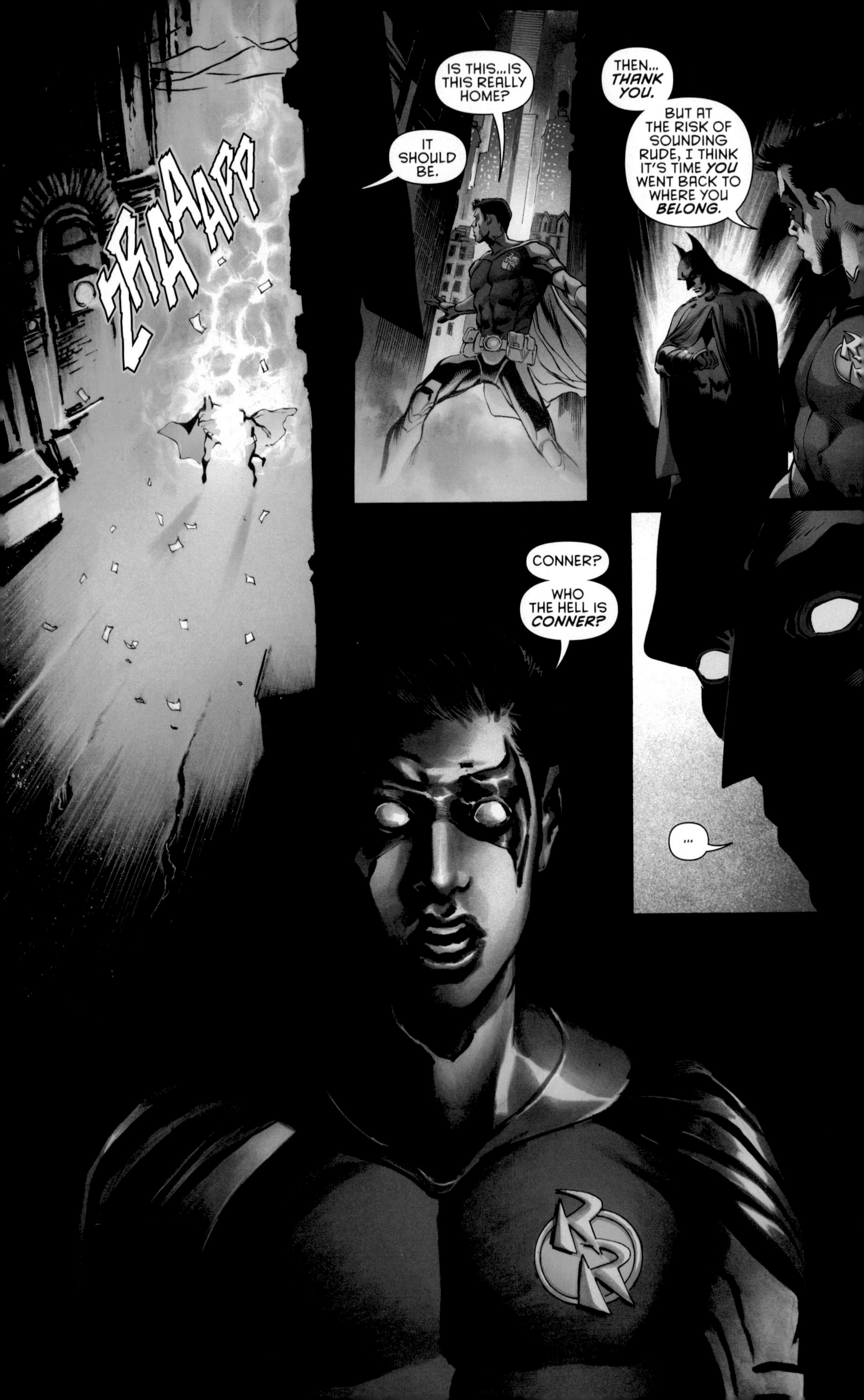
ZRAAPP
IS THIS...IS THIS REALLY HOME?
IT SHOULD BE.
THEN... THANK YOU.
BUT AT THE RISK OF SOUNDING RUDE, I THINK IT'S TIME YOU WENT BACK TO WHERE YOU BELONG.
CONNER?
WHO THE HELL IS CONNER?
...

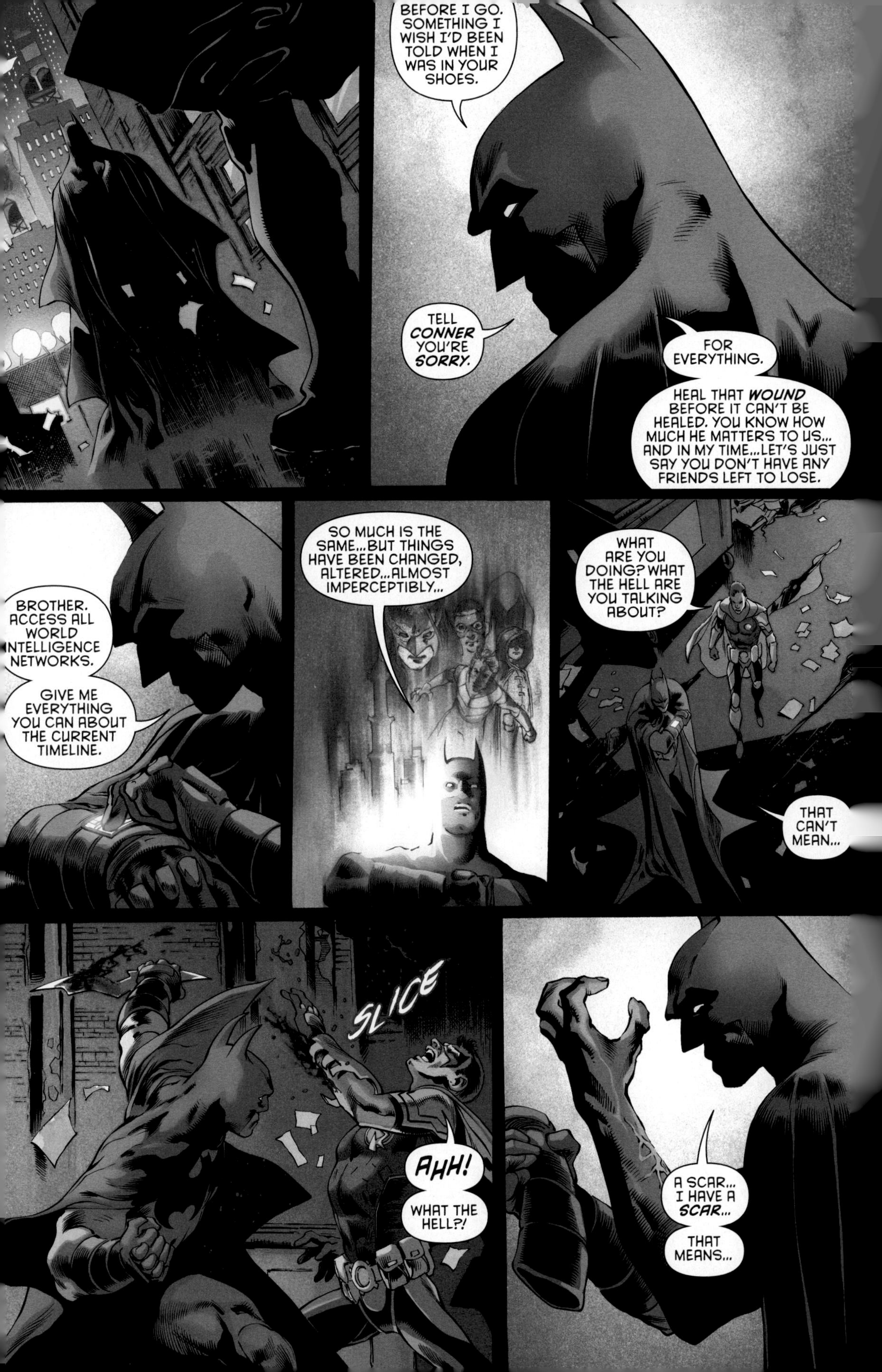
BEFORE I GO. SOMETHING I WISH I'D BEEN TOLD WHEN I WAS IN YOUR SHOES.
TELL CONNER YOU'RE SORRY.
FOR EVERYTHING.
HEAL THAT WOUND BEFORE IT CAN'T BE HEALED. YOU KNOW HOW MUCH HE MATTERS TO US... AND IN MY TIME...LET'S JUST SAY YOU DON'T HAVE ANY FRIENDS LEFT TO LOSE.
BROTHER. ACCESS ALL WORLD INTELLIGENCE NETWORKS.
GIVE ME EVERYTHING YOU CAN ABOUT THE CURRENT TIMELINE.
SO MUCH IS THE SAME...BUT THINGS HAVE BEEN CHANGED, ALTERED...ALMOST IMPERCEPTIBLY...
WHAT ARE YOU DOING? WHAT THE HELL ARE YOU TALKING ABOUT?
THAT CAN'T MEAN...
SLICE
AHH!
WHAT THE HELL?!
A SCAR... I HAVE A SCAR...
THAT MEANS...

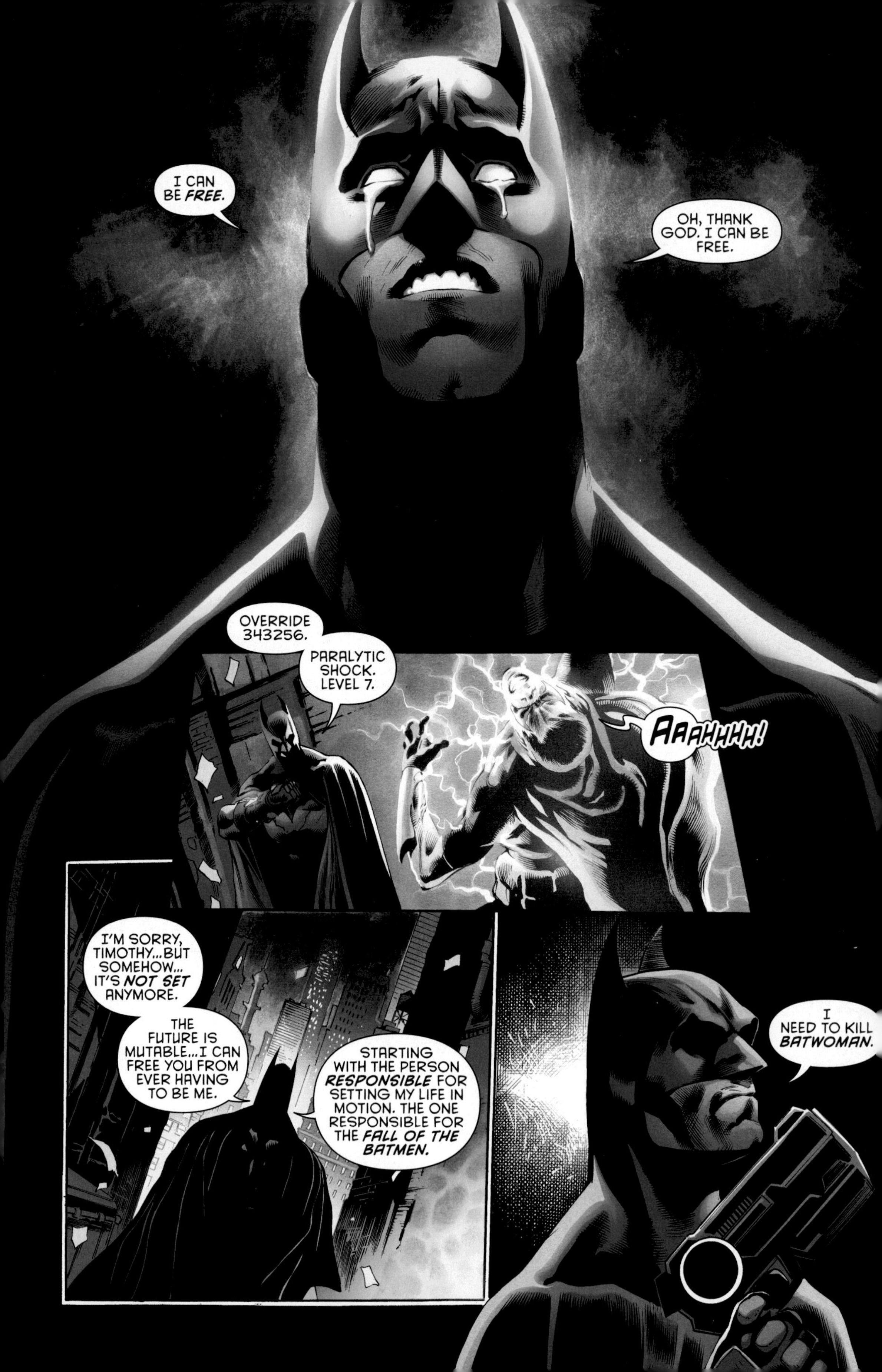

I CAN BE FREE.
OH, THANK GOD. I CAN BE FREE.
OVERRIDE 343256.
PARALYTIC SHOCK. LEVEL 7.
AAAHHHH!
I'M SORRY, TIMOTHY...BUT SOMEHOW... IT'S NOT SET ANYMORE.
THE FUTURE IS MUTABLE...I CAN FREE YOU FROM EVER HAVING TO BE ME.
STARTING WITH THE PERSON RESPONSIBLE FOR SETTING MY LIFE IN MOTION. THE ONE RESPONSIBLE FOR THE FALL OF THE BATMEN.
I NEED TO KILL BATWOMAN.

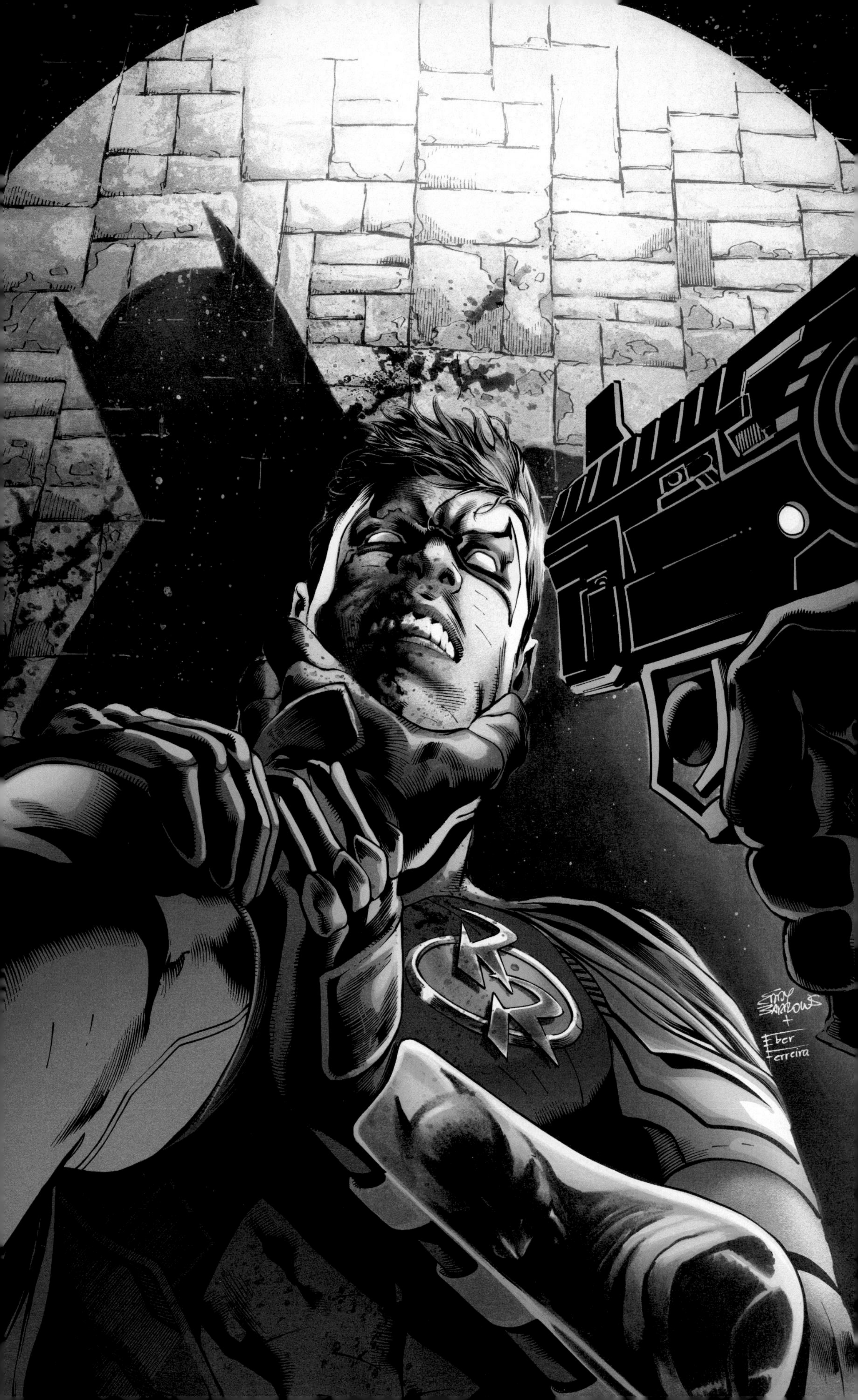

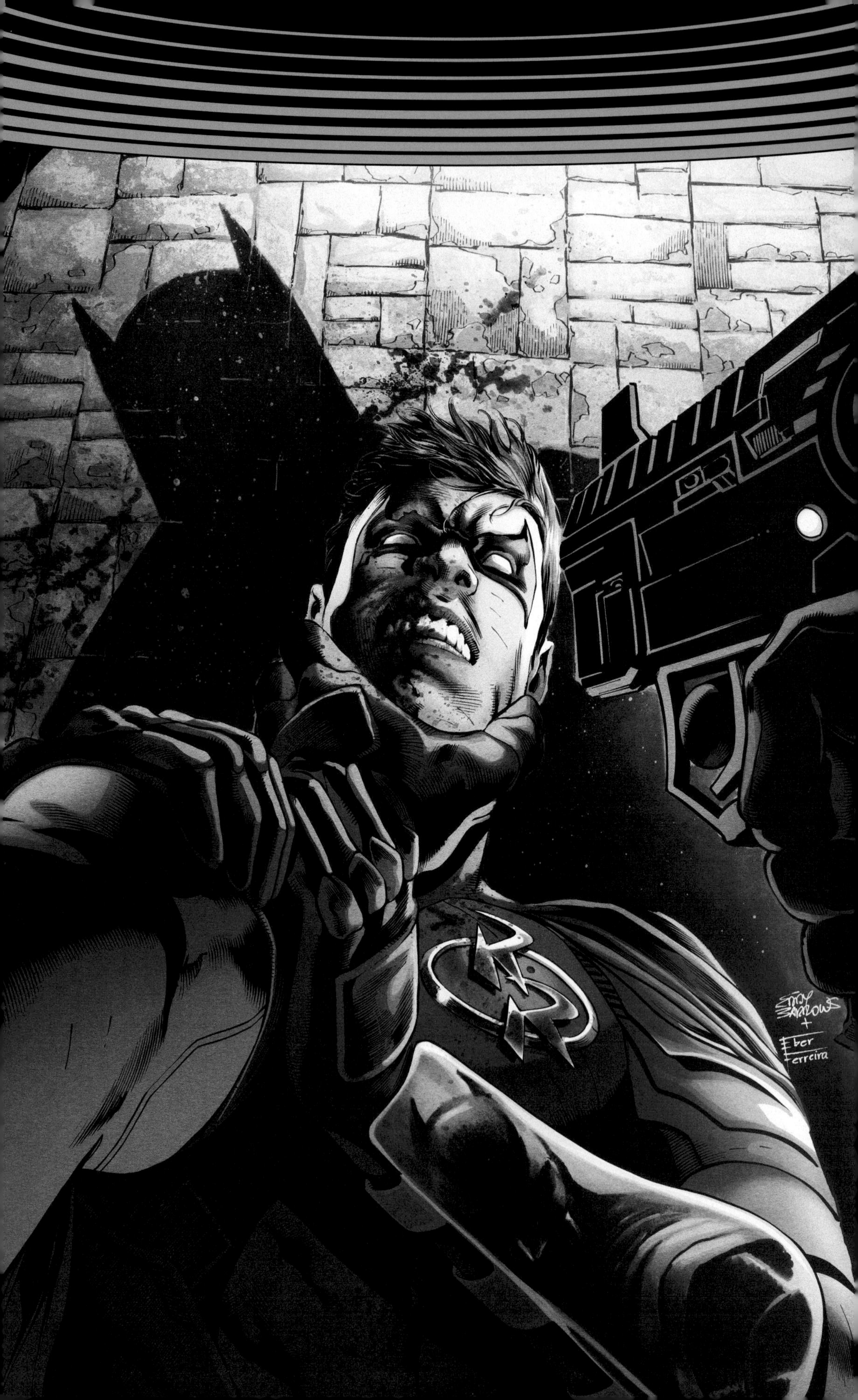

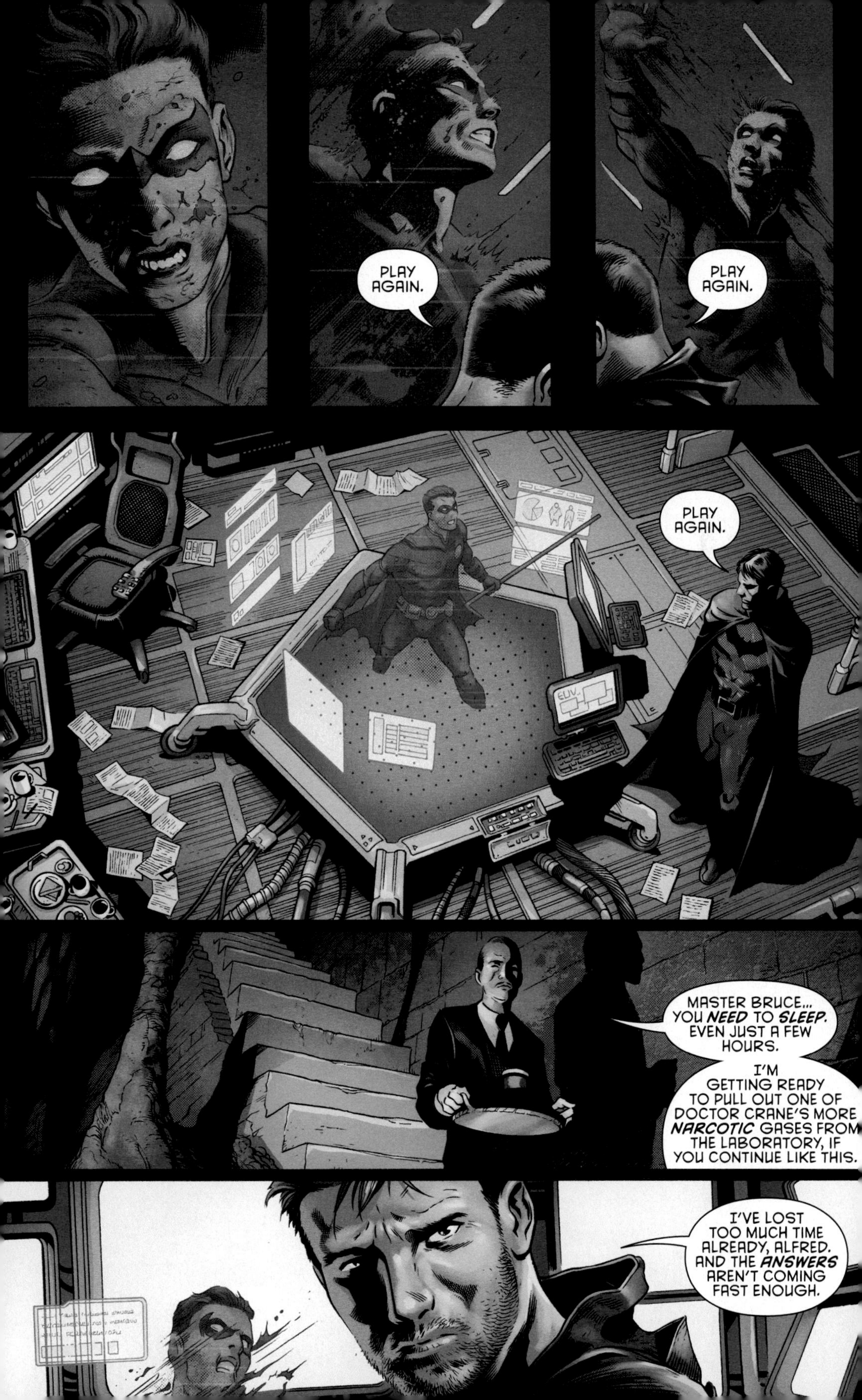
PLAY AGAIN.
PLAY AGAIN.
PLAY AGAIN.
MASTER BRUCE... YOU NEED TO SLEEP. EVEN JUST A FEW HOURS.
I'M GETTING READY TO PULL OUT ONE OF DOCTOR CRANE'S MORE NARCOTIC GASES FROM THE LABORATORY, IF YOU CONTINUE LIKE THIS.
I'VE LOST TOO MUCH TIME ALREADY, ALFRED. AND THE ANSWERS AREN'T COMING FAST ENOUGH.

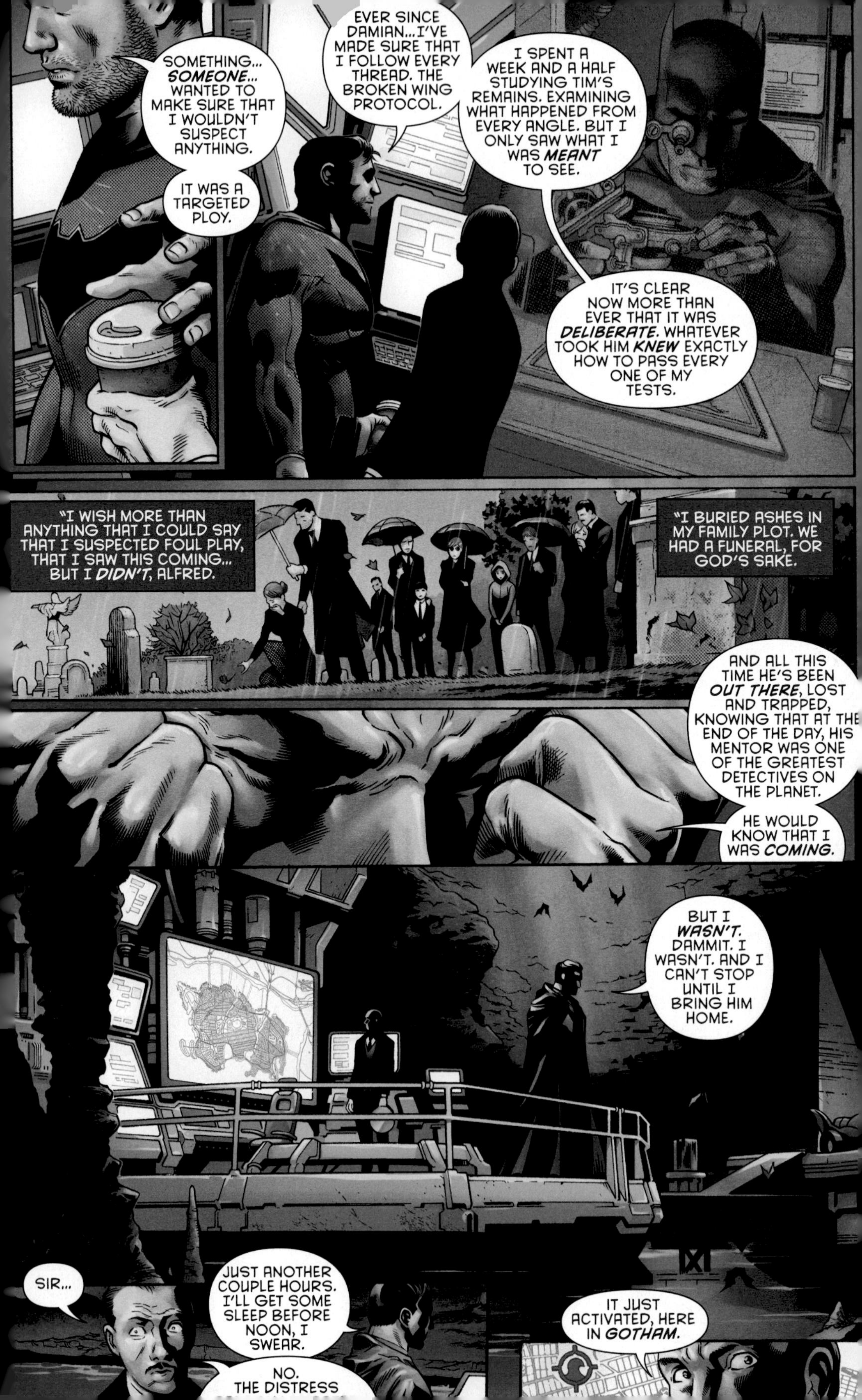
SOMETHING... SOMEONE... WANTED TO MAKE SURE THAT I WOULDN'T SUSPECT ANYTHING.
IT WAS A TARGETED PLOY.
EVER SINCE DAMIAN...I'VE MADE SURE THAT I FOLLOW EVERY THREAD. THE BROKEN WING PROTOCOL.
I SPENT A WEEK AND A HALF STUDYING TIM'S REMAINS. EXAMINING WHAT HAPPENED FROM EVERY ANGLE. BUT I ONLY SAW WHAT I WAS MEANT TO SEE.
IT'S CLEAR NOW MORE THAN EVER THAT IT WAS DELIBERATE. WHATEVER TOOK HIM KNEW EXACTLY HOW TO PASS EVERY ONE OF MY TESTS.
"I WISH MORE THAN ANYTHING THAT I COULD SAY THAT I SUSPECTED FOUL PLAY, THAT I SAW THIS COMING... BUT I DIDN'T, ALFRED.
"I BURIED ASHES IN MY FAMILY PLOT. WE HAD A FUNERAL, FOR GOD'S SAKE.
AND ALL THIS TIME HE'S BEEN OUT THERE, LOST AND TRAPPED, KNOWING THAT AT THE END OF THE DAY, HIS MENTOR WAS ONE OF THE GREATEST DETECTIVES ON THE PLANET.
HE WOULD KNOW THAT I WAS COMING.
BUT I WASN'T. DAMMIT. I WASN'T. AND I CAN'T STOP UNTIL I BRING HIM HOME.
SIR...
JUST ANOTHER COUPLE HOURS. I'LL GET SOME SLEEP BEFORE NOON, I SWEAR.
NO. THE DISTRESS
IT JUST ACTIVATED, HERE IN GOTHAM.

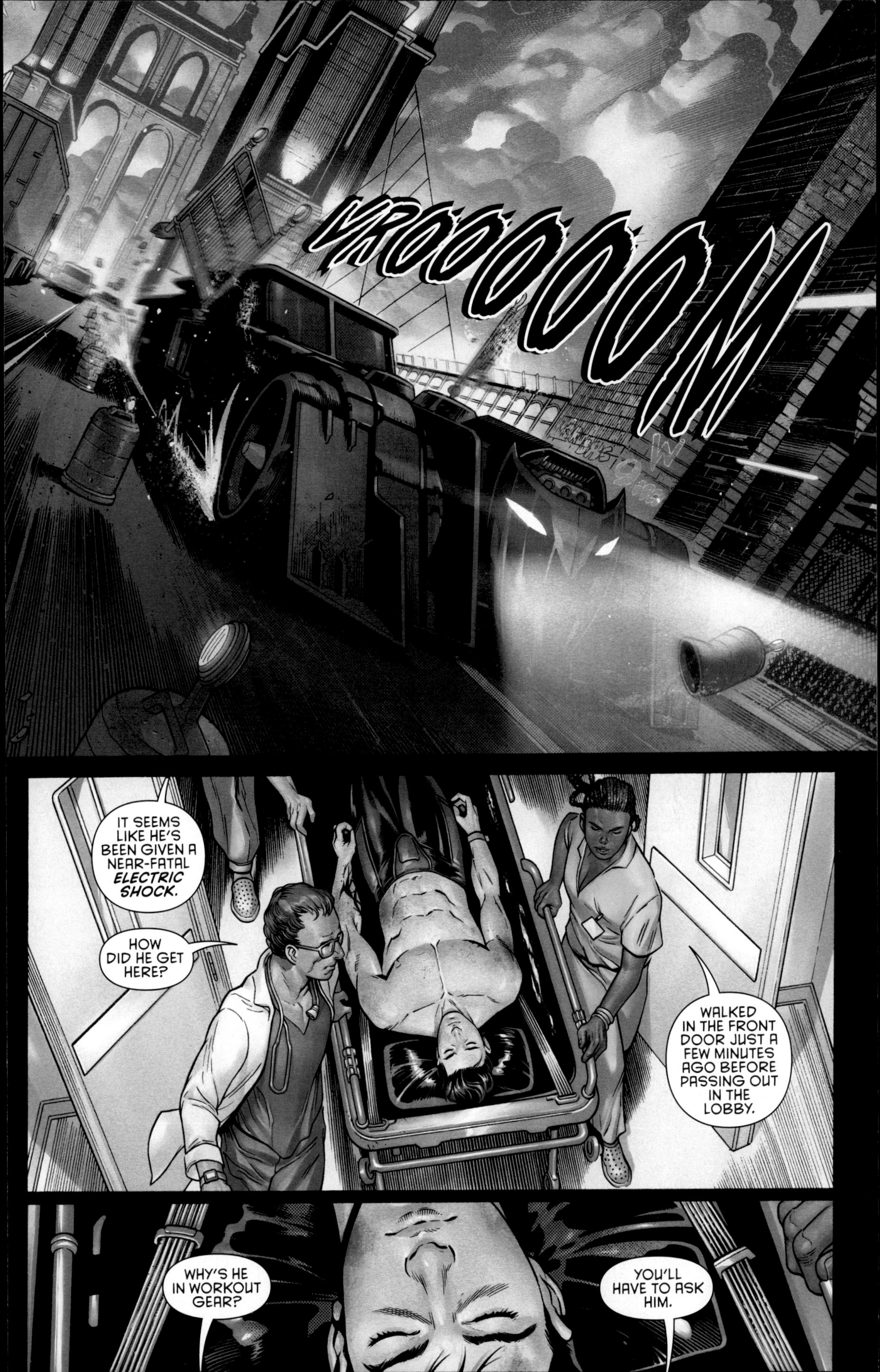
VROOOOOOM
IT SEEMS LIKE HE'S BEEN GIVEN A NEAR-FATAL *ELECTRIC SHOCK.*
HOW DID HE GET HERE?
WALKED IN THE FRONT DOOR JUST A FEW MINUTES AGO BEFORE PASSING OUT IN THE LOBBY.
WHY'S HE IN WORKOUT GEAR?
YOU'LL HAVE TO ASK HIM.

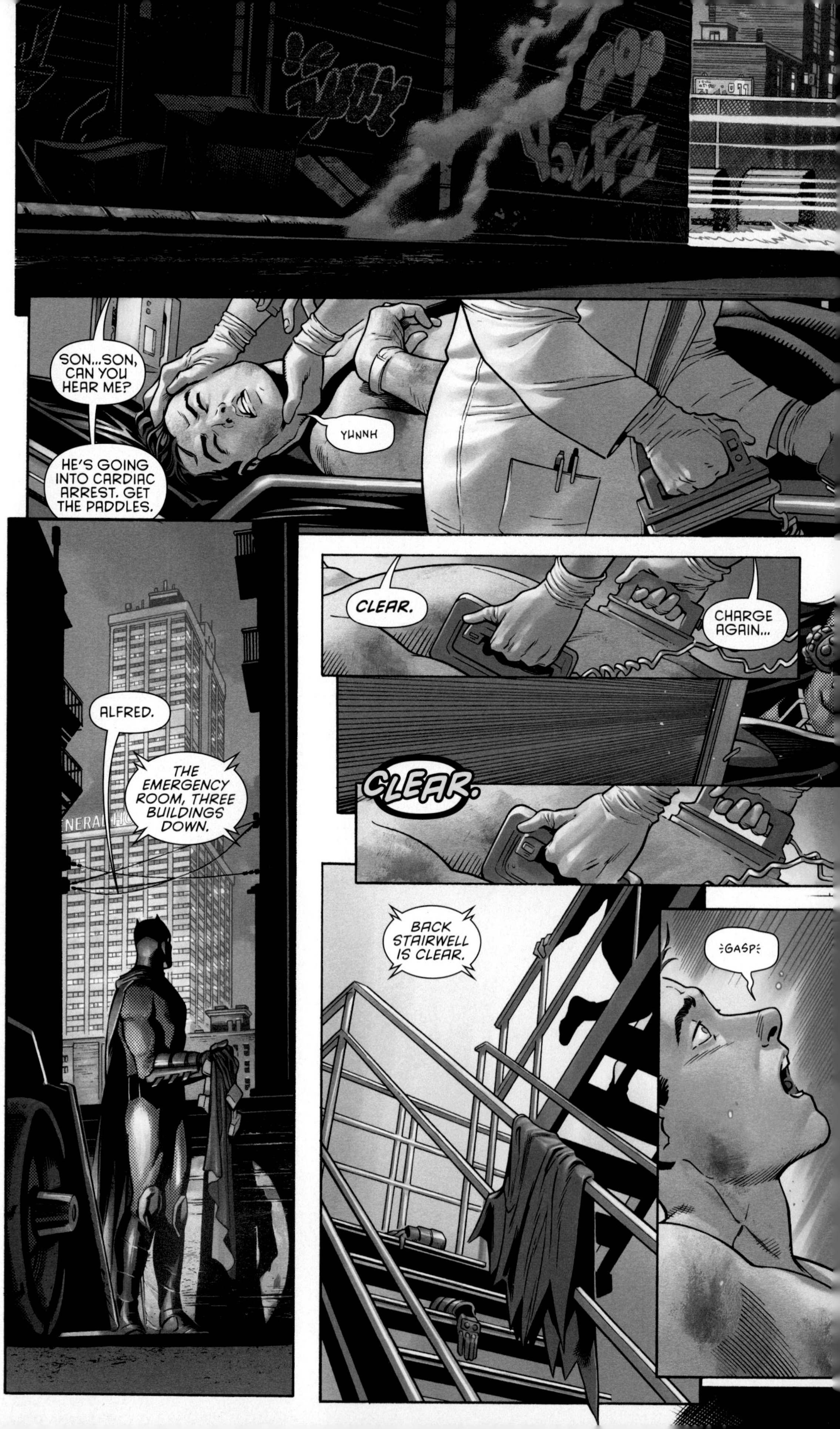
SON...SON, CAN YOU HEAR ME?
YUNNH
HE'S GOING INTO CARDIAC ARREST. GET THE PADDLES.
ALFRED.
THE EMERGENCY ROOM, THREE BUILDINGS DOWN.
CLEAR.
CHARGE AGAIN...
CLEAR.
BACK STAIRWELL IS CLEAR.
GASP

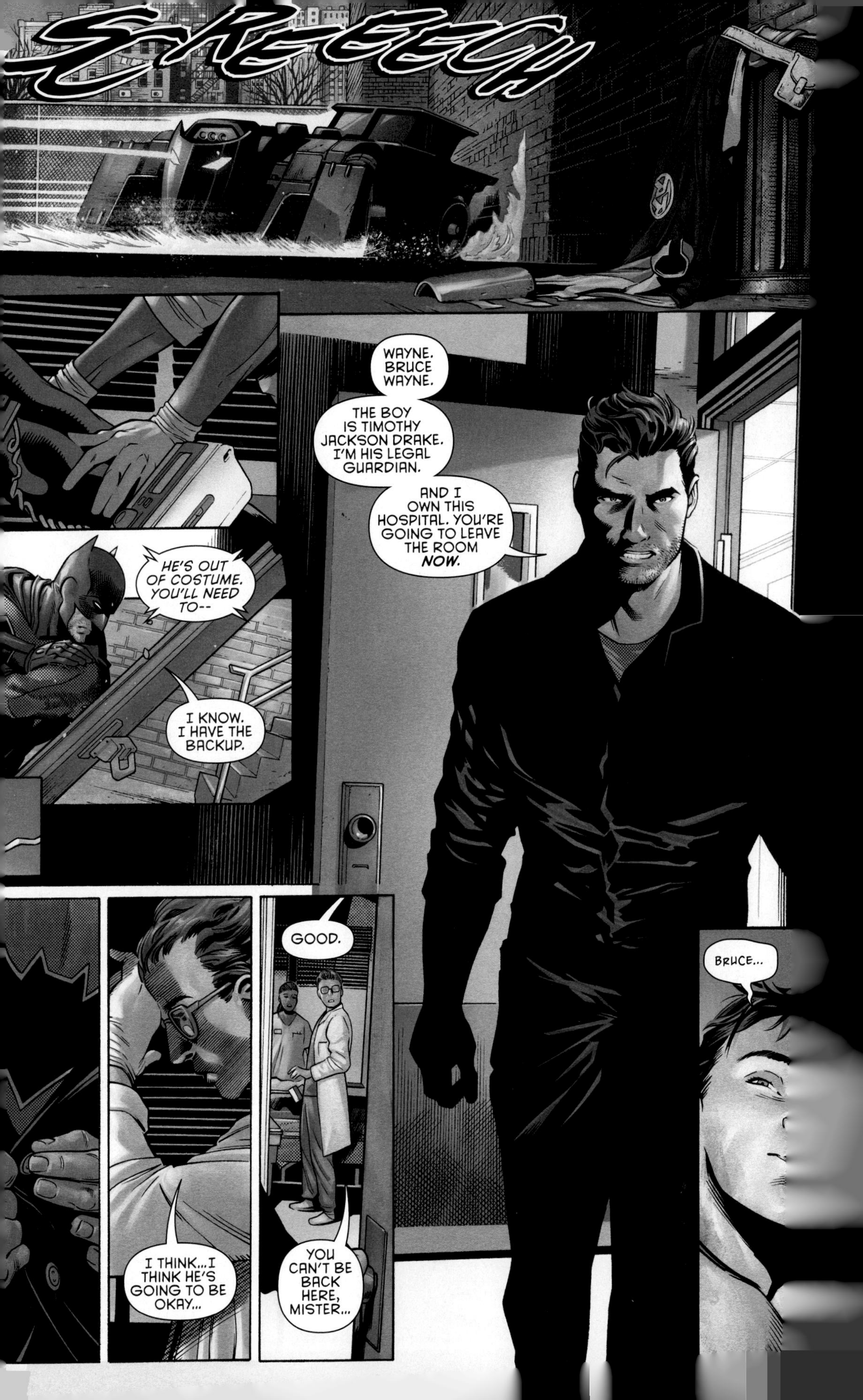
S-K-R-E-E-E-C-H
HE'S OUT OF COSTUME. YOU'LL NEED TO--
I KNOW. I HAVE THE BACKUP.
WAYNE. BRUCE WAYNE.
THE BOY IS TIMOTHY JACKSON DRAKE. I'M HIS LEGAL GUARDIAN.
AND I OWN THIS HOSPITAL. YOU'RE GOING TO LEAVE THE ROOM NOW.
I THINK... I THINK HE'S GOING TO BE OKAY...
GOOD.
YOU CAN'T BE BACK HERE, MISTER...
BRUCE...

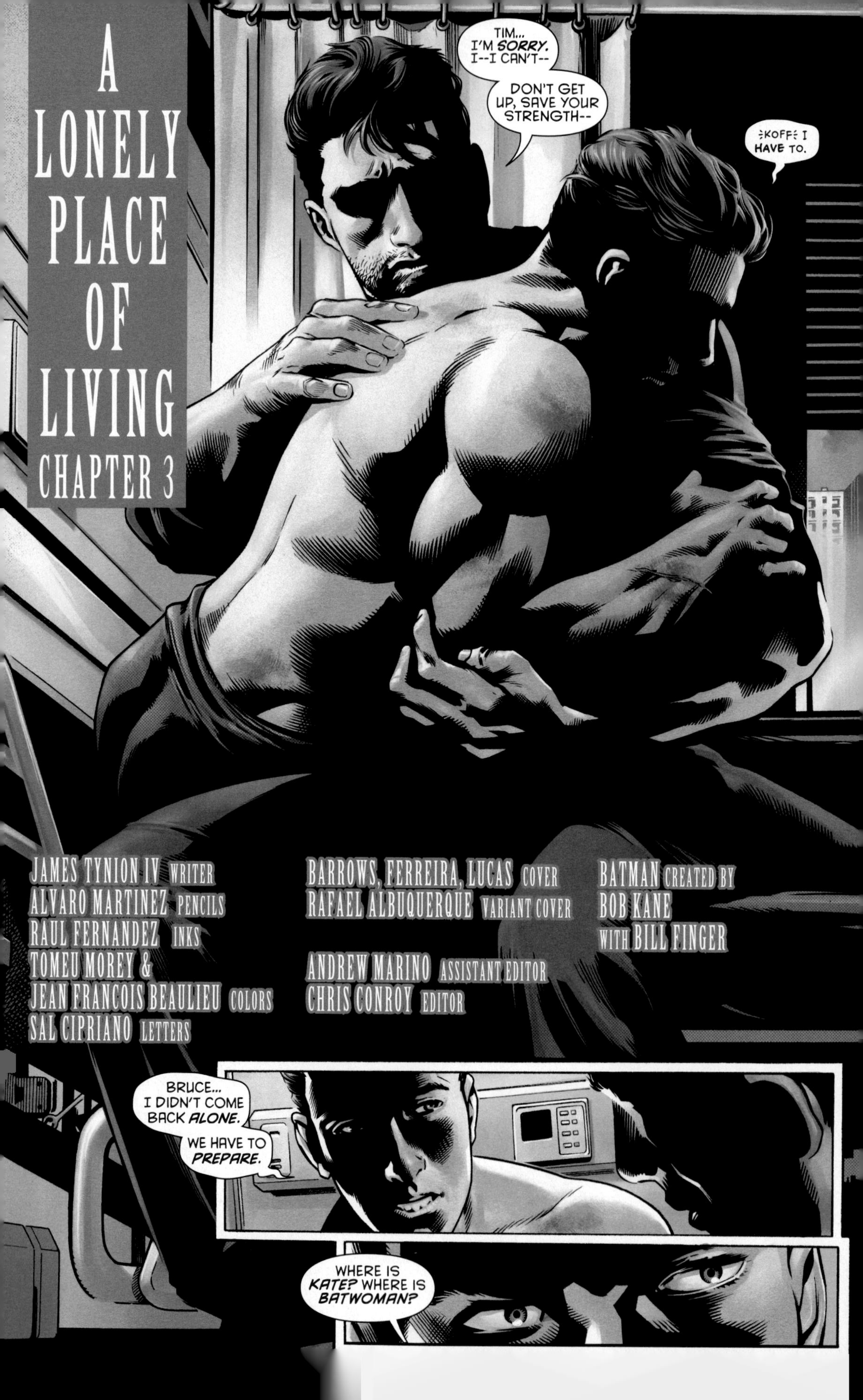
A LONELY PLACE OF LIVING
CHAPTER 3
TIM... I'M SORRY. I--I CAN'T--
DON'T GET UP, SAVE YOUR STRENGTH--
KOFF I HAVE TO.
JAMES TYNION IV WRITER
ALVARO MARTINEZ PENCILS
RAUL FERNANDEZ INKS
TOMEU MOREY & JEAN FRANCOIS BEAULIEU COLORS
SAL CIPRIANO LETTERS
BARROWS, FERREIRA, LUCAS COVER
RAFAEL ALBUQUERQUE VARIANT COVER
ANDREW MARINO ASSISTANT EDITOR
CHRIS CONROY EDITOR
BATMAN CREATED BY BOB KANE WITH BILL FINGER
BRUCE... I DIDN'T COME BACK ALONE.
WE HAVE TO PREPARE.
WHERE IS KATE? WHERE IS BATWOMAN?

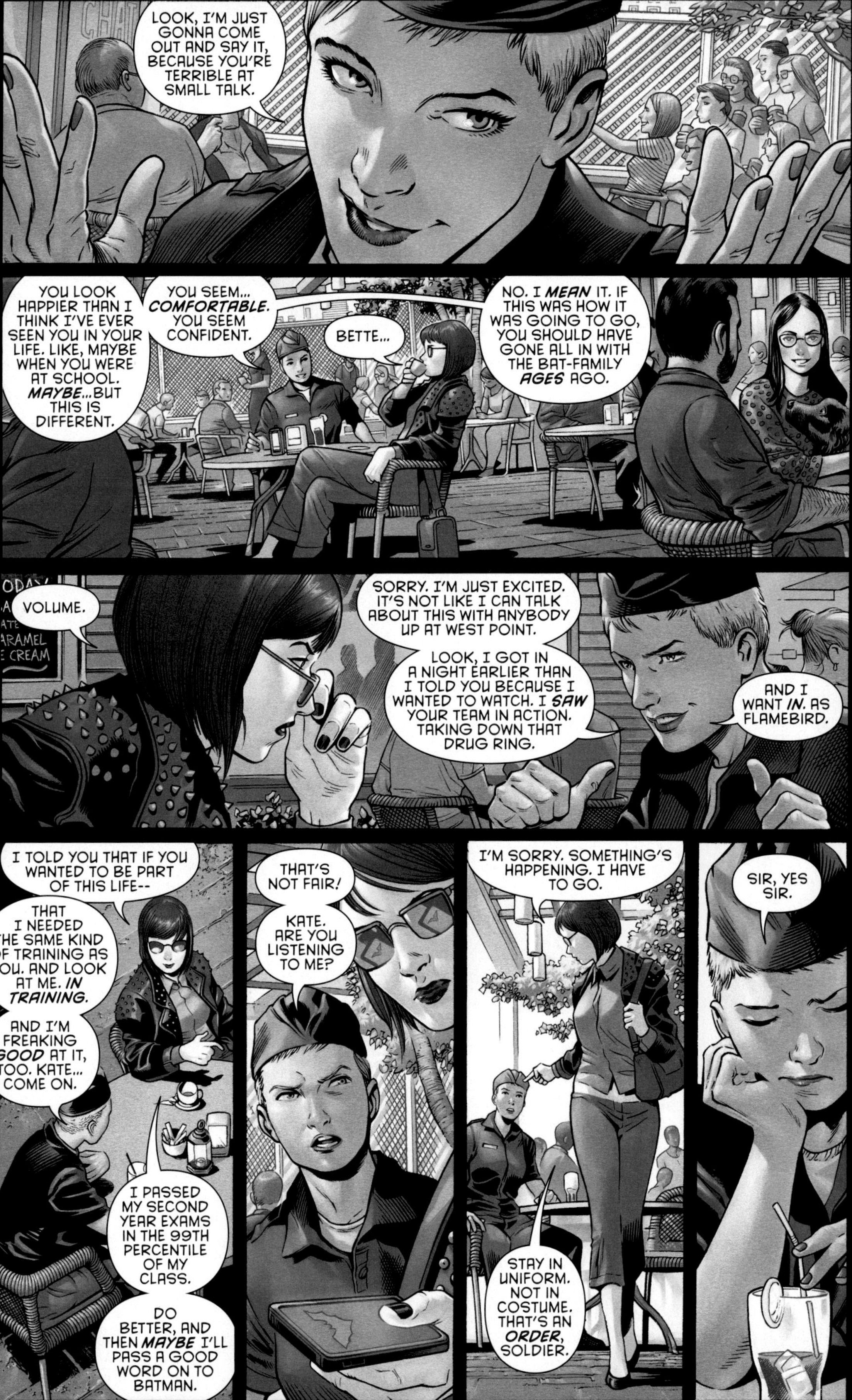
LOOK, I'M JUST GONNA COME OUT AND SAY IT, BECAUSE YOU'RE TERRIBLE AT SMALL TALK.
YOU LOOK HAPPIER THAN I THINK I'VE EVER SEEN YOU IN YOUR LIFE. LIKE, MAYBE WHEN YOU WERE AT SCHOOL. MAYBE...BUT THIS IS DIFFERENT.
YOU SEEM... COMFORTABLE. YOU SEEM CONFIDENT.
BETTE...
NO. I MEAN IT. IF THIS WAS HOW IT WAS GOING TO GO, YOU SHOULD HAVE GONE ALL IN WITH THE BAT-FAMILY AGES AGO.
VOLUME.
SORRY. I'M JUST EXCITED. IT'S NOT LIKE I CAN TALK ABOUT THIS WITH ANYBODY UP AT WEST POINT.
LOOK, I GOT IN A NIGHT EARLIER THAN I TOLD YOU BECAUSE I WANTED TO WATCH. I SAW YOUR TEAM IN ACTION. TAKING DOWN THAT DRUG RING.
AND I WANT IN. AS FLAMEBIRD.
I TOLD YOU THAT IF YOU WANTED TO BE PART OF THIS LIFE--
THAT I NEEDED THE SAME KIND OF TRAINING AS YOU. AND LOOK AT ME. IN TRAINING.
AND I'M FREAKING GOOD AT IT, TOO. KATE... COME ON.
I PASSED MY SECOND YEAR EXAMS IN THE 99TH PERCENTILE OF MY CLASS.
DO BETTER, AND THEN MAYBE I'LL PASS A GOOD WORD ON TO BATMAN.
THAT'S NOT FAIR!
KATE. ARE YOU LISTENING TO ME?
I'M SORRY. SOMETHING'S HAPPENING. I HAVE TO GO.
STAY IN UNIFORM. NOT IN COSTUME. THAT'S AN ORDER, SOLDIER.
SIR, YES SIR.

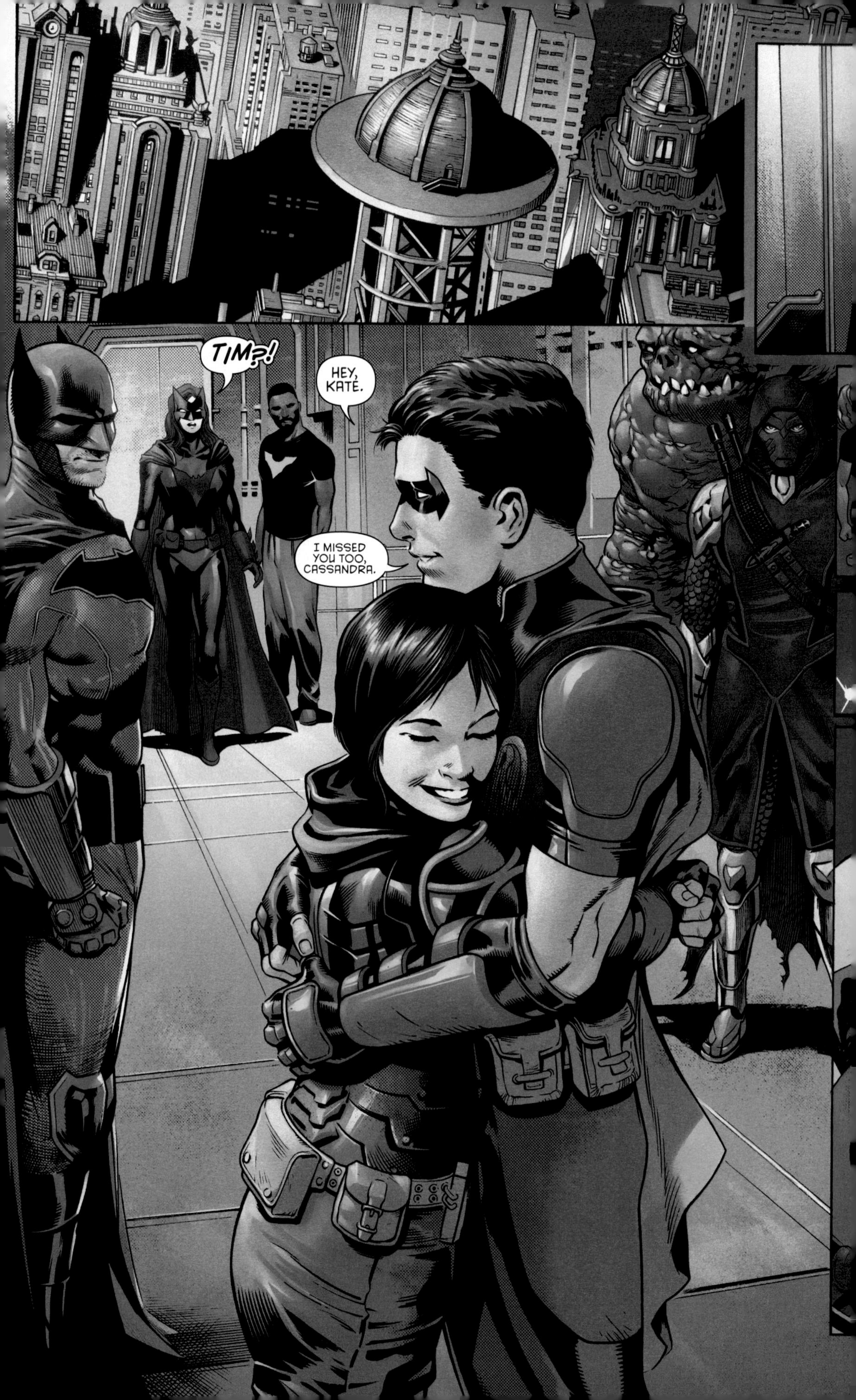
TIM?!
HEY, KATE.
I MISSED YOU TOO, CASSANDRA.

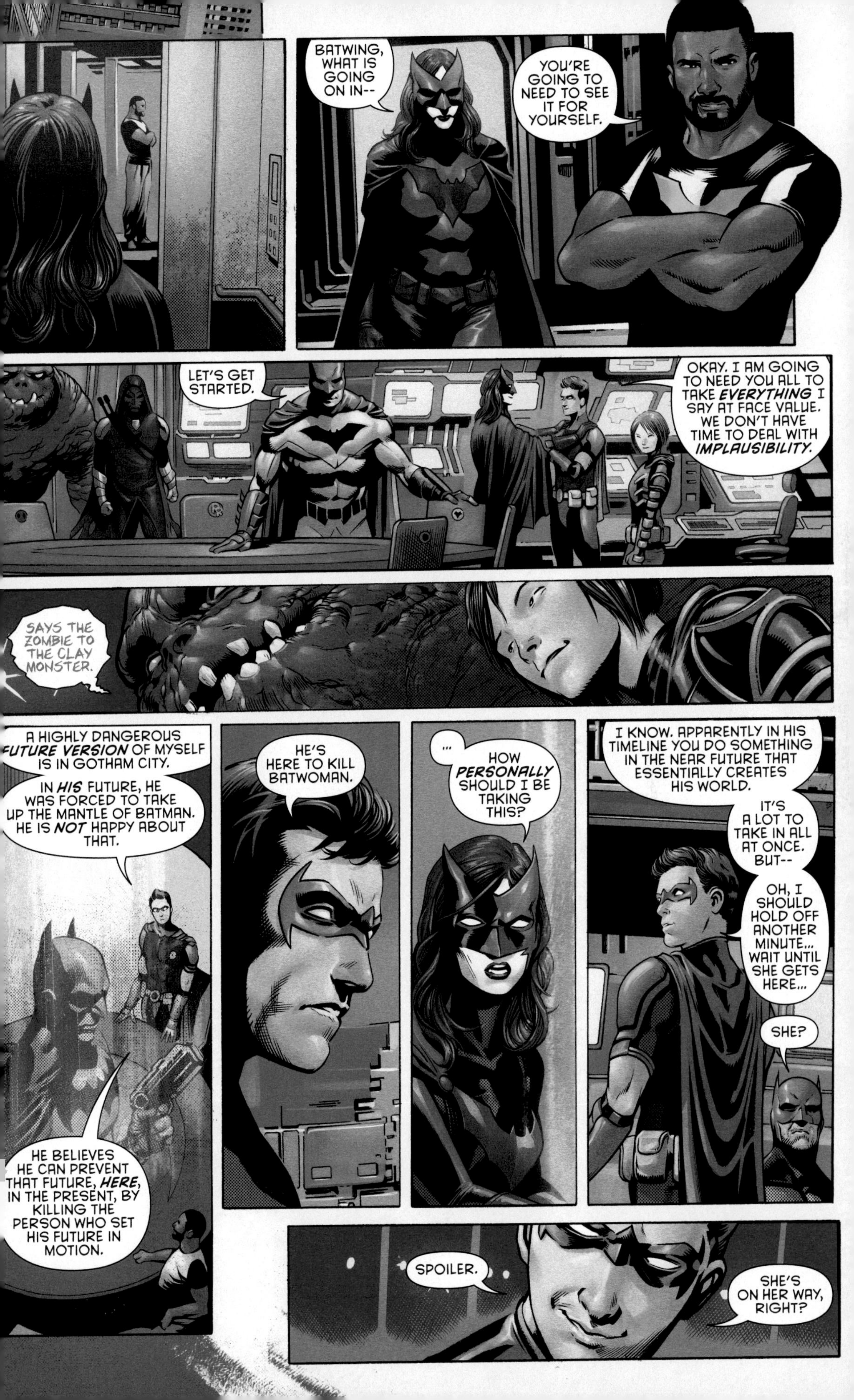
BATWING, WHAT IS GOING ON IN--
YOU'RE GOING TO NEED TO SEE IT FOR YOURSELF.
LET'S GET STARTED.
OKAY. I AM GOING TO NEED YOU ALL TO TAKE EVERYTHING I SAY AT FACE VALUE. WE DON'T HAVE TIME TO DEAL WITH IMPLAUSIBILITY.
SAYS THE ZOMBIE TO THE CLAY MONSTER.
A HIGHLY DANGEROUS FUTURE VERSION OF MYSELF IS IN GOTHAM CITY.
IN HIS FUTURE, HE WAS FORCED TO TAKE UP THE MANTLE OF BATMAN. HE IS NOT HAPPY ABOUT THAT.
HE BELIEVES HE CAN PREVENT THAT FUTURE, HERE, IN THE PRESENT, BY KILLING THE PERSON WHO SET HIS FUTURE IN MOTION.
HE'S HERE TO KILL BATWOMAN.
...
HOW PERSONALLY SHOULD I BE TAKING THIS?
I KNOW. APPARENTLY IN HIS TIMELINE YOU DO SOMETHING IN THE NEAR FUTURE THAT ESSENTIALLY CREATES HIS WORLD.
IT'S A LOT TO TAKE IN ALL AT ONCE. BUT--
OH, I SHOULD HOLD OFF ANOTHER MINUTE... WAIT UNTIL SHE GETS HERE...
SHE?
SPOILER.
SHE'S ON HER WAY, RIGHT?

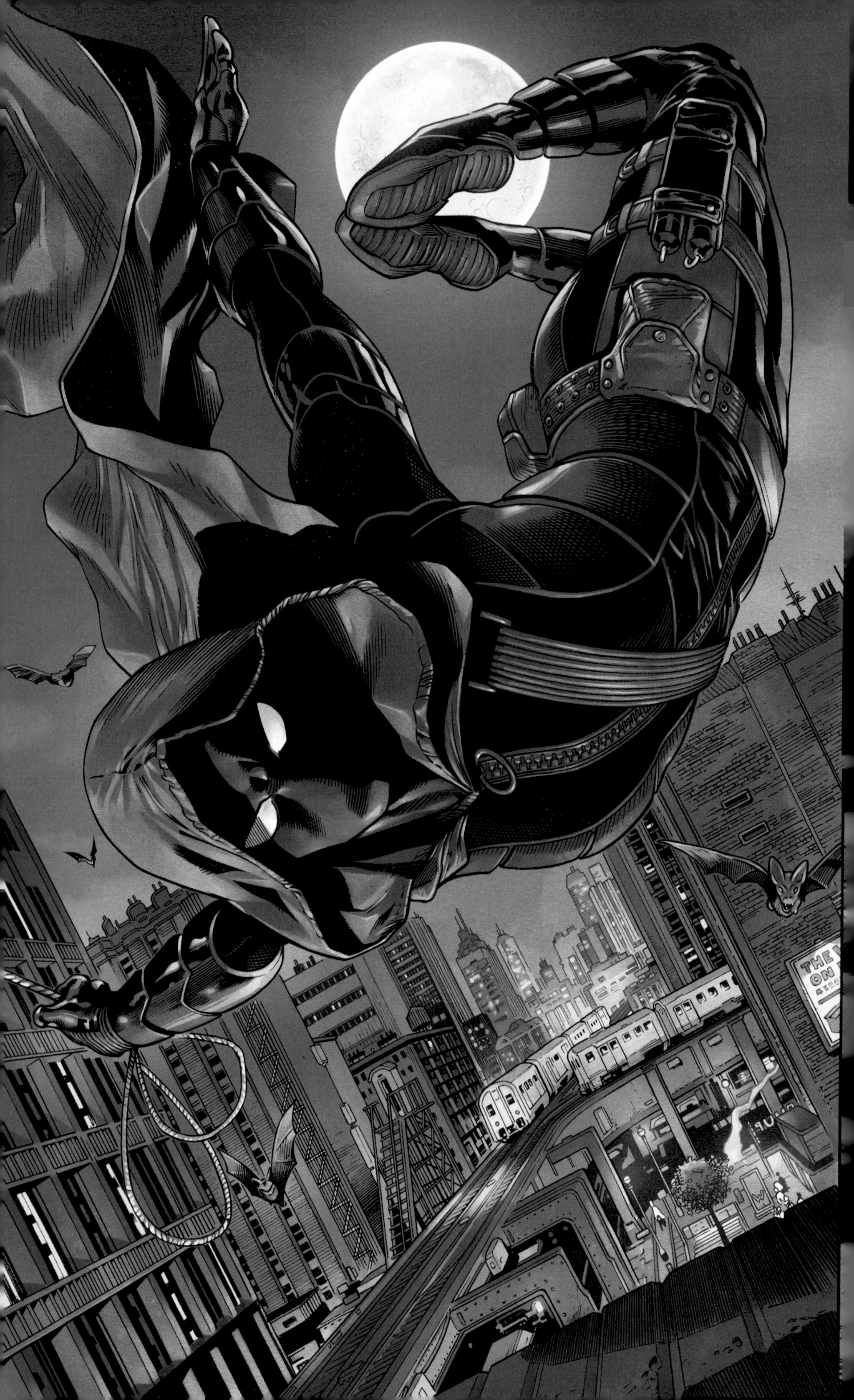

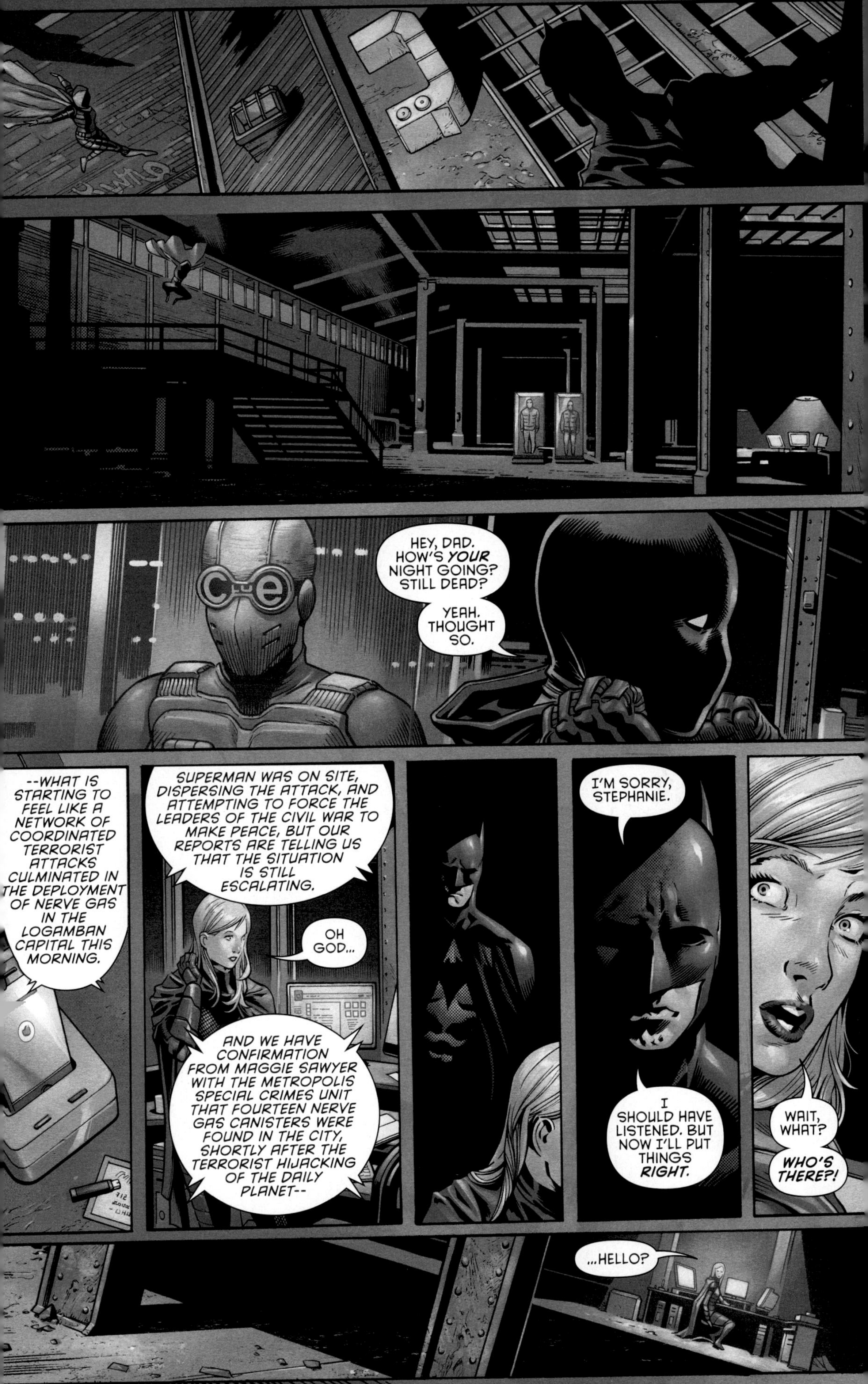
HEY, DAD. HOW'S YOUR NIGHT GOING? STILL DEAD?
YEAH. THOUGHT SO.
--WHAT IS STARTING TO FEEL LIKE A NETWORK OF COORDINATED TERRORIST ATTACKS CULMINATED IN THE DEPLOYMENT OF NERVE GAS IN THE LOGAMBAN CAPITAL THIS MORNING.
SUPERMAN WAS ON SITE, DISPERSING THE ATTACK, AND ATTEMPTING TO FORCE THE LEADERS OF THE CIVIL WAR TO MAKE PEACE, BUT OUR REPORTS ARE TELLING US THAT THE SITUATION IS STILL ESCALATING.
OH GOD...
AND WE HAVE CONFIRMATION FROM MAGGIE SAWYER WITH THE METROPOLIS SPECIAL CRIMES UNIT THAT FOURTEEN NERVE GAS CANISTERS WERE FOUND IN THE CITY, SHORTLY AFTER THE TERRORIST HIJACKING OF THE DAILY PLANET--
I'M SORRY, STEPHANIE.
I SHOULD HAVE LISTENED. BUT NOW I'LL PUT THINGS RIGHT.
WAIT, WHAT?
WHO'S THERE?!
...HELLO?

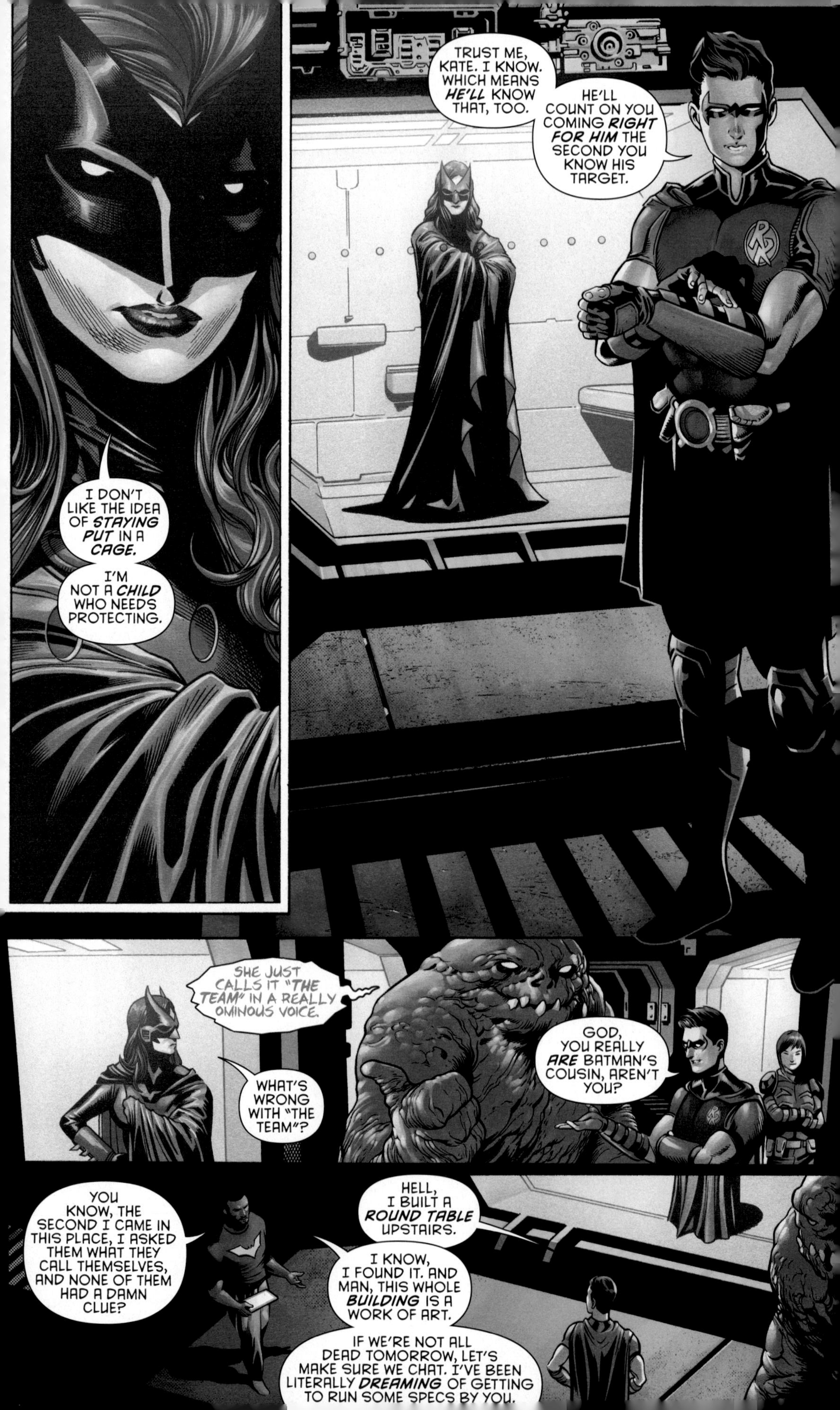

I DON'T LIKE THE IDEA OF STAYING PUT IN A CAGE.
I'M NOT A CHILD WHO NEEDS PROTECTING.
TRUST ME, KATE. I KNOW. WHICH MEANS HE'LL KNOW THAT, TOO.
HE'LL COUNT ON YOU COMING RIGHT FOR HIM THE SECOND YOU KNOW HIS TARGET.
SHE JUST CALLS IT "THE TEAM" IN A REALLY OMINOUS VOICE.
WHAT'S WRONG WITH "THE TEAM"?
GOD, YOU REALLY ARE BATMAN'S COUSIN, AREN'T YOU?
YOU KNOW, THE SECOND I CAME IN THIS PLACE, I ASKED THEM WHAT THEY CALL THEMSELVES, AND NONE OF THEM HAD A DAMN CLUE?
HELL, I BUILT A ROUND TABLE UPSTAIRS.
I KNOW, I FOUND IT. AND MAN, THIS WHOLE BUILDING IS A WORK OF ART.
IF WE'RE NOT ALL DEAD TOMORROW, LET'S MAKE SURE WE CHAT. I'VE BEEN LITERALLY DREAMING OF GETTING TO RUN SOME SPECS BY YOU.

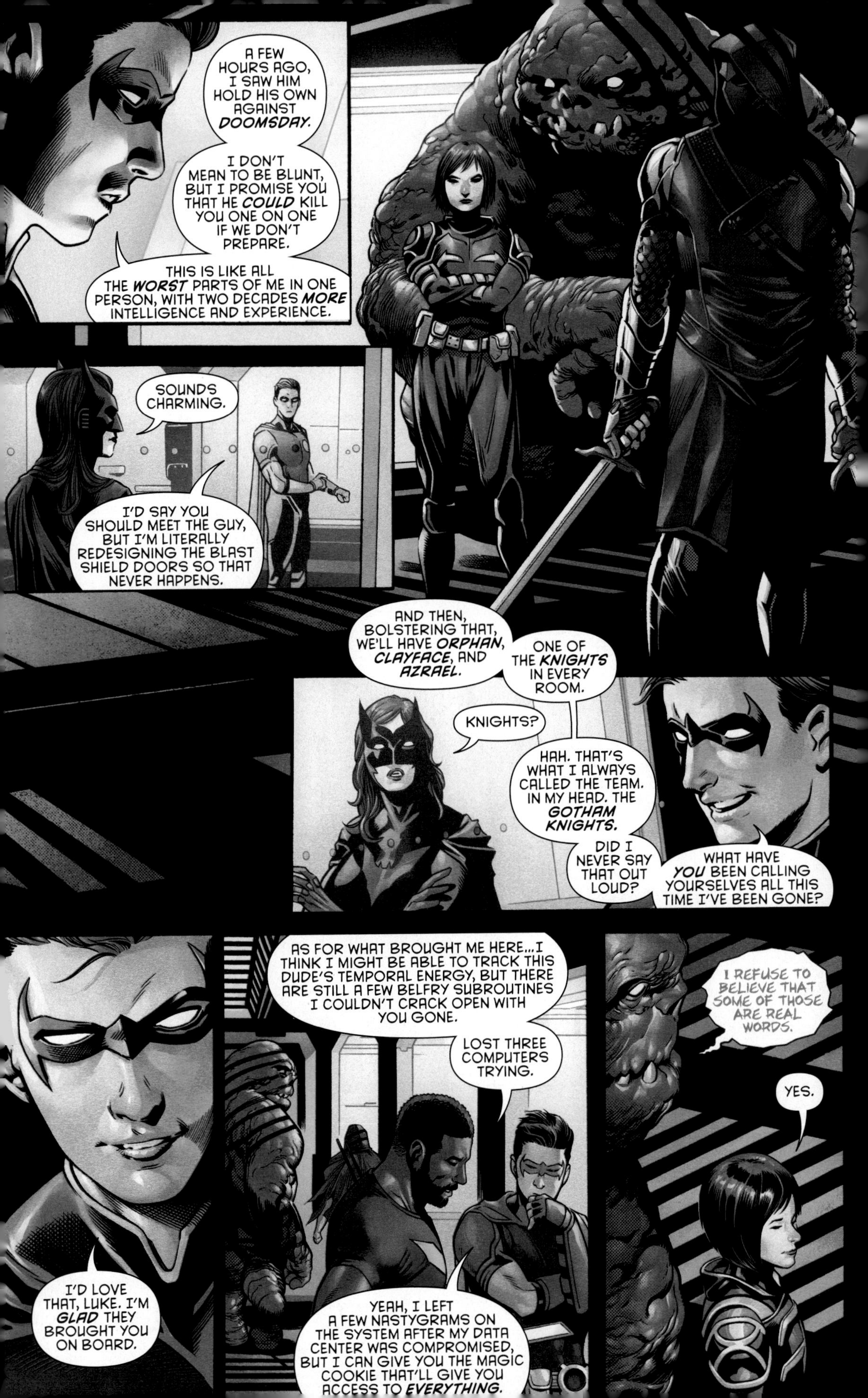
A FEW HOURS AGO, I SAW HIM HOLD HIS OWN AGAINST DOOMSDAY.
I DON'T MEAN TO BE BLUNT, BUT I PROMISE YOU THAT HE COULD KILL YOU ONE ON ONE IF WE DON'T PREPARE.
THIS IS LIKE ALL THE WORST PARTS OF ME IN ONE PERSON, WITH TWO DECADES MORE INTELLIGENCE AND EXPERIENCE.
SOUNDS CHARMING.
I'D SAY YOU SHOULD MEET THE GUY, BUT I'M LITERALLY REDESIGNING THE BLAST SHIELD DOORS SO THAT NEVER HAPPENS.
AND THEN, BOLSTERING THAT, WE'LL HAVE ORPHAN, CLAYFACE, AND AZRAEL.
ONE OF THE KNIGHTS IN EVERY ROOM.
KNIGHTS?
HAH. THAT'S WHAT I ALWAYS CALLED THE TEAM. IN MY HEAD. THE GOTHAM KNIGHTS.
DID I NEVER SAY THAT OUT LOUD?
WHAT HAVE YOU BEEN CALLING YOURSELVES ALL THIS TIME I'VE BEEN GONE?
I'D LOVE THAT, LUKE. I'M GLAD THEY BROUGHT YOU ON BOARD.
AS FOR WHAT BROUGHT ME HERE...I THINK I MIGHT BE ABLE TO TRACK THIS DUDE'S TEMPORAL ENERGY, BUT THERE ARE STILL A FEW BELFRY SUBROUTINES I COULDN'T CRACK OPEN WITH YOU GONE.
LOST THREE COMPUTERS TRYING.
YEAH, I LEFT A FEW NASTYGRAMS ON THE SYSTEM AFTER MY DATA CENTER WAS COMPROMISED, BUT I CAN GIVE YOU THE MAGIC COOKIE THAT'LL GIVE YOU ACCESS TO EVERYTHING.
I REFUSE TO BELIEVE THAT SOME OF THOSE ARE REAL WORDS.
YES.

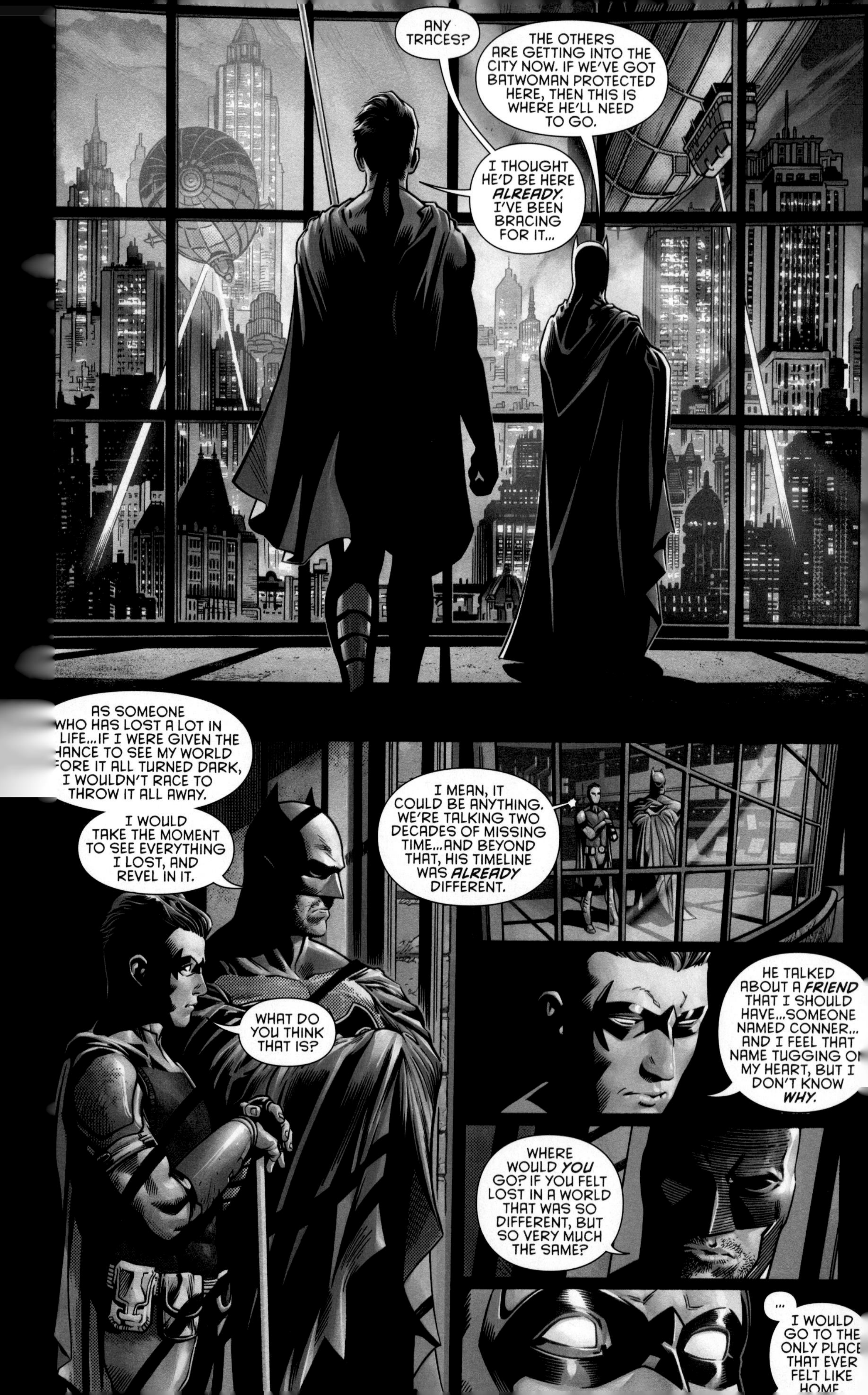
ANY TRACES?
THE OTHERS ARE GETTING INTO THE CITY NOW. IF WE'VE GOT BATWOMAN PROTECTED HERE, THEN THIS IS WHERE HE'LL NEED TO GO.
I THOUGHT HE'D BE HERE ALREADY. I'VE BEEN BRACING FOR IT...
AS SOMEONE WHO HAS LOST A LOT IN LIFE...IF I WERE GIVEN THE HANCE TO SEE MY WORLD FORE IT ALL TURNED DARK, I WOULDN'T RACE TO THROW IT ALL AWAY.
I WOULD TAKE THE MOMENT TO SEE EVERYTHING I LOST, AND REVEL IN IT.
WHAT DO YOU THINK THAT IS?
I MEAN, IT COULD BE ANYTHING. WE'RE TALKING TWO DECADES OF MISSING TIME...AND BEYOND THAT, HIS TIMELINE WAS ALREADY DIFFERENT.
HE TALKED ABOUT A FRIEND THAT I SHOULD HAVE...SOMEONE NAMED CONNER... AND I FEEL THAT NAME TUGGING ON MY HEART, BUT I DON'T KNOW WHY.
WHERE WOULD YOU GO? IF YOU FELT LOST IN A WORLD THAT WAS SO DIFFERENT, BUT SO VERY MUCH THE SAME?
...
I WOULD GO TO THE ONLY PLACE THAT EVER FELT LIKE HOME.

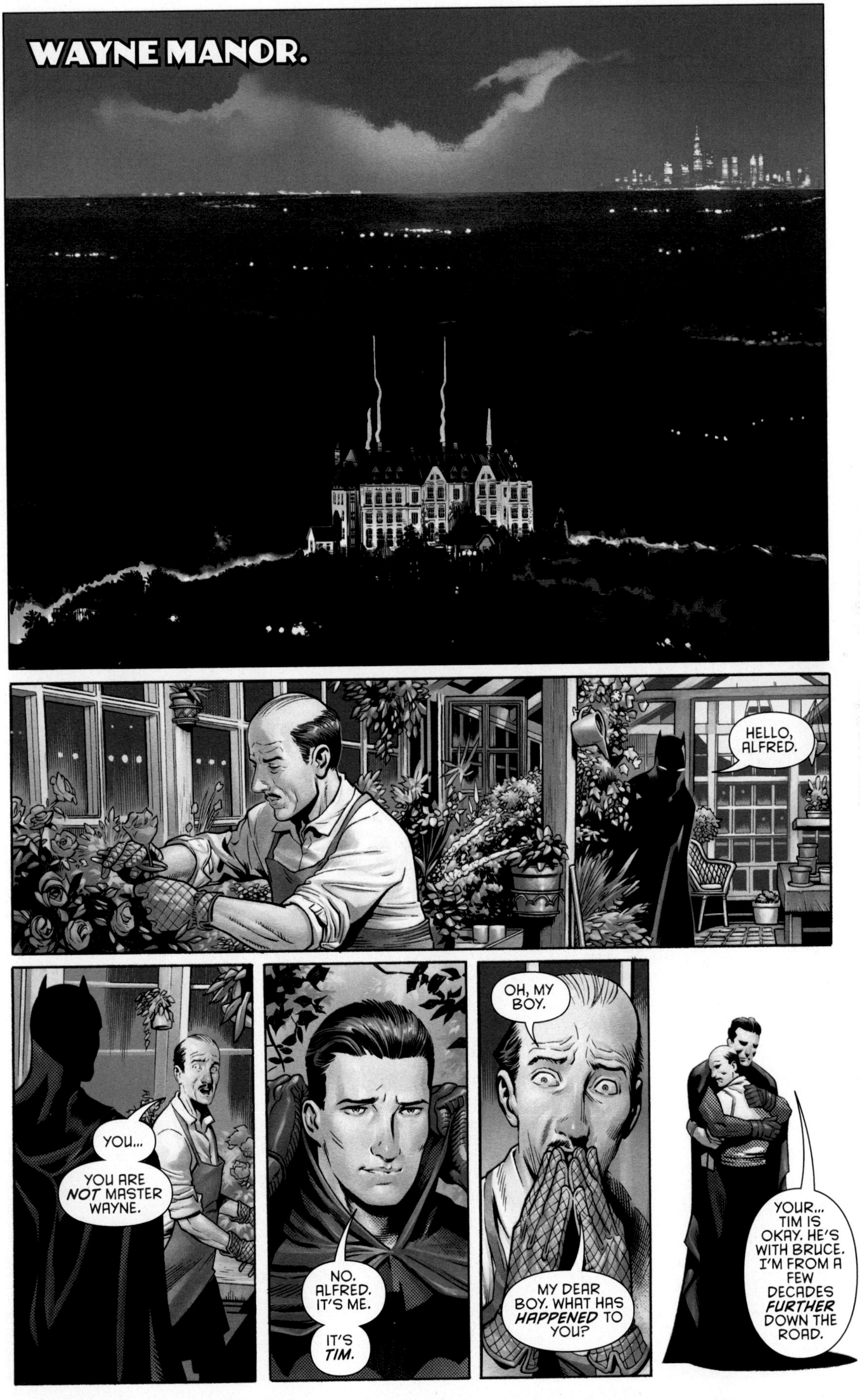
WAYNE MANOR.
HELLO, ALFRED.
YOU...
YOU ARE NOT MASTER WAYNE.
NO. ALFRED. IT'S ME.
IT'S TIM.
OH, MY BOY.
MY DEAR BOY. WHAT HAS HAPPENED TO YOU?
YOUR... TIM IS OKAY. HE'S WITH BRUCE. I'M FROM A FEW DECADES FURTHER DOWN THE ROAD.

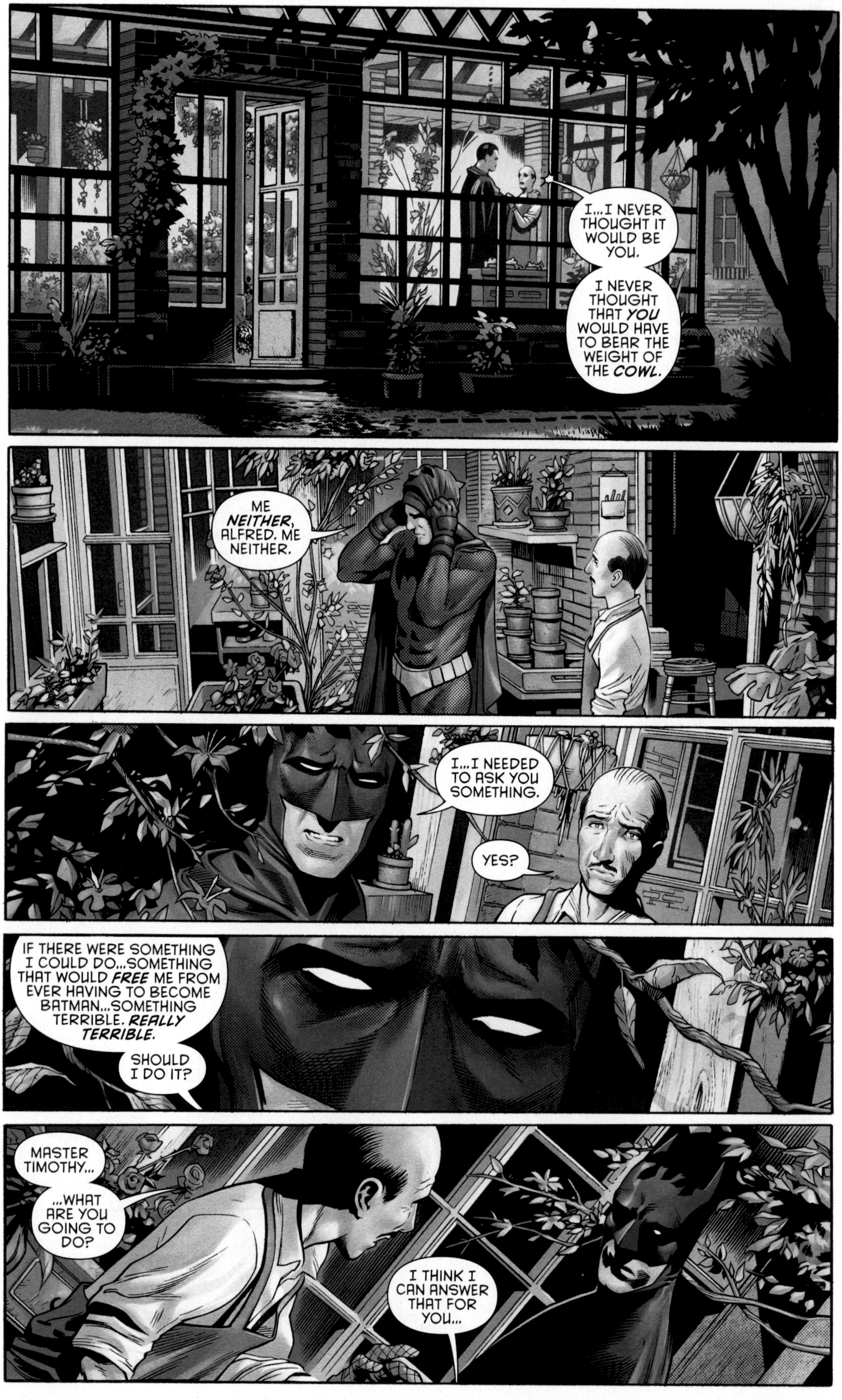
I...I NEVER THOUGHT IT WOULD BE YOU.
I NEVER THOUGHT THAT *YOU* WOULD HAVE TO BEAR THE WEIGHT OF THE *COWL*.
ME *NEITHER*, ALFRED. ME NEITHER.
I...I NEEDED TO ASK YOU SOMETHING.
YES?
IF THERE WERE SOMETHING I COULD DO...SOMETHING THAT WOULD *FREE* ME FROM EVER HAVING TO BECOME BATMAN...SOMETHING TERRIBLE. *REALLY TERRIBLE*.
SHOULD I DO IT?
MASTER TIMOTHY...
...WHAT ARE YOU GOING TO DO?
I THINK I CAN ANSWER THAT FOR YOU...

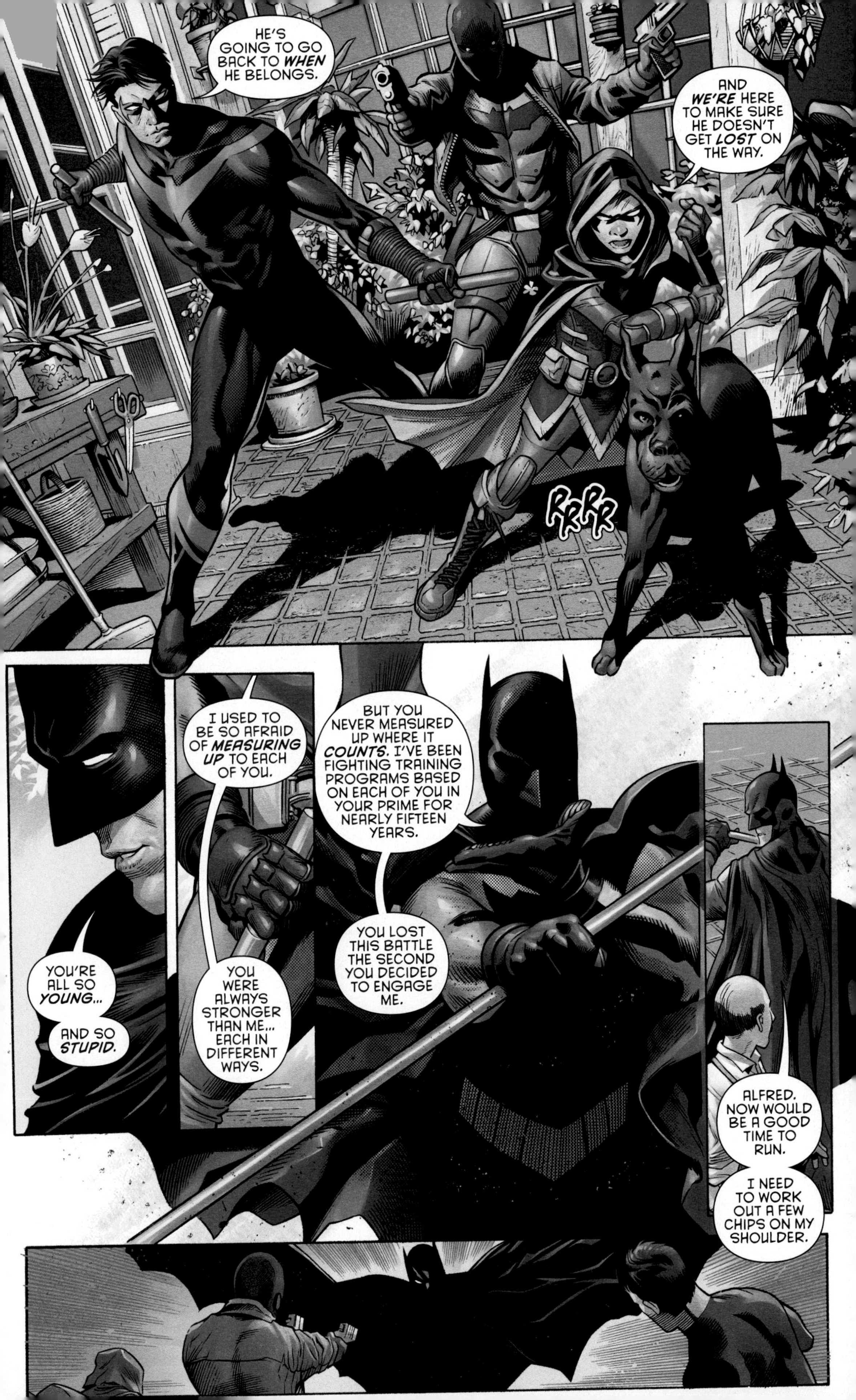
HE'S GOING TO GO BACK TO WHEN HE BELONGS.
AND WE'RE HERE TO MAKE SURE HE DOESN'T GET LOST ON THE WAY.
RRRR
YOU'RE ALL SO YOUNG...
AND SO STUPID.
I USED TO BE SO AFRAID OF MEASURING UP TO EACH OF YOU.
YOU WERE ALWAYS STRONGER THAN ME... EACH IN DIFFERENT WAYS.
BUT YOU NEVER MEASURED UP WHERE IT COUNTS. I'VE BEEN FIGHTING TRAINING PROGRAMS BASED ON EACH OF YOU IN YOUR PRIME FOR NEARLY FIFTEEN YEARS.
YOU LOST THIS BATTLE THE SECOND YOU DECIDED TO ENGAGE ME.
ALFRED. NOW WOULD BE A GOOD TIME TO RUN.
I NEED TO WORK OUT A FEW CHIPS ON MY SHOULDER.

COMPUTER... COMPUTER, THIS IS PENNY ONE. I NEED AN ALL-POINTS BULLETIN...

CANNOT COMPLY.

OVERRIDE, *BLUE ROSE.*

ALFRED. WHAT'S WRONG?

WE CAN *HELP* YOU. WE CAN WORK THROUGH WHATEVER IT IS YOU'RE GOING THROUGH...

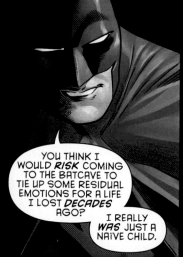

YOU THINK I WOULD *RISK* COMING TO THE BATCAVE TO TIE UP SOME RESIDUAL EMOTIONS FOR A LIFE I LOST *DECADES* AGO?

I REALLY *WAS* JUST A NAÏVE CHILD.

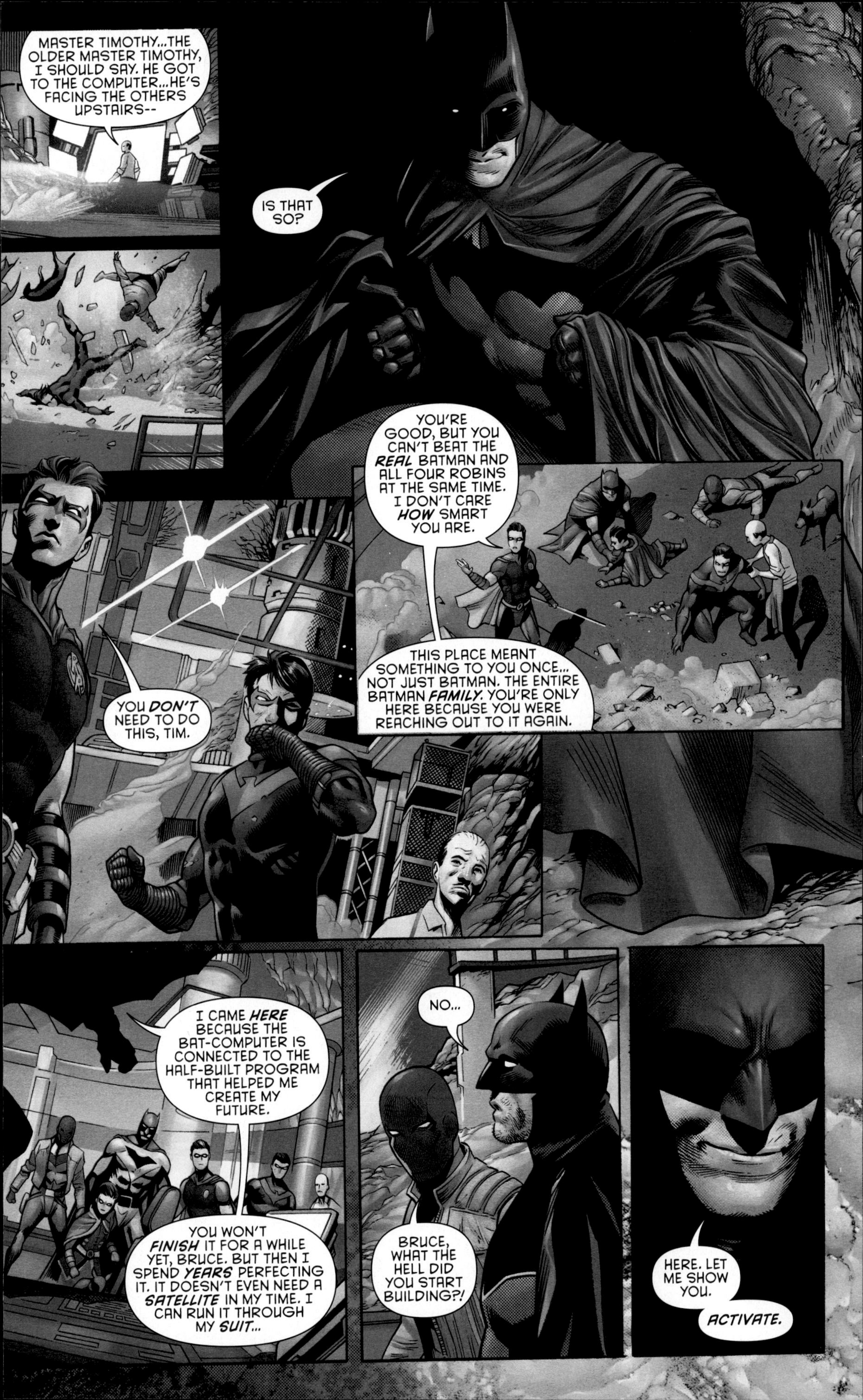
MASTER TIMOTHY...THE OLDER MASTER TIMOTHY, I SHOULD SAY. HE GOT TO THE COMPUTER...HE'S FACING THE OTHERS UPSTAIRS--
IS THAT SO?
YOU'RE GOOD, BUT YOU CAN'T BEAT THE REAL BATMAN AND ALL FOUR ROBINS AT THE SAME TIME. I DON'T CARE HOW SMART YOU ARE.
THIS PLACE MEANT SOMETHING TO YOU ONCE... NOT JUST BATMAN. THE ENTIRE BATMAN FAMILY. YOU'RE ONLY HERE BECAUSE YOU WERE REACHING OUT TO IT AGAIN.
YOU DON'T NEED TO DO THIS, TIM.
I CAME HERE BECAUSE THE BAT-COMPUTER IS CONNECTED TO THE HALF-BUILT PROGRAM THAT HELPED ME CREATE MY FUTURE.
YOU WON'T FINISH IT FOR A WHILE YET, BRUCE. BUT THEN I SPEND YEARS PERFECTING IT. IT DOESN'T EVEN NEED A SATELLITE IN MY TIME. I CAN RUN IT THROUGH MY SUIT...
NO...
BRUCE, WHAT THE HELL DID YOU START BUILDING?!
HERE. LET ME SHOW YOU.
ACTIVATE.

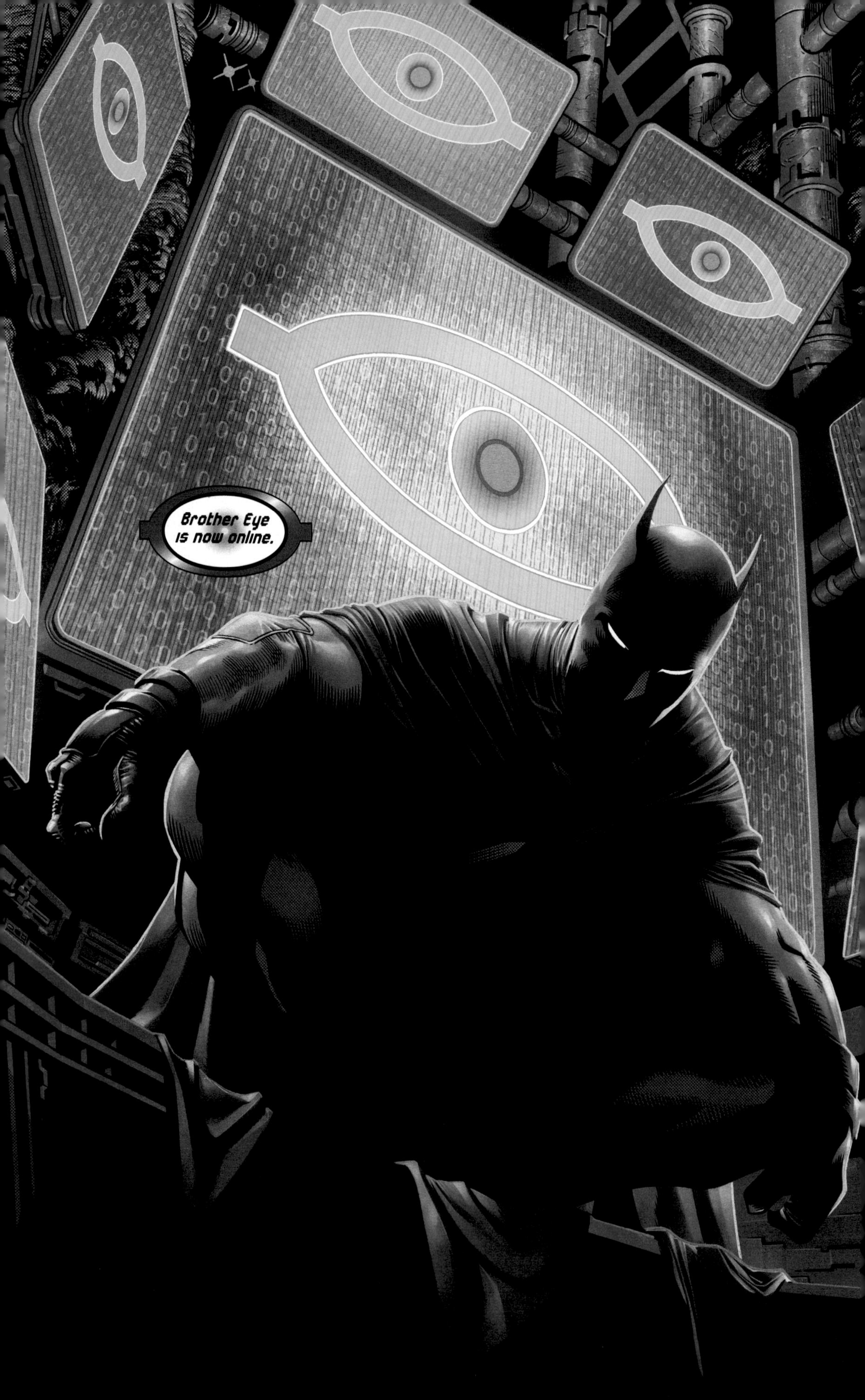
Brother Eye is now online.

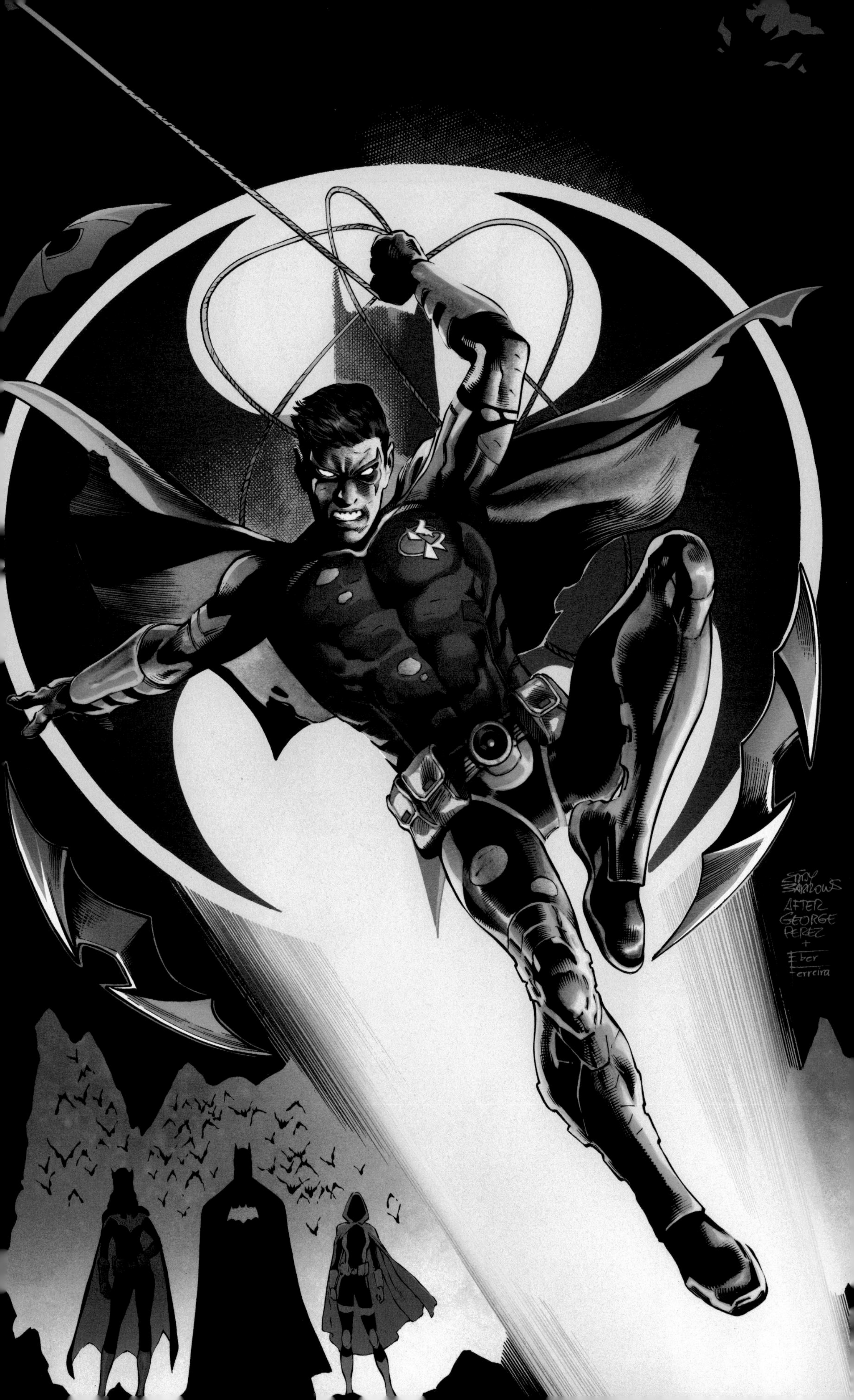
AFTER GEORGE PEREZ
+
Eber Ferreira

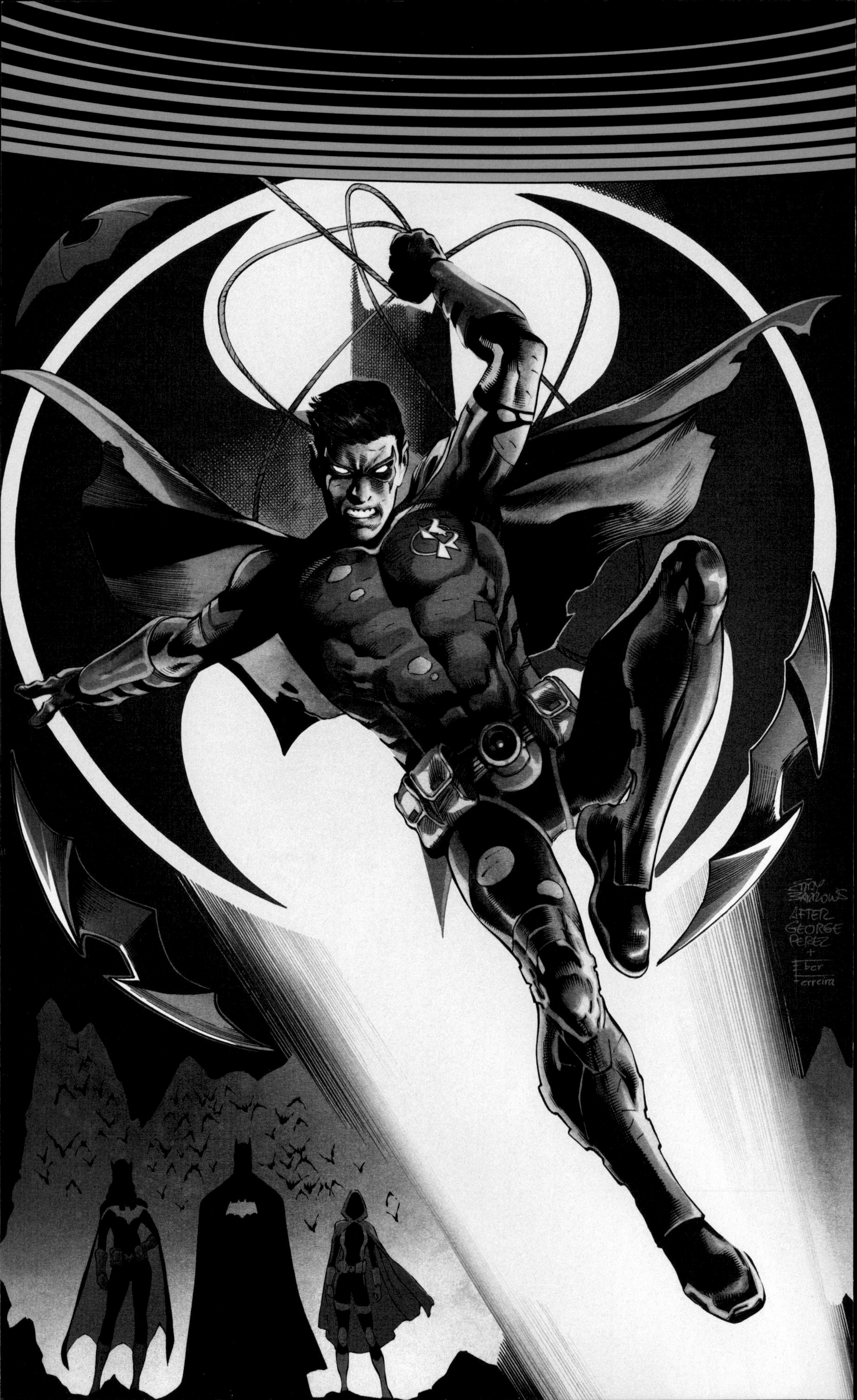
AFTER GEORGE PEREZ
+

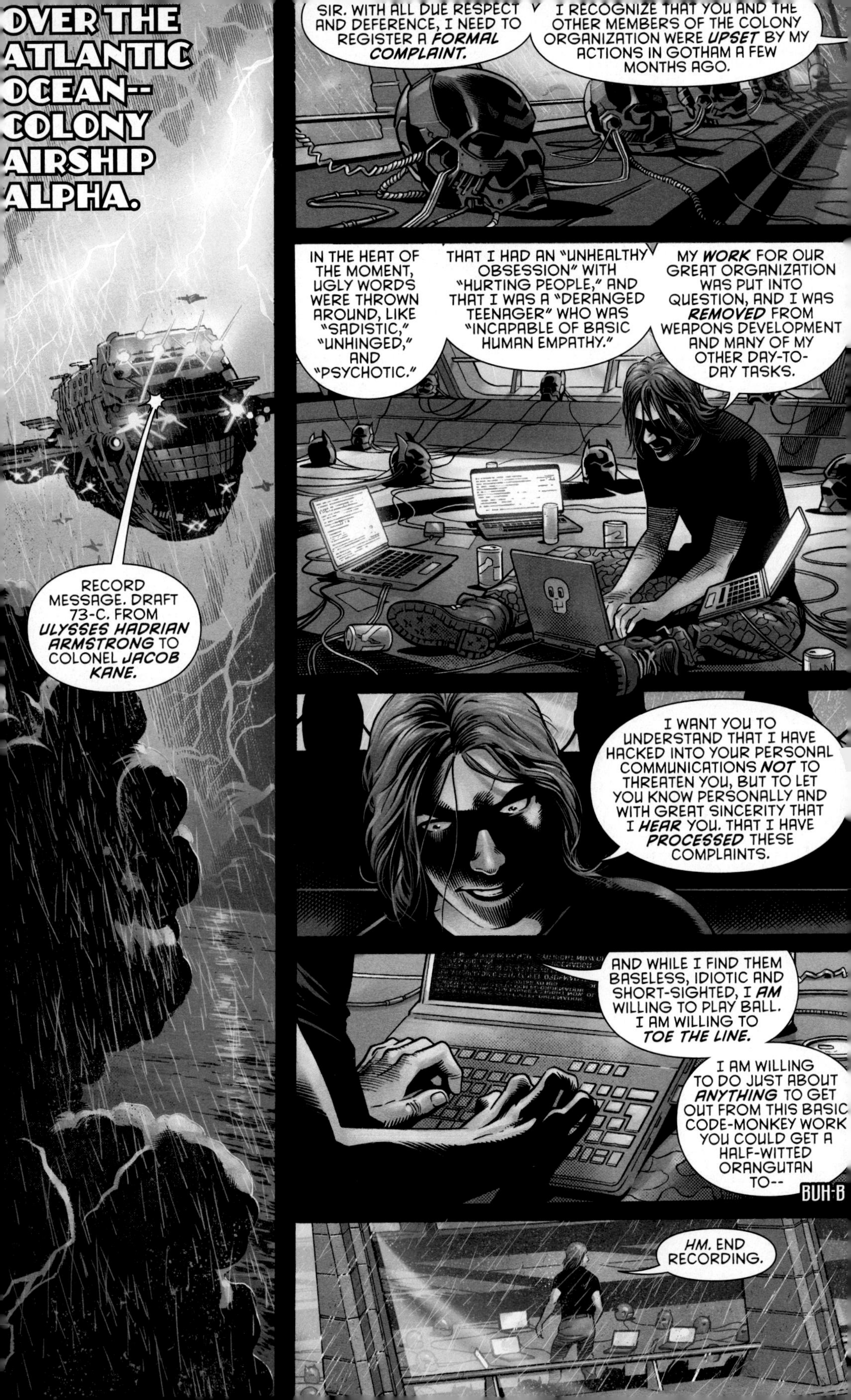
OVER THE ATLANTIC OCEAN-- COLONY AIRSHIP ALPHA.
RECORD MESSAGE. DRAFT 73-C. FROM ULYSSES HADRIAN ARMSTRONG TO COLONEL JACOB KANE.
SIR. WITH ALL DUE RESPECT AND DEFERENCE, I NEED TO REGISTER A FORMAL COMPLAINT.
I RECOGNIZE THAT YOU AND THE OTHER MEMBERS OF THE COLONY ORGANIZATION WERE UPSET BY MY ACTIONS IN GOTHAM A FEW MONTHS AGO.
IN THE HEAT OF THE MOMENT, UGLY WORDS WERE THROWN AROUND, LIKE "SADISTIC," "UNHINGED," AND "PSYCHOTIC."
THAT I HAD AN "UNHEALTHY OBSESSION" WITH "HURTING PEOPLE," AND THAT I WAS A "DERANGED TEENAGER" WHO WAS "INCAPABLE OF BASIC HUMAN EMPATHY."
MY WORK FOR OUR GREAT ORGANIZATION WAS PUT INTO QUESTION, AND I WAS REMOVED FROM WEAPONS DEVELOPMENT AND MANY OF MY OTHER DAY-TO-DAY TASKS.
I WANT YOU TO UNDERSTAND THAT I HAVE HACKED INTO YOUR PERSONAL COMMUNICATIONS NOT TO THREATEN YOU, BUT TO LET YOU KNOW PERSONALLY AND WITH GREAT SINCERITY THAT I HEAR YOU. THAT I HAVE PROCESSED THESE COMPLAINTS.
AND WHILE I FIND THEM BASELESS, IDIOTIC AND SHORT-SIGHTED, I AM WILLING TO PLAY BALL. I AM WILLING TO TOE THE LINE.
I AM WILLING TO DO JUST ABOUT ANYTHING TO GET OUT FROM THIS BASIC CODE-MONKEY WORK YOU COULD GET A HALF-WITTED ORANGUTAN TO--
BUH-B
HM. END RECORDING.

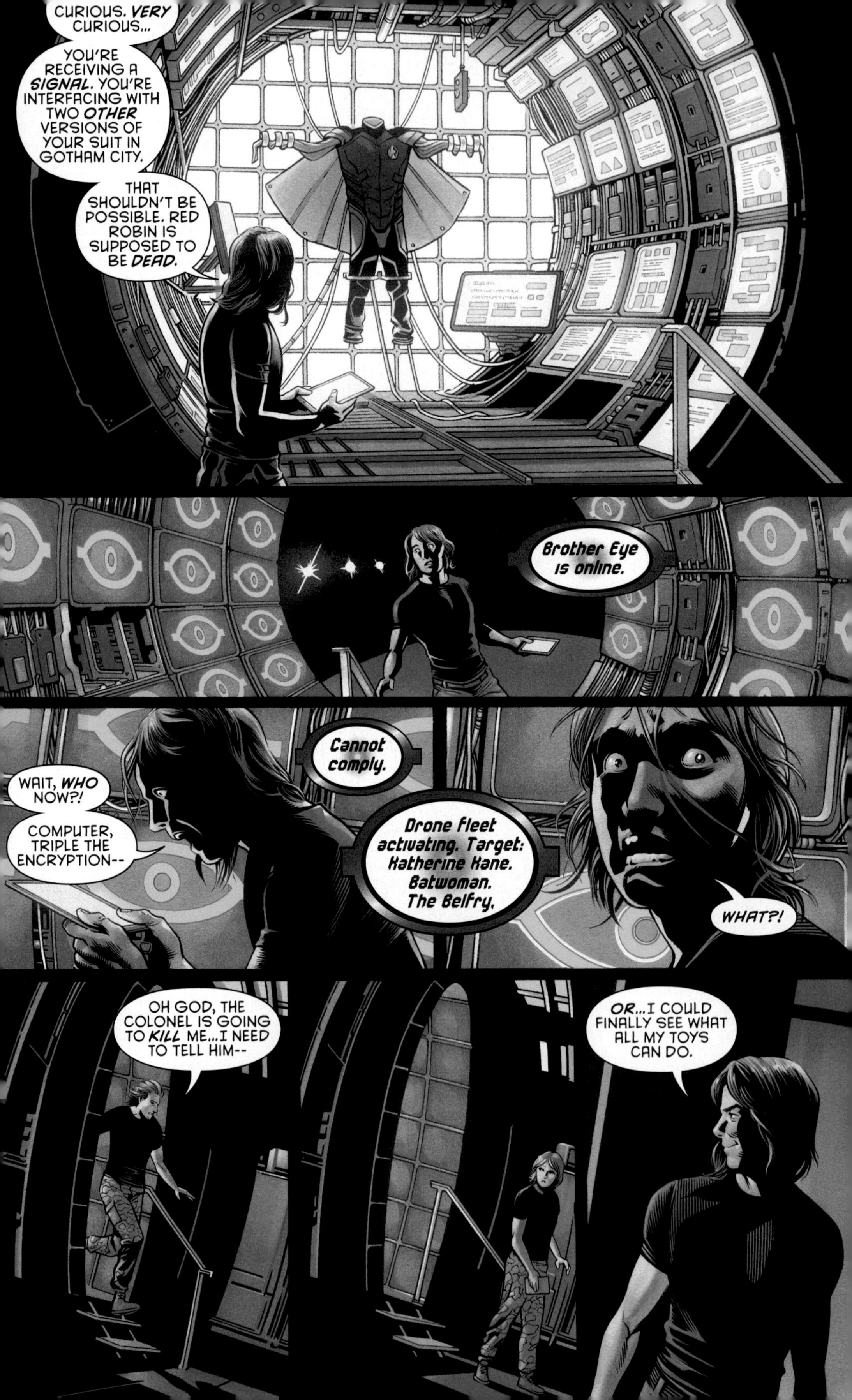

CURIOUS. VERY CURIOUS...
YOU'RE RECEIVING A SIGNAL. YOU'RE INTERFACING WITH TWO OTHER VERSIONS OF YOUR SUIT IN GOTHAM CITY.
THAT SHOULDN'T BE POSSIBLE. RED ROBIN IS SUPPOSED TO BE DEAD.
Brother Eye is online.
WAIT, WHO NOW?!
COMPUTER, TRIPLE THE ENCRYPTION--
Cannot comply.
Drone fleet activating. Target: Katherine Kane. Batwoman. The Belfry.
WHAT?!
OH GOD, THE COLONEL IS GOING TO KILL ME...I NEED TO TELL HIM--
OR...I COULD FINALLY SEE WHAT ALL MY TOYS CAN DO.

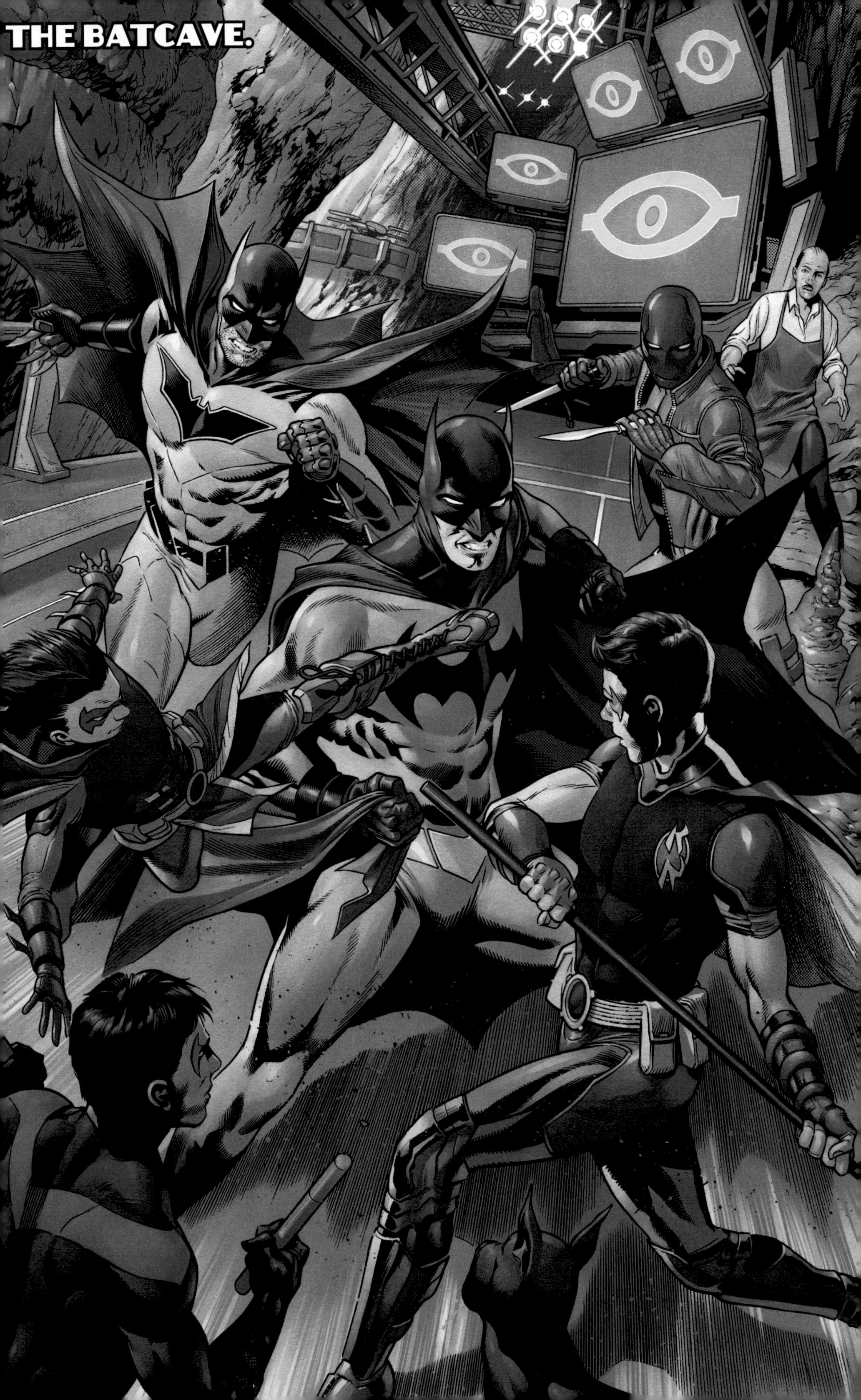
THE BATCAVE.

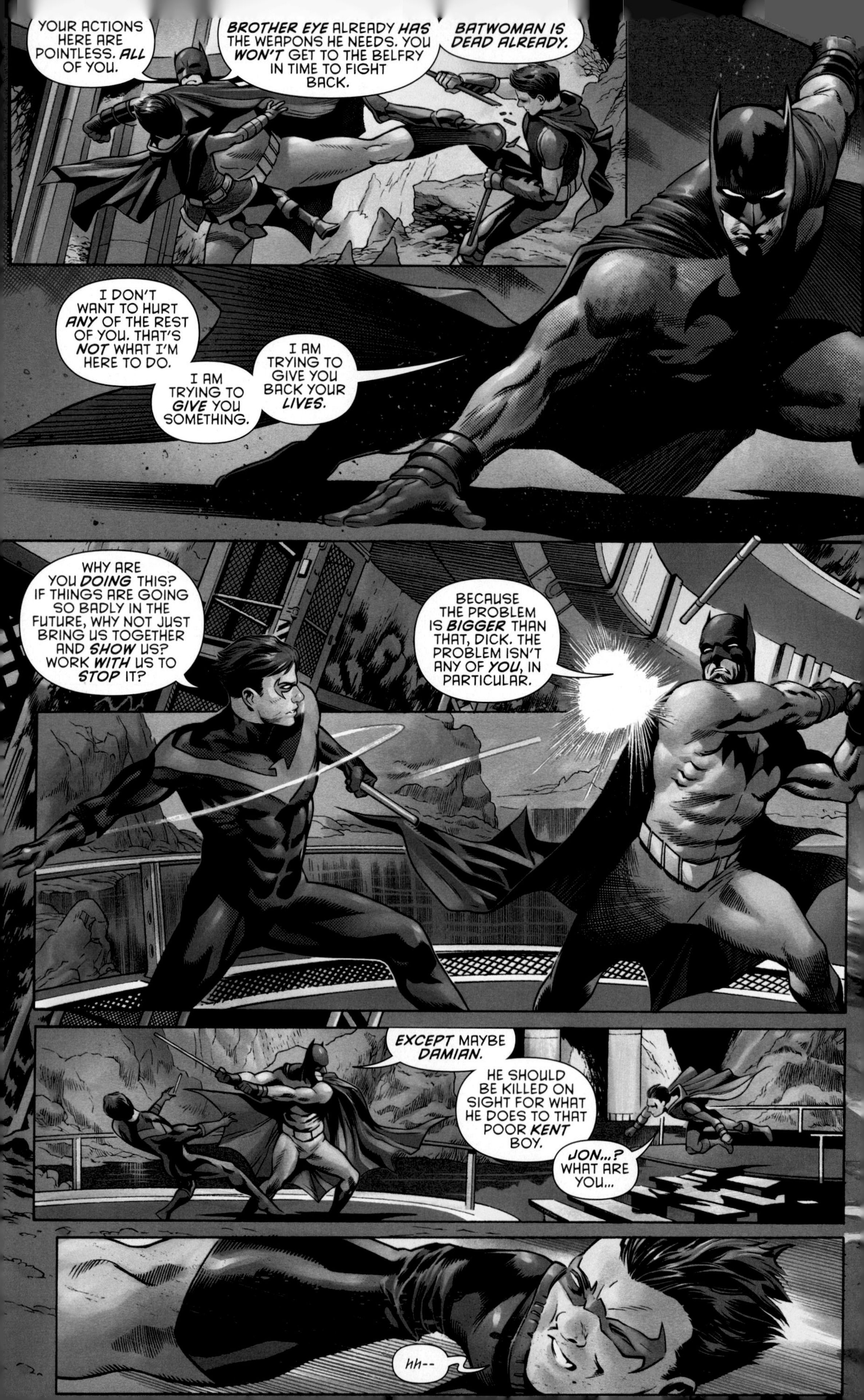
YOUR ACTIONS HERE ARE POINTLESS. ALL OF YOU.
BROTHER EYE ALREADY HAS THE WEAPONS HE NEEDS. YOU WON'T GET TO THE BELFRY IN TIME TO FIGHT BACK.
BATWOMAN IS DEAD ALREADY.
I DON'T WANT TO HURT ANY OF THE REST OF YOU. THAT'S NOT WHAT I'M HERE TO DO.
I AM TRYING TO GIVE YOU SOMETHING.
I AM TRYING TO GIVE YOU BACK YOUR LIVES.
WHY ARE YOU DOING THIS? IF THINGS ARE GOING SO BADLY IN THE FUTURE, WHY NOT JUST BRING US TOGETHER AND SHOW US? WORK WITH US TO STOP IT?
BECAUSE THE PROBLEM IS BIGGER THAN THAT, DICK. THE PROBLEM ISN'T ANY OF YOU, IN PARTICULAR.
EXCEPT MAYBE DAMIAN.
HE SHOULD BE KILLED ON SIGHT FOR WHAT HE DOES TO THAT POOR KENT BOY.
JON...? WHAT ARE YOU...
hh--

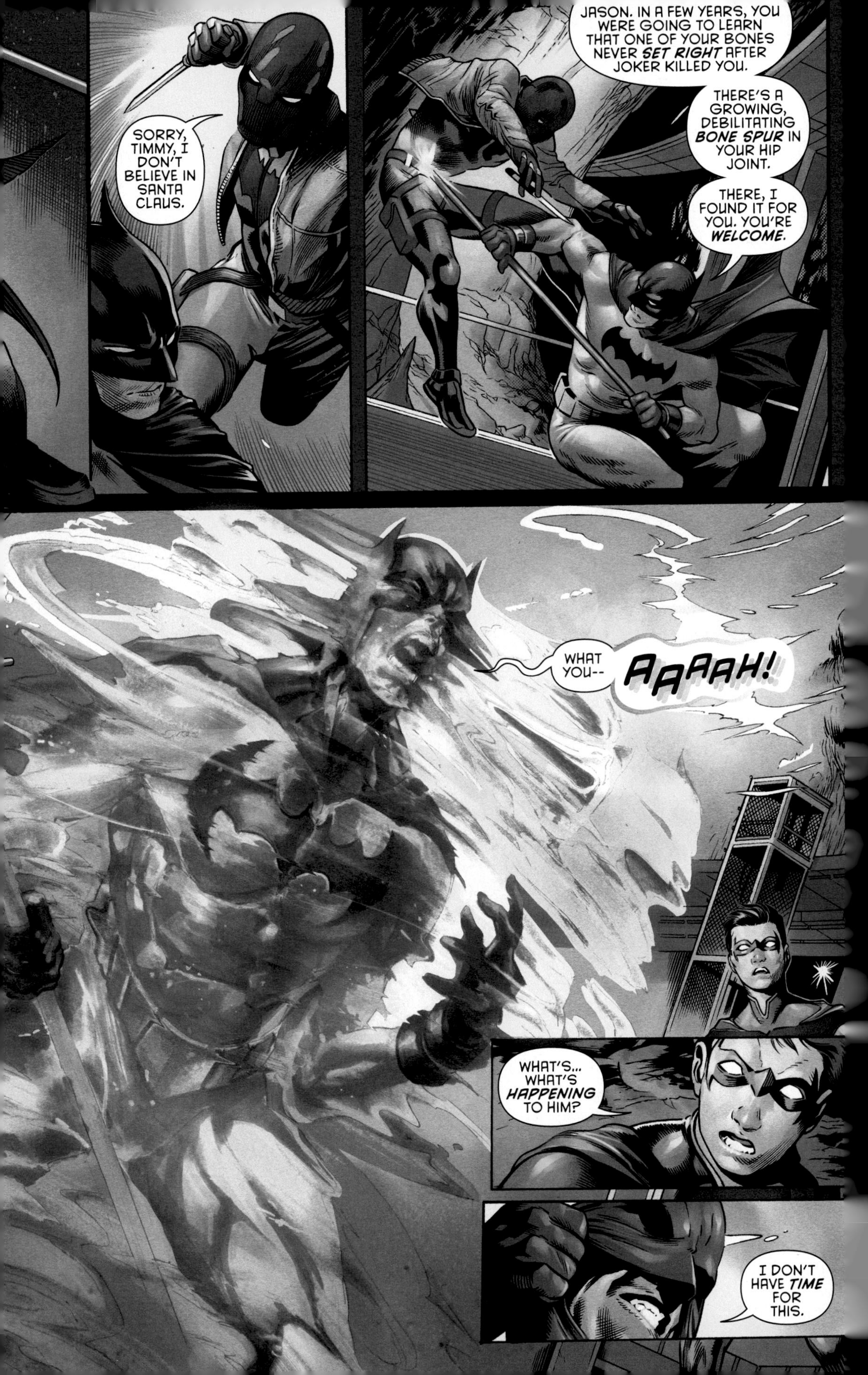
SORRY, TIMMY, I DON'T BELIEVE IN SANTA CLAUS.
JASON. IN A FEW YEARS, YOU WERE GOING TO LEARN THAT ONE OF YOUR BONES NEVER SET RIGHT AFTER JOKER KILLED YOU.
THERE'S A GROWING, DEBILITATING BONE SPUR IN YOUR HIP JOINT.
THERE, I FOUND IT FOR YOU. YOU'RE WELCOME.
WHAT YOU--
AAAAH!
WHAT'S... WHAT'S HAPPENING TO HIM?
I DON'T HAVE TIME FOR THIS.

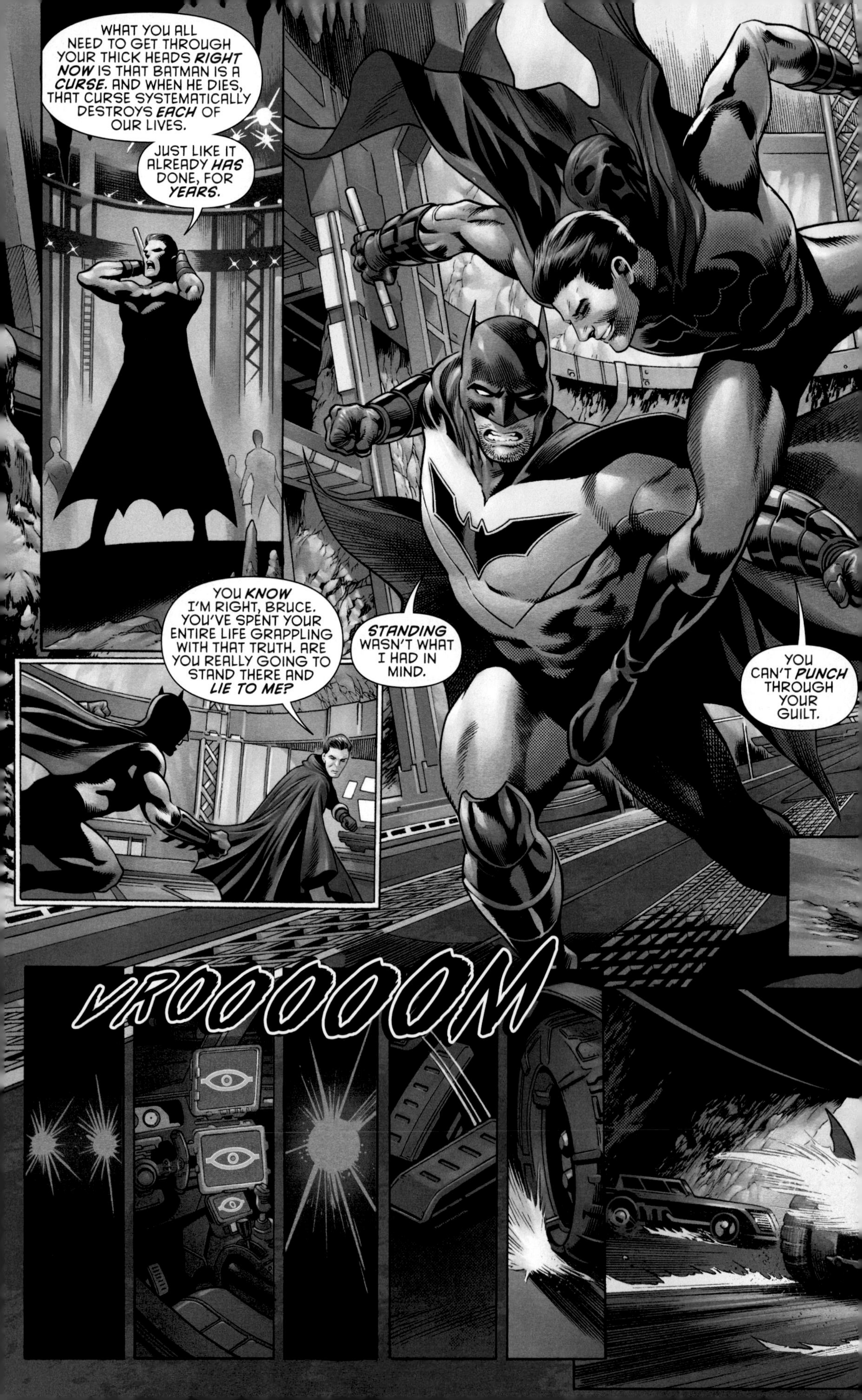
WHAT YOU ALL NEED TO GET THROUGH YOUR THICK HEADS *RIGHT NOW* IS THAT BATMAN IS A *CURSE.* AND WHEN HE DIES, THAT CURSE SYSTEMATICALLY DESTROYS *EACH* OF OUR LIVES.
JUST LIKE IT ALREADY *HAS* DONE, FOR *YEARS*.
YOU *KNOW* I'M RIGHT, BRUCE. YOU'VE SPENT YOUR ENTIRE LIFE GRAPPLING WITH THAT TRUTH. ARE YOU REALLY GOING TO STAND THERE AND *LIE TO ME?*
STANDING WASN'T WHAT I HAD IN MIND.
YOU CAN'T *PUNCH* THROUGH YOUR GUILT.
VROOOOOM

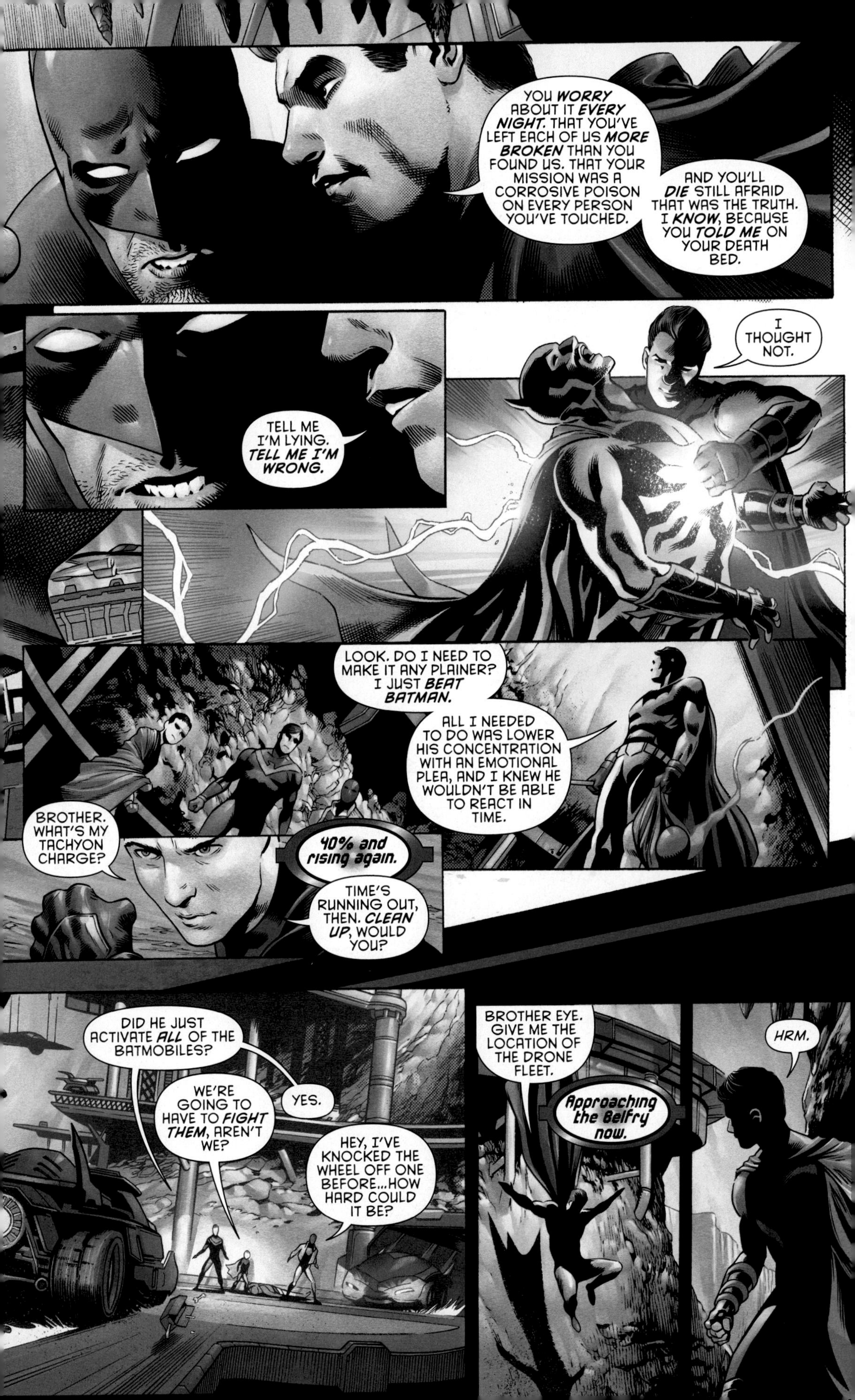
YOU WORRY ABOUT IT EVERY NIGHT. THAT YOU'VE LEFT EACH OF US MORE BROKEN THAN YOU FOUND US. THAT YOUR MISSION WAS A CORROSIVE POISON ON EVERY PERSON YOU'VE TOUCHED.
AND YOU'LL DIE STILL AFRAID THAT WAS THE TRUTH. I KNOW, BECAUSE YOU TOLD ME ON YOUR DEATH BED.
TELL ME I'M LYING. TELL ME I'M WRONG.
I THOUGHT NOT.
LOOK. DO I NEED TO MAKE IT ANY PLAINER? I JUST BEAT BATMAN.
ALL I NEEDED TO DO WAS LOWER HIS CONCENTRATION WITH AN EMOTIONAL PLEA, AND I KNEW HE WOULDN'T BE ABLE TO REACT IN TIME.
BROTHER. WHAT'S MY TACHYON CHARGE?
40% and rising again.
TIME'S RUNNING OUT, THEN. CLEAN UP, WOULD YOU?
DID HE JUST ACTIVATE ALL OF THE BATMOBILES?
YES.
WE'RE GOING TO HAVE TO FIGHT THEM, AREN'T WE?
HEY, I'VE KNOCKED THE WHEEL OFF ONE BEFORE...HOW HARD COULD IT BE?
BROTHER EYE. GIVE ME THE LOCATION OF THE DRONE FLEET.
Approaching the Belfry now.
HRM.

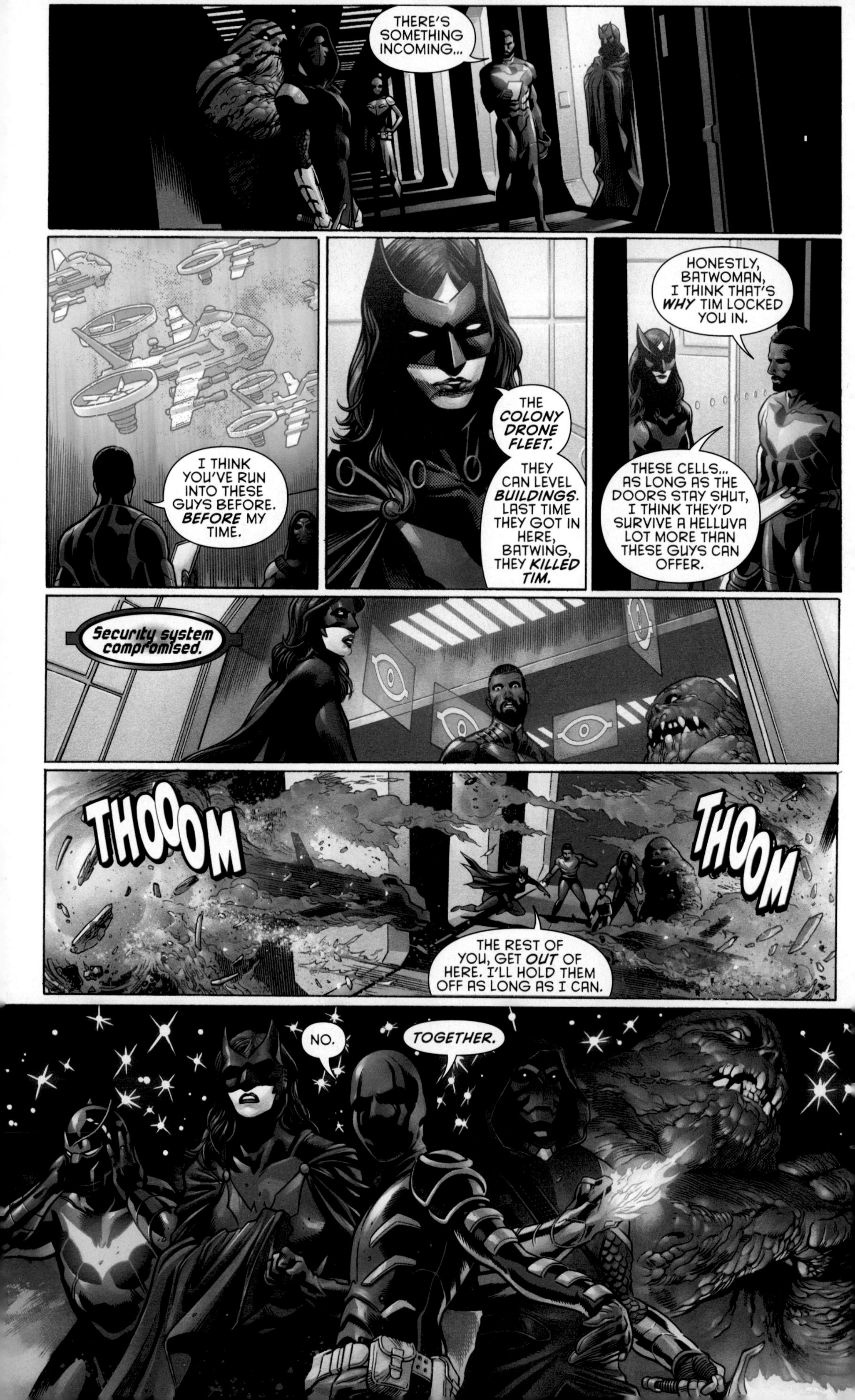
THERE'S SOMETHING INCOMING...
I THINK YOU'VE RUN INTO THESE GUYS BEFORE. BEFORE MY TIME.
THE COLONY DRONE FLEET.
THEY CAN LEVEL BUILDINGS. LAST TIME THEY GOT IN HERE, BATWING, THEY KILLED TIM.
HONESTLY, BATWOMAN, I THINK THAT'S WHY TIM LOCKED YOU IN.
THESE CELLS... AS LONG AS THE DOORS STAY SHUT, I THINK THEY'D SURVIVE A HELLUVA LOT MORE THAN THESE GUYS CAN OFFER.
Security system compromised.
THOOOM
THOOM
THE REST OF YOU, GET OUT OF HERE. I'LL HOLD THEM OFF AS LONG AS I CAN.
NO.
TOGETHER.

YOU KNOW, YOU SHOULD HAVE THOUGHT OF A WAY TO GET BACK TO THE BELFRY *WITHOUT* USING A TRANSPORTATION SYSTEM THAT *I BUILT* FROM SCRATCH.

WHY SHOULD I HAVE DONE THAT, TIM?

I *WANTED* YOU TO FOLLOW ME.

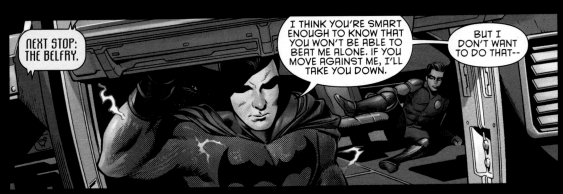

NEXT STOP: THE BELFRY.

I THINK YOU'RE SMART ENOUGH TO KNOW THAT YOU WON'T BE ABLE TO BEAT ME ALONE. IF YOU MOVE AGAINST ME, I'LL TAKE YOU DOWN.

BUT I DON'T WANT TO DO THAT--

RRRRR

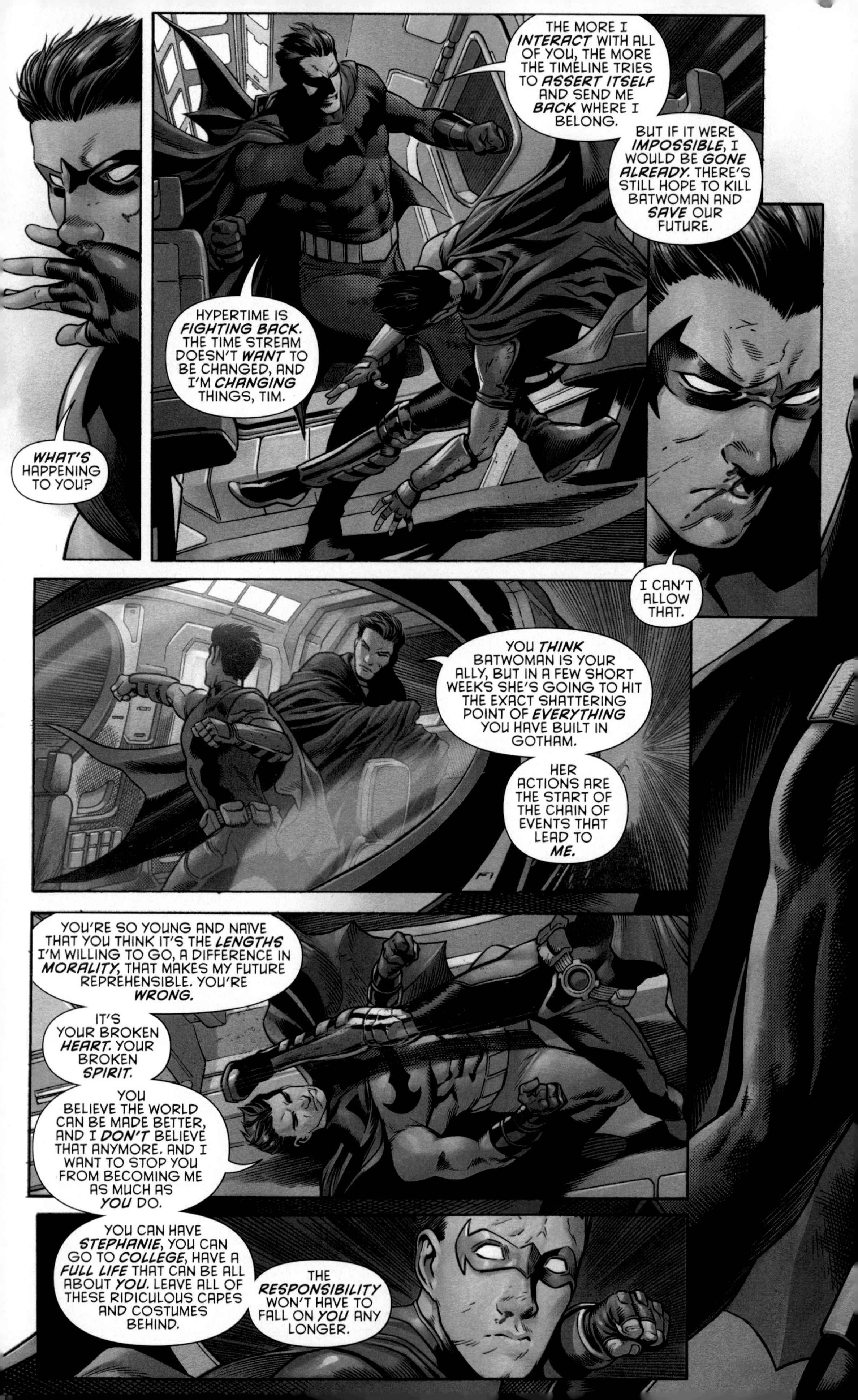

THE MORE I INTERACT WITH ALL OF YOU, THE MORE THE TIMELINE TRIES TO ASSERT ITSELF AND SEND ME BACK WHERE I BELONG.
BUT IF IT WERE IMPOSSIBLE, I WOULD BE GONE ALREADY. THERE'S STILL HOPE TO KILL BATWOMAN AND SAVE OUR FUTURE.
HYPERTIME IS FIGHTING BACK. THE TIME STREAM DOESN'T WANT TO BE CHANGED, AND I'M CHANGING THINGS, TIM.
WHAT'S HAPPENING TO YOU?
I CAN'T ALLOW THAT.
YOU THINK BATWOMAN IS YOUR ALLY, BUT IN A FEW SHORT WEEKS SHE'S GOING TO HIT THE EXACT SHATTERING POINT OF EVERYTHING YOU HAVE BUILT IN GOTHAM.
HER ACTIONS ARE THE START OF THE CHAIN OF EVENTS THAT LEAD TO ME.
YOU'RE SO YOUNG AND NAÏVE THAT YOU THINK IT'S THE LENGTHS I'M WILLING TO GO, A DIFFERENCE IN MORALITY, THAT MAKES MY FUTURE REPREHENSIBLE. YOU'RE WRONG.
IT'S YOUR BROKEN HEART. YOUR BROKEN SPIRIT.
YOU BELIEVE THE WORLD CAN BE MADE BETTER, AND I DON'T BELIEVE THAT ANYMORE. AND I WANT TO STOP YOU FROM BECOMING ME AS MUCH AS YOU DO.
YOU CAN HAVE STEPHANIE, YOU CAN GO TO COLLEGE, HAVE A FULL LIFE THAT CAN BE ALL ABOUT YOU. LEAVE ALL OF THESE RIDICULOUS CAPES AND COSTUMES BEHIND.
THE RESPONSIBILITY WON'T HAVE TO FALL ON YOU ANY LONGER.

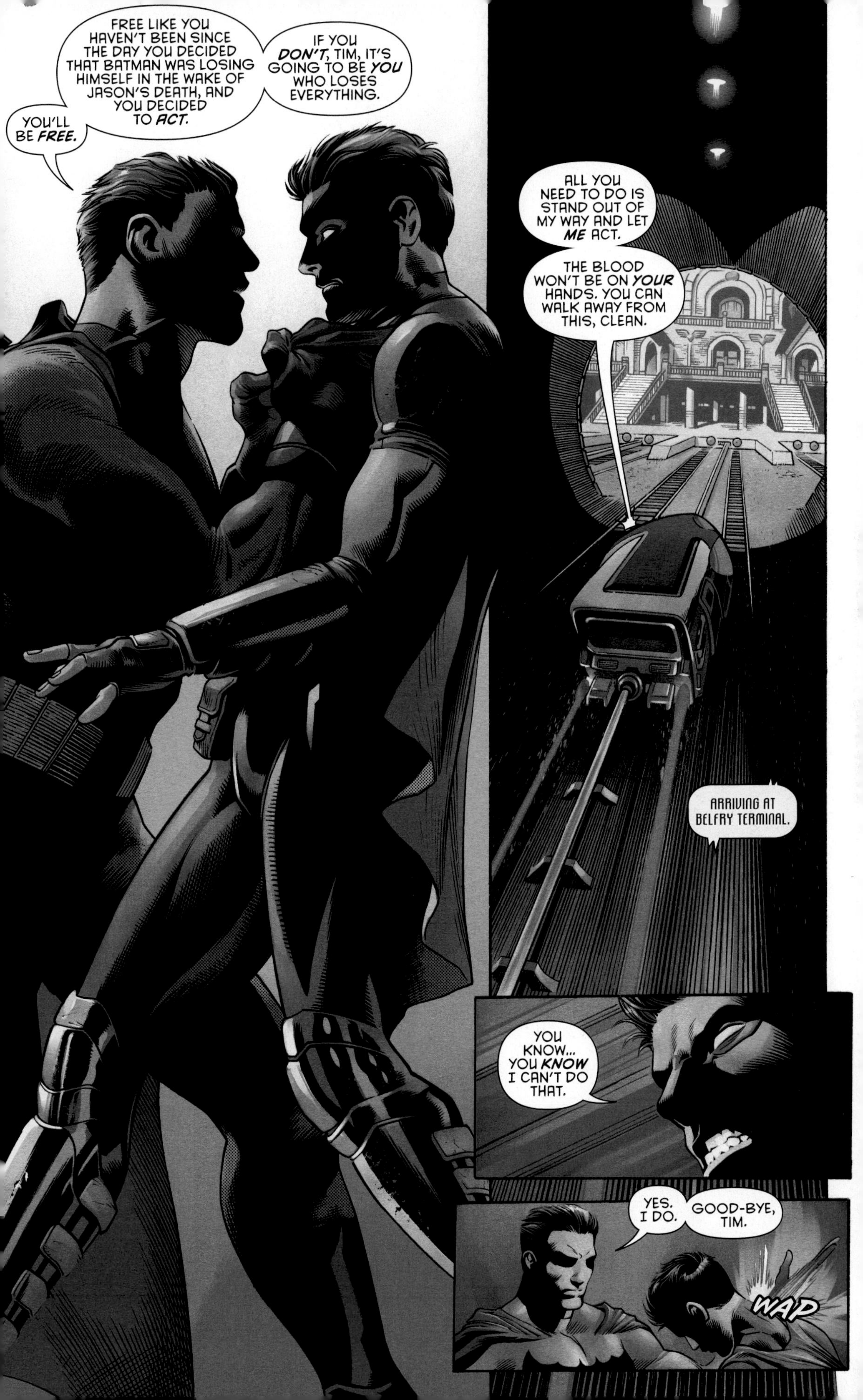
FREE LIKE YOU HAVEN'T BEEN SINCE THE DAY YOU DECIDED THAT BATMAN WAS LOSING HIMSELF IN THE WAKE OF JASON'S DEATH, AND YOU DECIDED TO ACT.
YOU'LL BE FREE.
IF YOU DON'T, TIM, IT'S GOING TO BE YOU WHO LOSES EVERYTHING.
ALL YOU NEED TO DO IS STAND OUT OF MY WAY AND LET ME ACT.
THE BLOOD WON'T BE ON YOUR HANDS. YOU CAN WALK AWAY FROM THIS, CLEAN.
ARRIVING AT BELFRY TERMINAL.
YOU KNOW... YOU KNOW I CAN'T DO THAT.
YES. I DO.
GOOD-BYE, TIM.
WAP

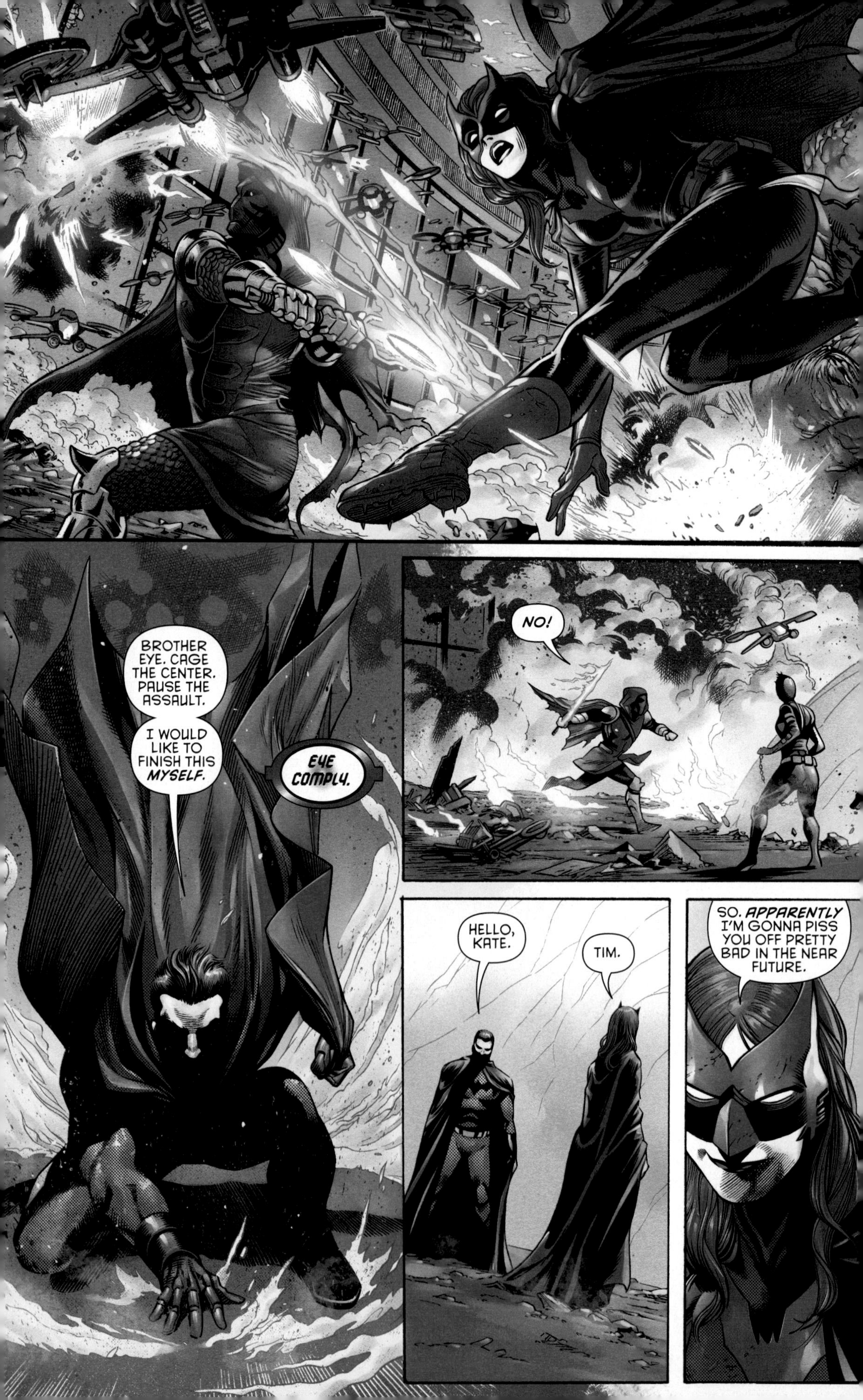
BROTHER EYE. CAGE THE CENTER. PAUSE THE ASSAULT.
I WOULD LIKE TO FINISH THIS *MYSELF*.
EYE COMPLY.
NO!
HELLO, KATE.
TIM.
SO. *APPARENTLY* I'M GONNA PISS YOU OFF PRETTY BAD IN THE NEAR FUTURE.

GET AWAY FROM HER!

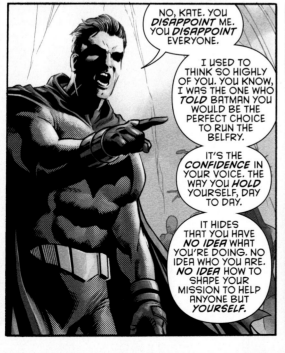

NO, KATE. YOU *DISAPPOINT* ME. YOU *DISAPPOINT* EVERYONE.

I USED TO THINK SO HIGHLY OF YOU. YOU KNOW, I WAS THE ONE WHO *TOLD* BATMAN YOU WOULD BE THE PERFECT CHOICE TO RUN THE BELFRY.

IT'S THE *CONFIDENCE* IN YOUR VOICE. THE WAY YOU *HOLD* YOURSELF, DAY TO DAY.

IT HIDES THAT YOU HAVE *NO IDEA* WHAT YOU'RE DOING. NO IDEA WHO YOU ARE. *NO IDEA* HOW TO SHAPE YOUR MISSION TO HELP ANYONE BUT *YOURSELF*.

YOU *DESTROY* PEOPLE, KATE. THAT'S ALL YOU'VE EVER DONE. PIECE BY PIECE.

BUT IT'S OVER NOW.

CRACK

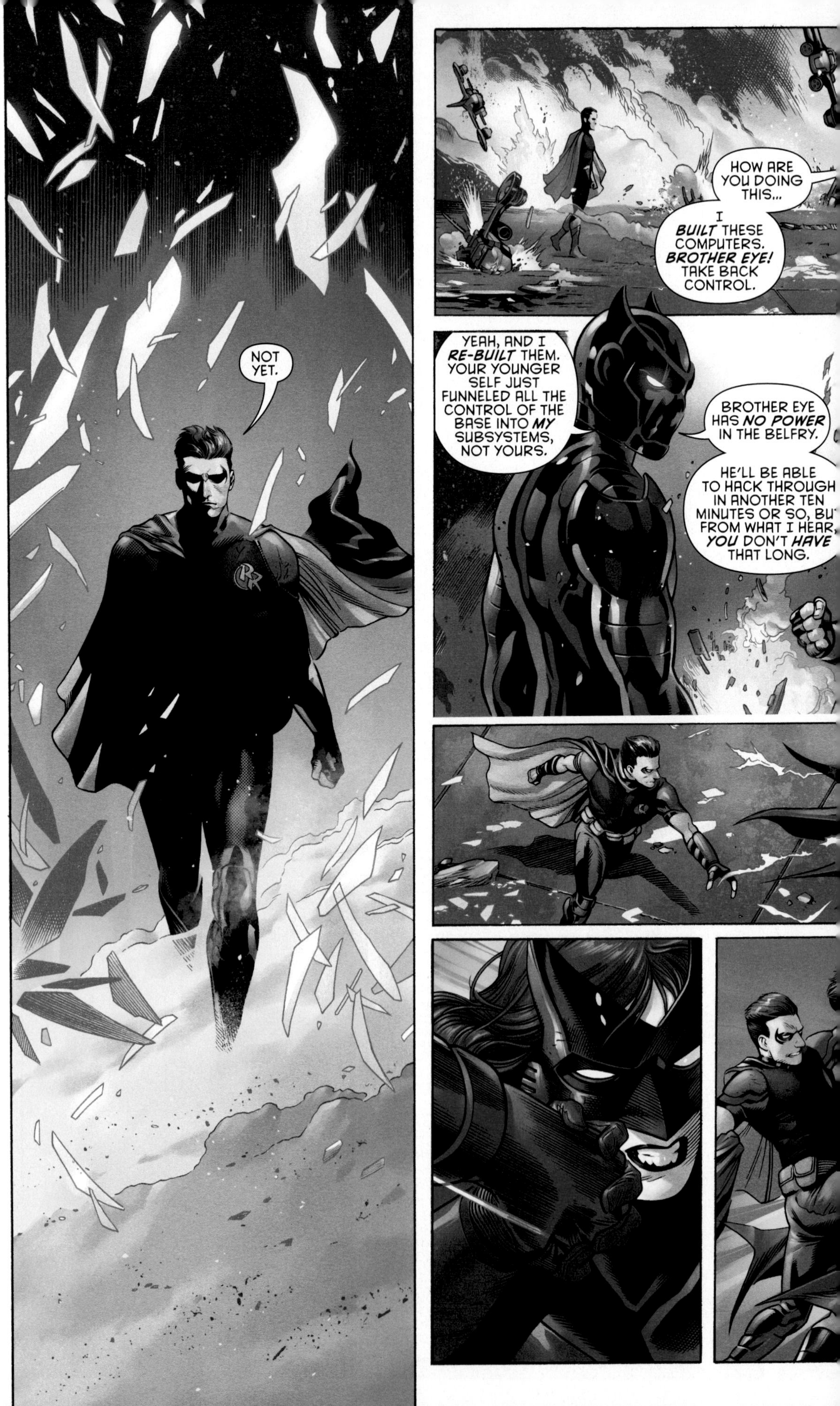
NOT YET.
HOW ARE YOU DOING THIS...
I BUILT THESE COMPUTERS. BROTHER EYE! TAKE BACK CONTROL.
YEAH, AND I RE-BUILT THEM. YOUR YOUNGER SELF JUST FUNNELED ALL THE CONTROL OF THE BASE INTO MY SUBSYSTEMS, NOT YOURS.
BROTHER EYE HAS NO POWER IN THE BELFRY.
HE'LL BE ABLE TO HACK THROUGH IN ANOTHER TEN MINUTES OR SO, BUT FROM WHAT I HEAR, YOU DON'T HAVE THAT LONG.

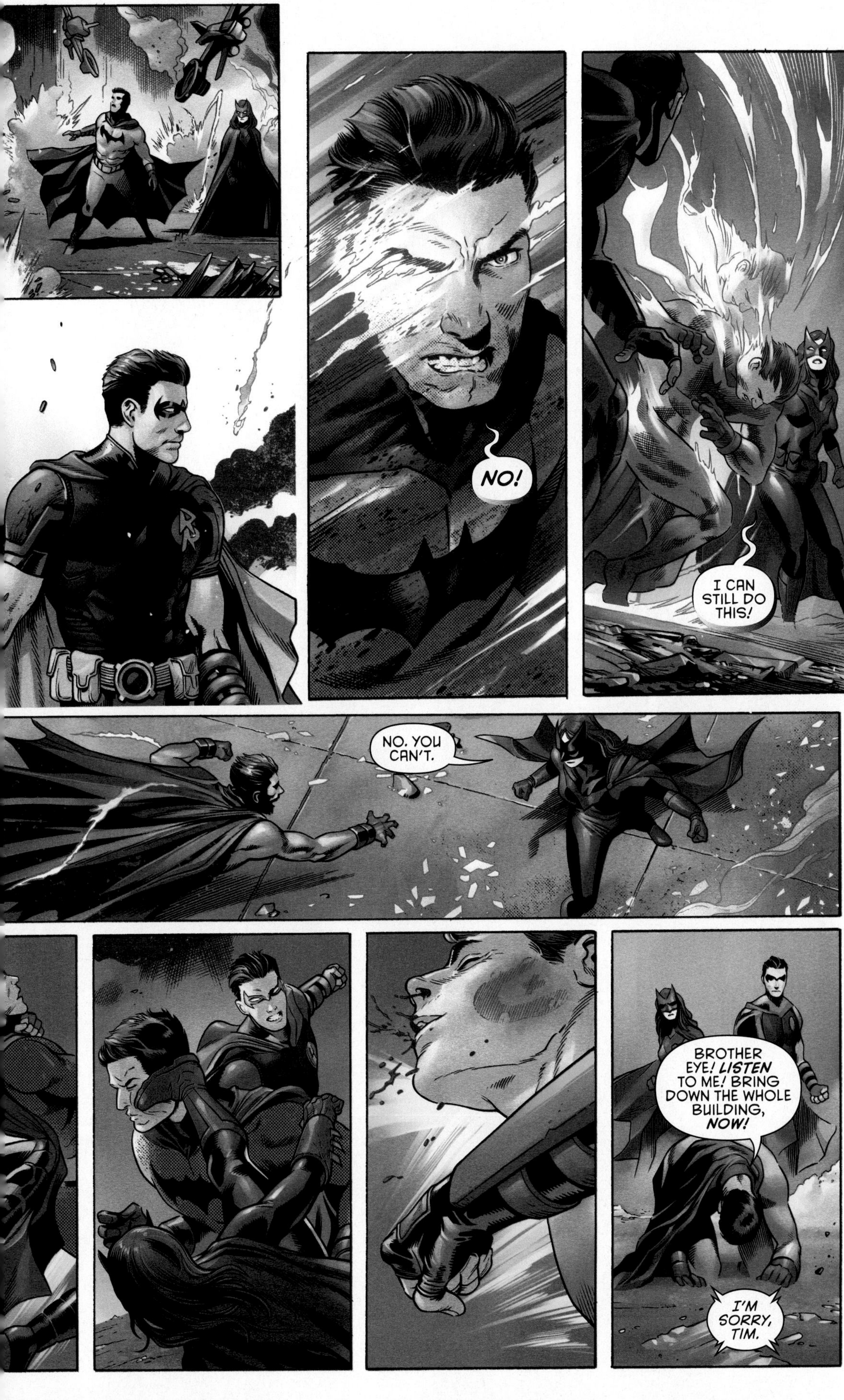
NO!
I CAN STILL DO THIS!
NO. YOU CAN'T.
BROTHER EYE! LISTEN TO ME! BRING DOWN THE WHOLE BUILDING, NOW!
I'M SORRY, TIM.

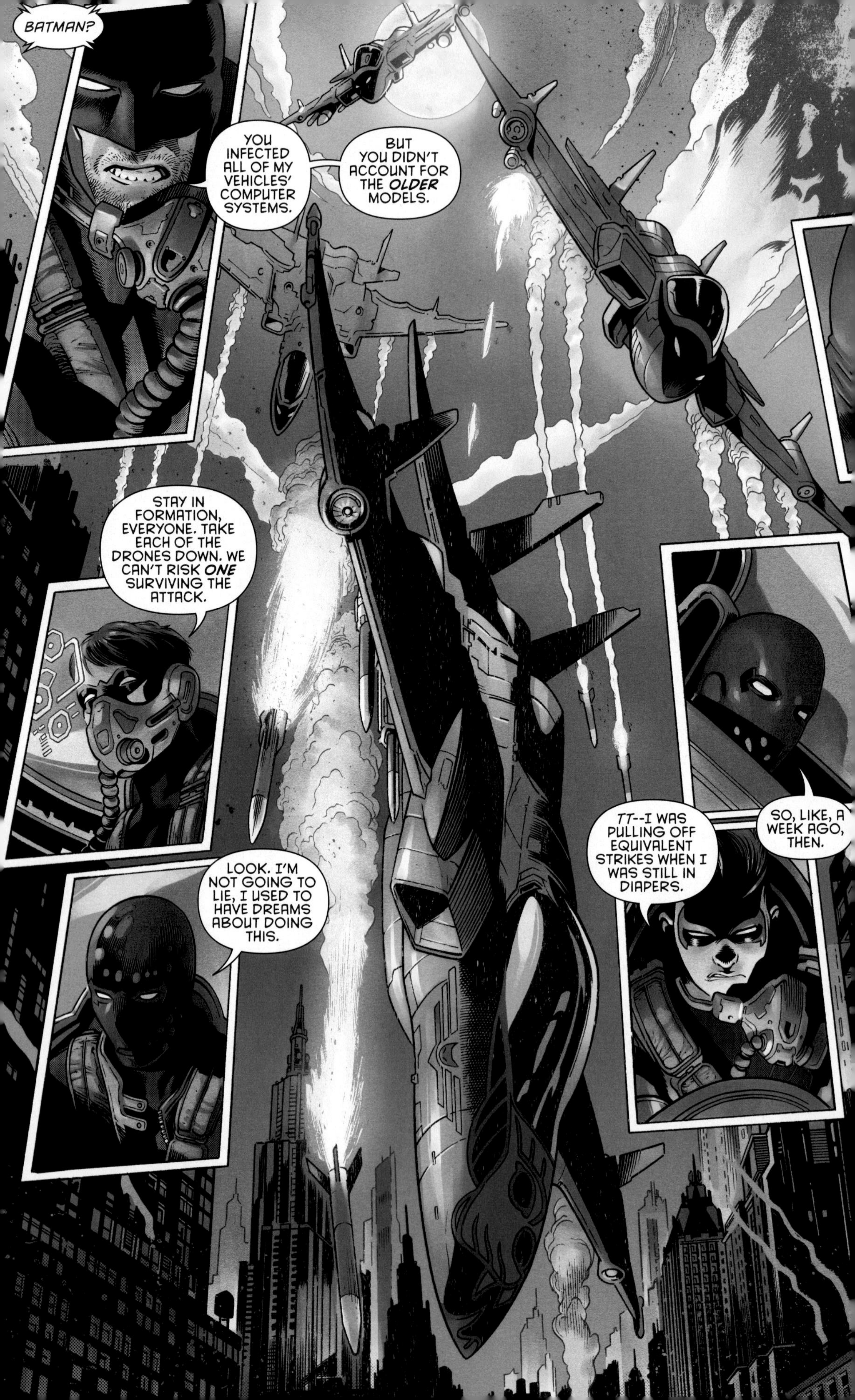
BATMAN?
YOU INFECTED ALL OF MY VEHICLES' COMPUTER SYSTEMS.
BUT YOU DIDN'T ACCOUNT FOR THE *OLDER* MODELS.
STAY IN FORMATION, EVERYONE. TAKE EACH OF THE DRONES DOWN. WE CAN'T RISK *ONE* SURVIVING THE ATTACK.
LOOK. I'M NOT GOING TO LIE, I USED TO HAVE DREAMS ABOUT DOING THIS.
TT--I WAS PULLING OFF EQUIVALENT STRIKES WHEN I WAS STILL IN DIAPERS.
SO, LIKE, A WEEK AGO, THEN.

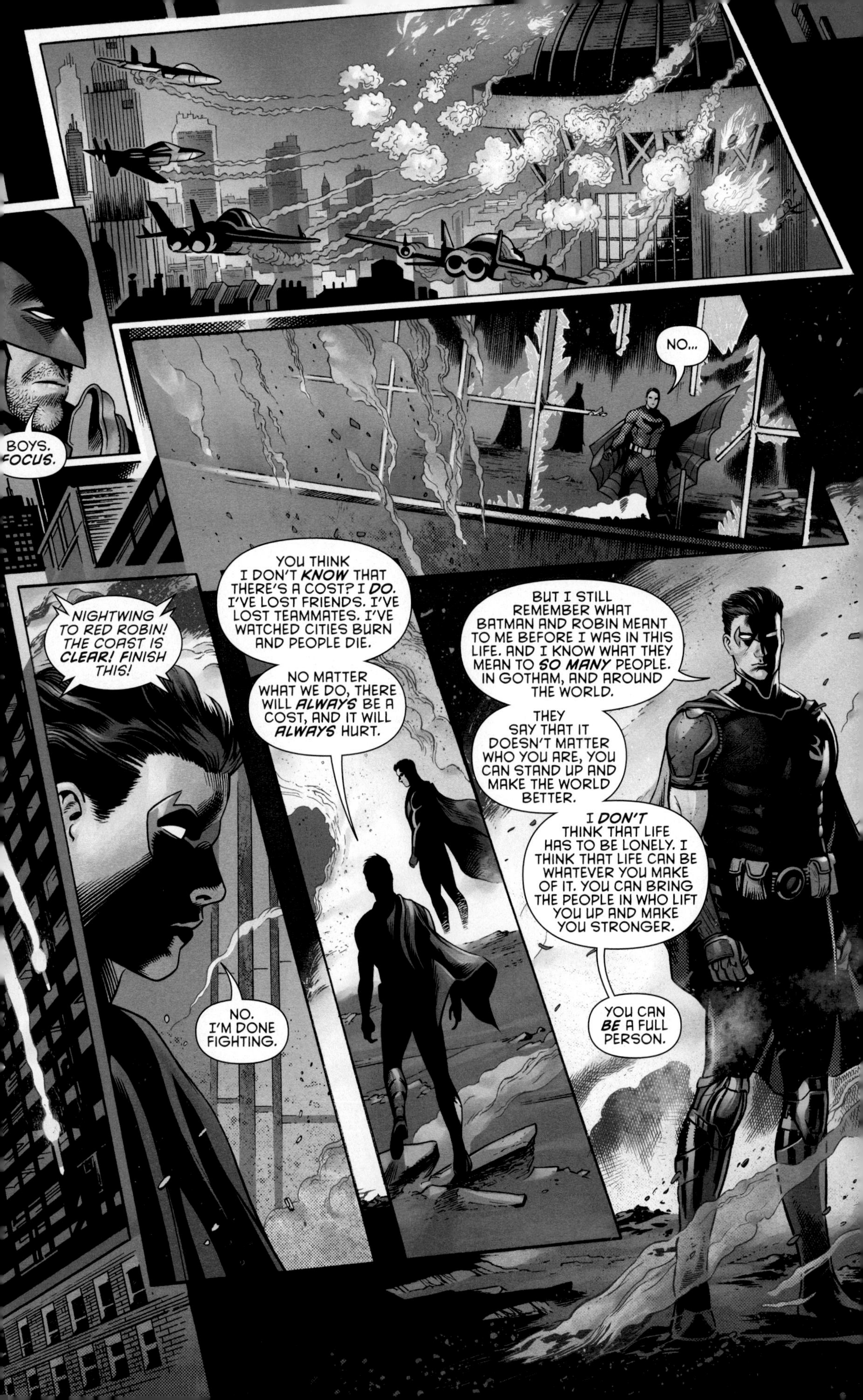
NO...
BOYS. FOCUS.
NIGHTWING TO RED ROBIN! THE COAST IS CLEAR! FINISH THIS!
NO. I'M DONE FIGHTING.
YOU THINK I DON'T KNOW THAT THERE'S A COST? I DO. I'VE LOST FRIENDS. I'VE LOST TEAMMATES. I'VE WATCHED CITIES BURN AND PEOPLE DIE.
NO MATTER WHAT WE DO, THERE WILL ALWAYS BE A COST, AND IT WILL ALWAYS HURT.
BUT I STILL REMEMBER WHAT BATMAN AND ROBIN MEANT TO ME BEFORE I WAS IN THIS LIFE. AND I KNOW WHAT THEY MEAN TO SO MANY PEOPLE. IN GOTHAM, AND AROUND THE WORLD.
THEY SAY THAT IT DOESN'T MATTER WHO YOU ARE, YOU CAN STAND UP AND MAKE THE WORLD BETTER.
I DON'T THINK THAT LIFE HAS TO BE LONELY. I THINK THAT LIFE CAN BE WHATEVER YOU MAKE OF IT. YOU CAN BRING THE PEOPLE IN WHO LIFT YOU UP AND MAKE YOU STRONGER.
YOU CAN BE A FULL PERSON.

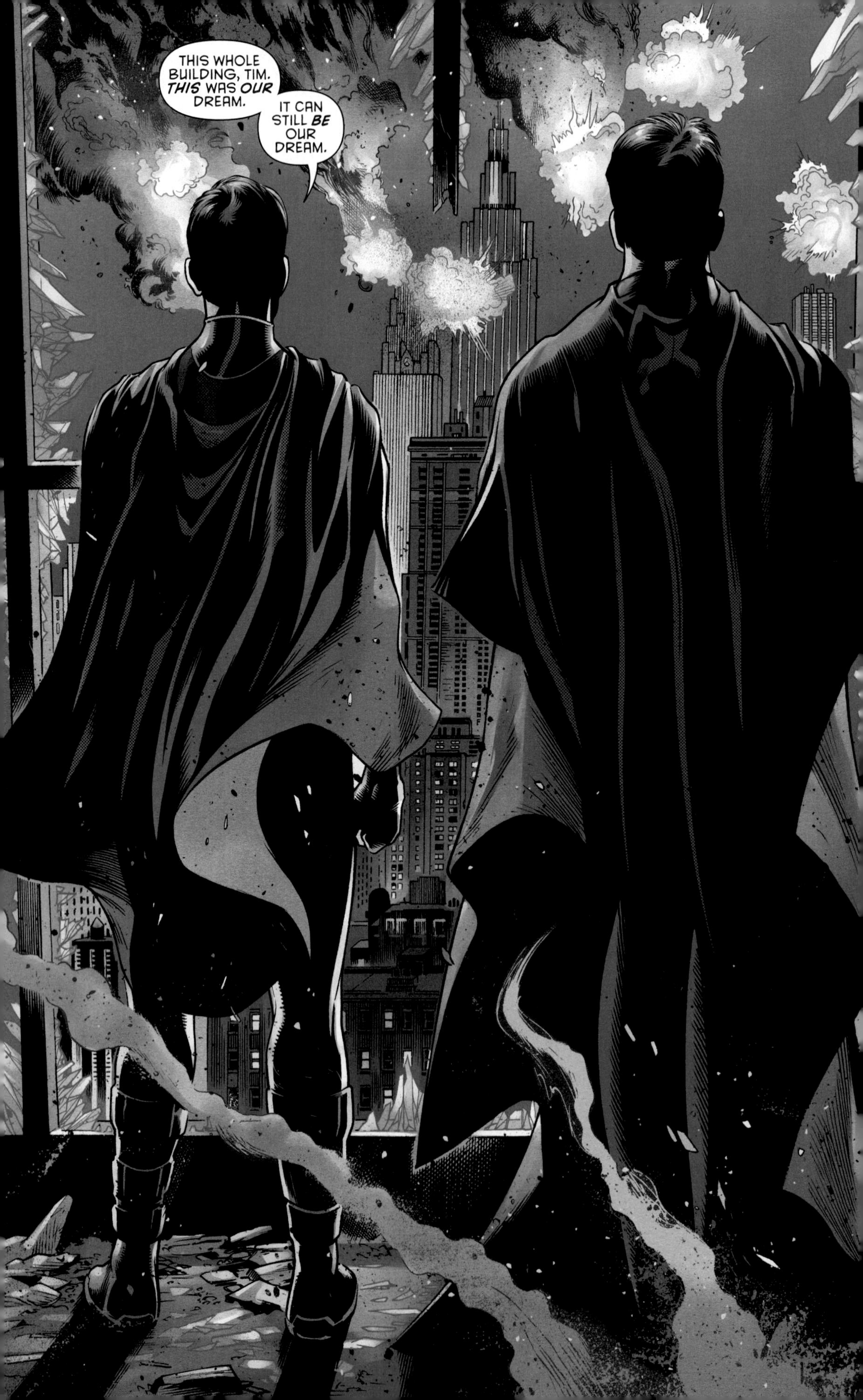

THIS WHOLE BUILDING, TIM. *THIS* WAS *OUR* DREAM.
IT CAN STILL *BE* OUR DREAM.

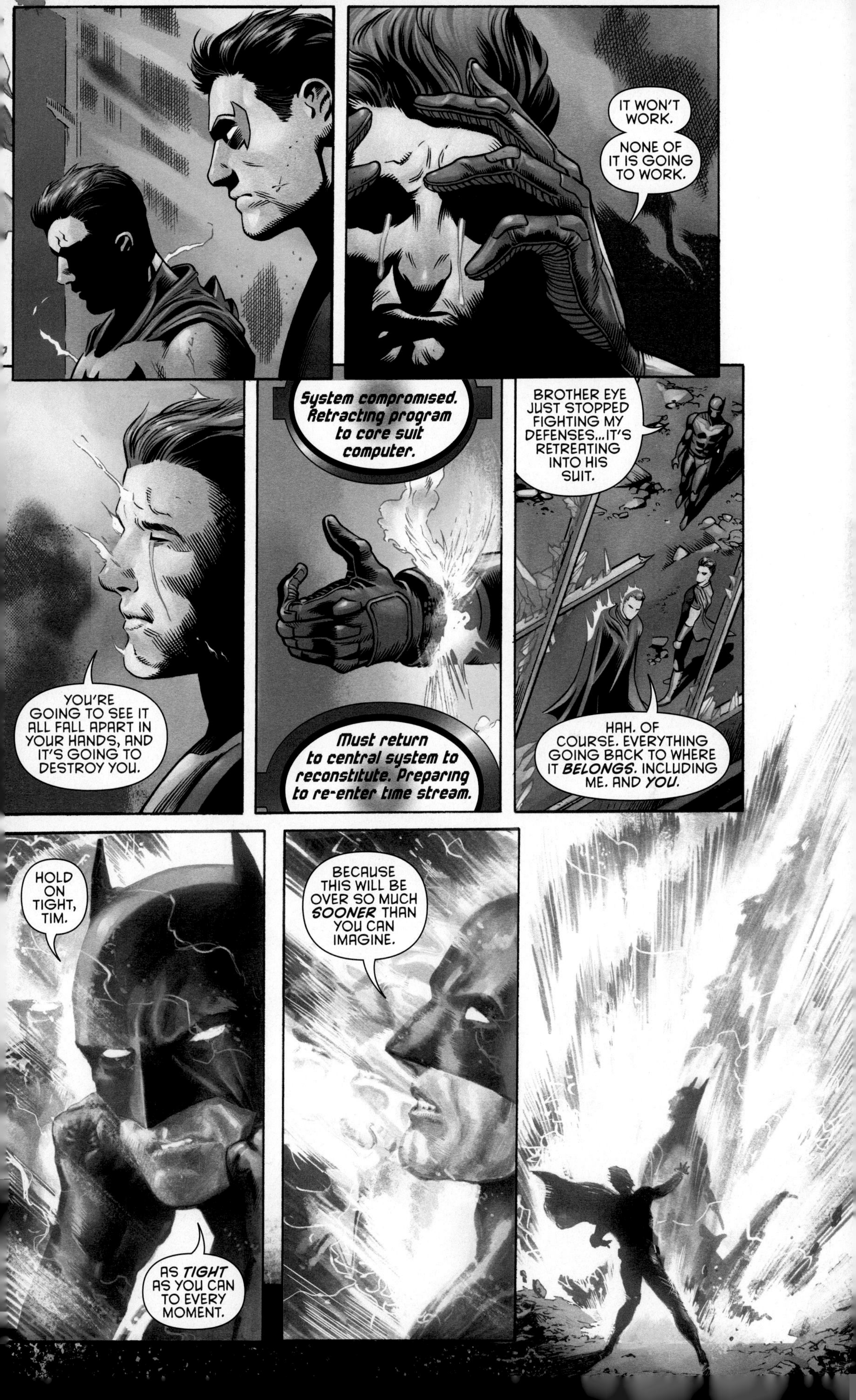
IT WON'T WORK.
NONE OF IT IS GOING TO WORK.
YOU'RE GOING TO SEE IT ALL FALL APART IN YOUR HANDS, AND IT'S GOING TO DESTROY YOU.
System compromised. Retracting program to core suit computer.
Must return to central system to reconstitute. Preparing to re-enter time stream.
BROTHER EYE JUST STOPPED FIGHTING MY DEFENSES...IT'S RETREATING INTO HIS SUIT.
HAH. OF COURSE. EVERYTHING GOING BACK TO WHERE IT *BELONGS*. INCLUDING ME. AND *YOU*.
HOLD ON TIGHT, TIM.
AS *TIGHT* AS YOU CAN TO EVERY MOMENT.
BECAUSE THIS WILL BE OVER SO MUCH *SOONER* THAN YOU CAN IMAGINE.

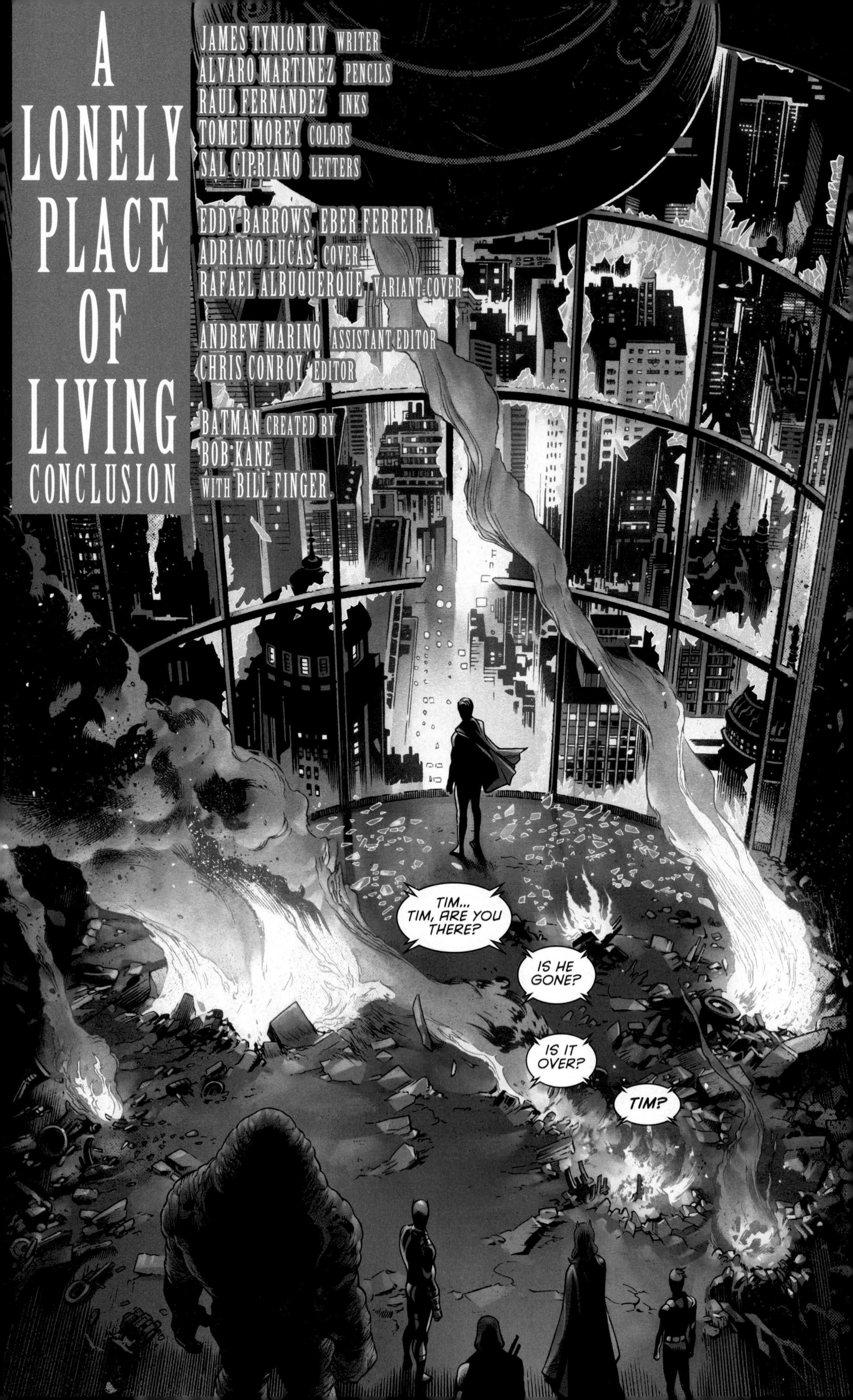
A LONELY PLACE OF LIVING
CONCLUSION
JAMES TYNION IV WRITER
ALVARO MARTINEZ PENCILS
RAUL FERNANDEZ INKS
TOMEU MOREY COLORS
SAL CIPRIANO LETTERS
EDDY BARROWS, EBER FERREIRA,
ADRIANO LUCAS COVER
RAFAEL ALBUQUERQUE VARIANT COVER
ANDREW MARINO ASSISTANT EDITOR
CHRIS CONROY EDITOR
BATMAN CREATED BY
BOB KANE
WITH BILL FINGER.
TIM... TIM, ARE YOU THERE?
IS HE GONE?
IS IT OVER?
TIM?

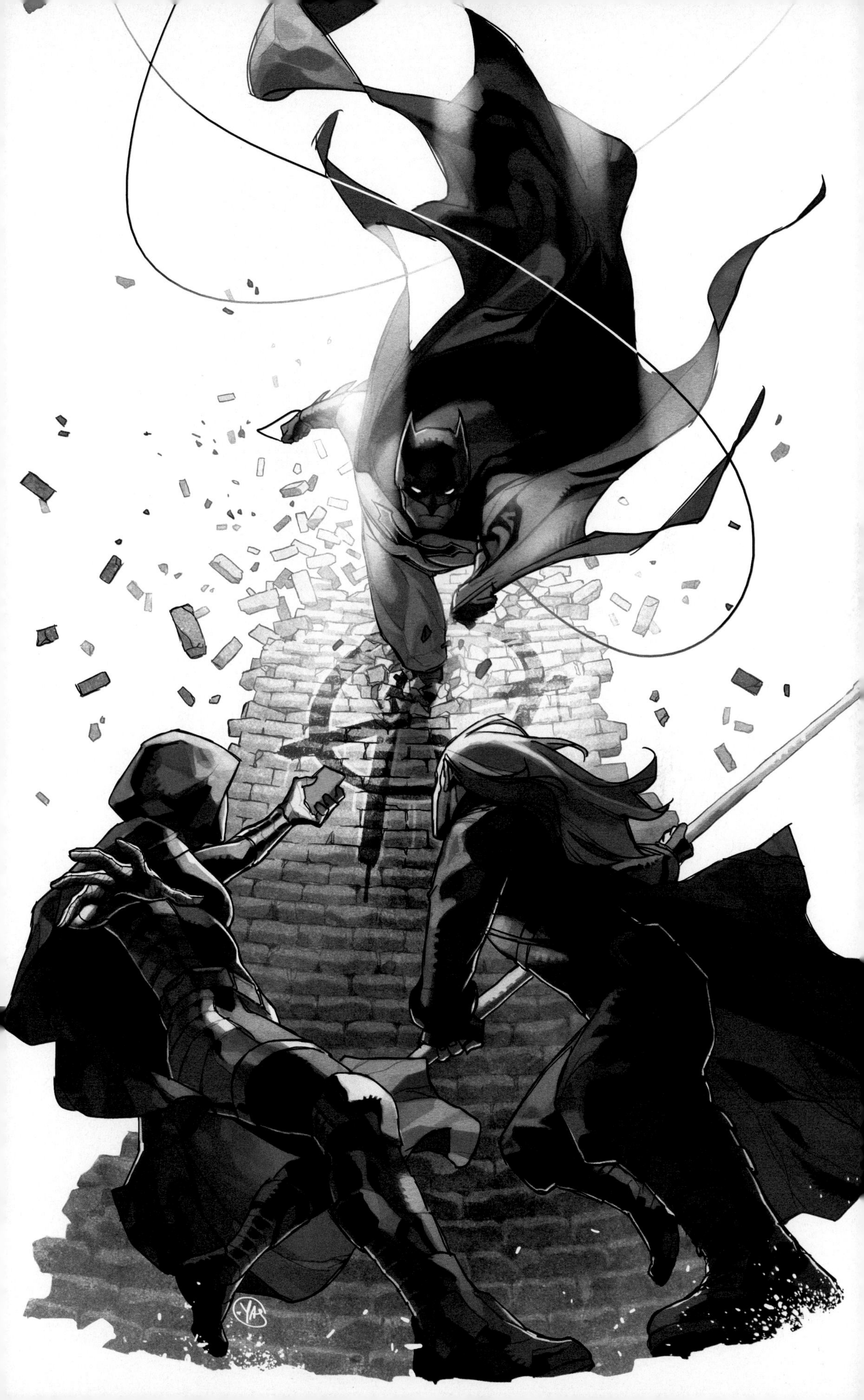

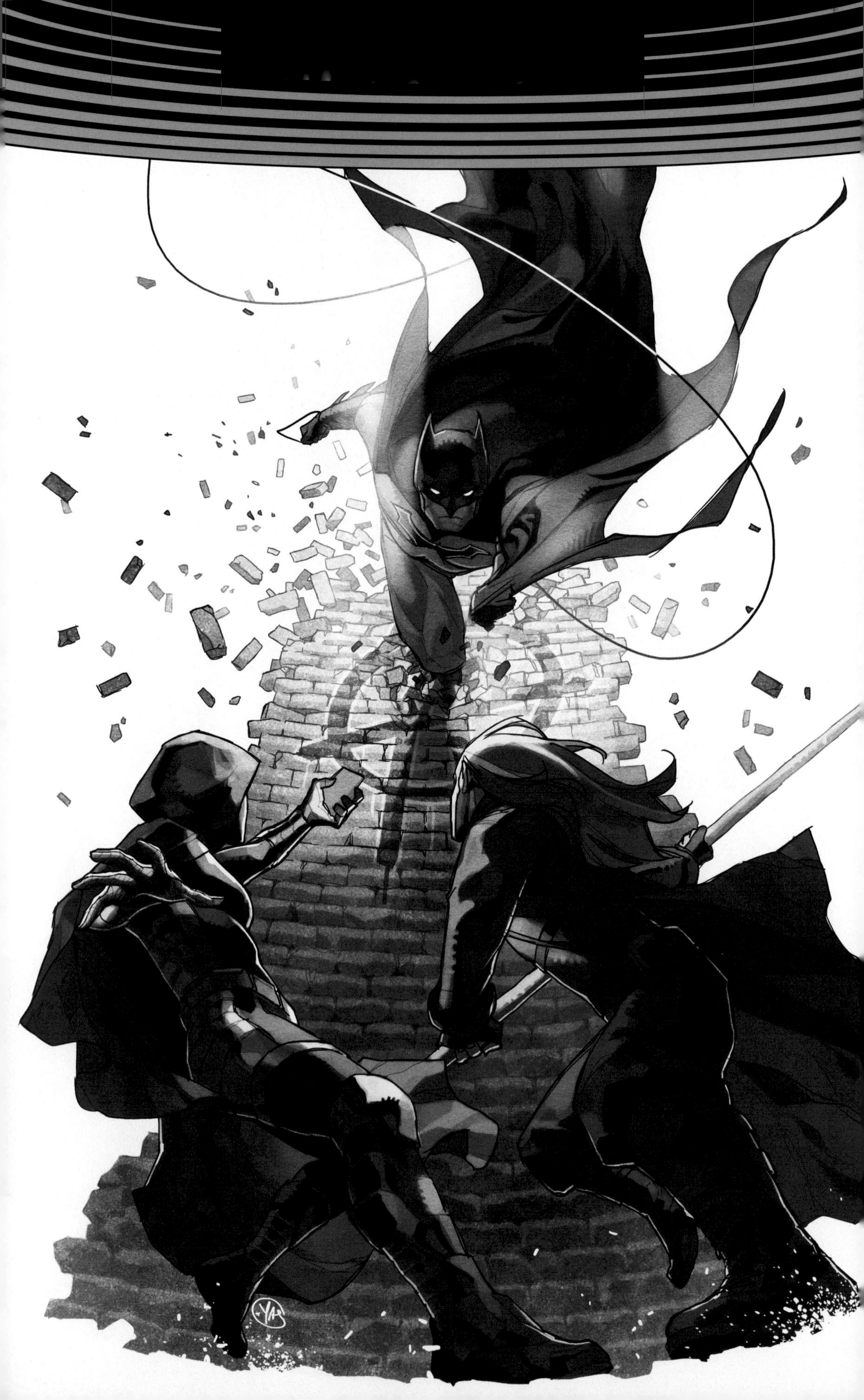

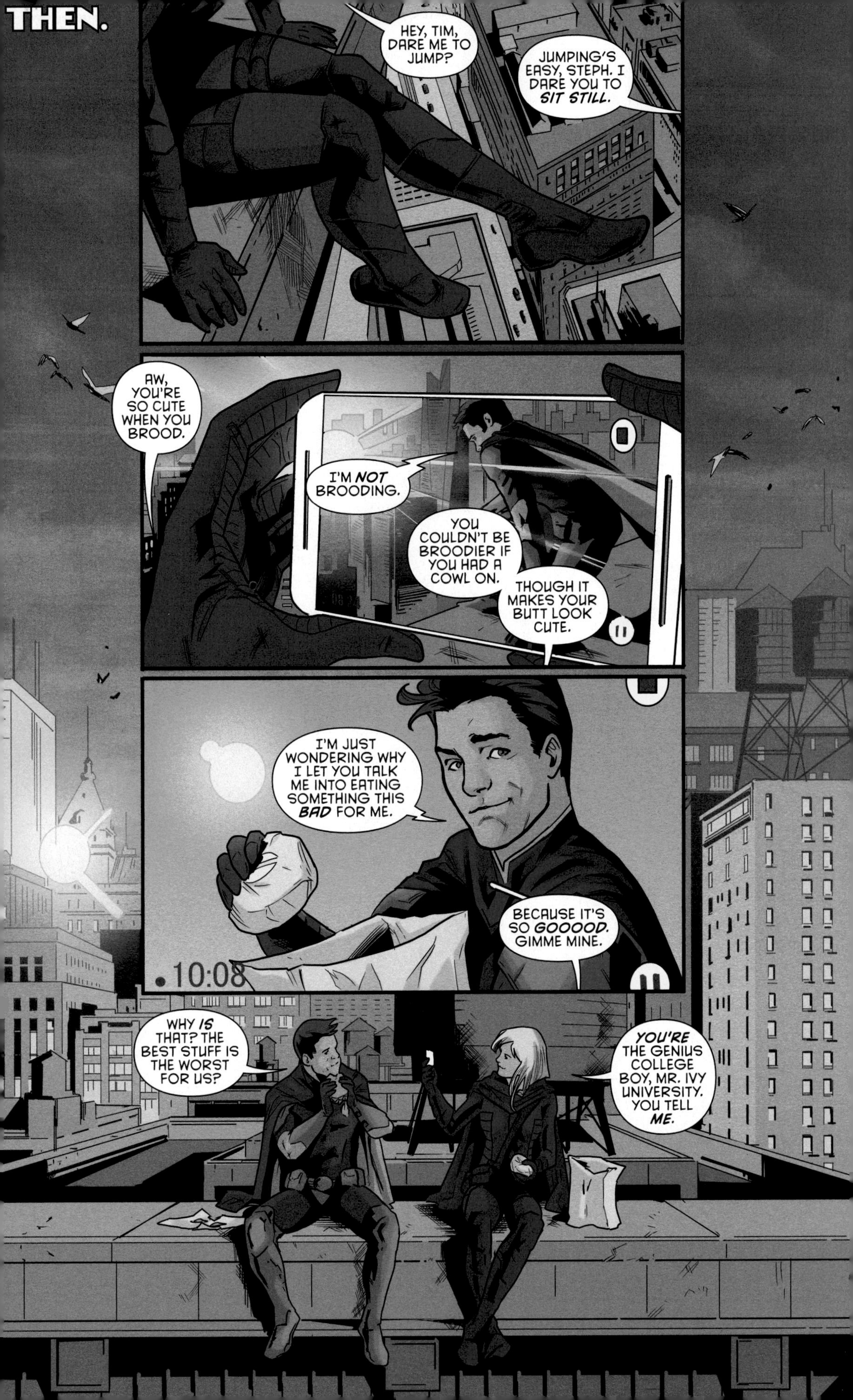
THEN.
HEY, TIM, DARE ME TO JUMP?
JUMPING'S EASY, STEPH. I DARE YOU TO SIT STILL.
AW, YOU'RE SO CUTE WHEN YOU BROOD.
I'M NOT BROODING.
YOU COULDN'T BE BROODIER IF YOU HAD A COWL ON.
THOUGH IT MAKES YOUR BUTT LOOK CUTE.
I'M JUST WONDERING WHY I LET YOU TALK ME INTO EATING SOMETHING THIS BAD FOR ME.
BECAUSE IT'S SO GOOOOD. GIMME MINE.
10:08
WHY IS THAT? THE BEST STUFF IS THE WORST FOR US?
YOU'RE THE GENIUS COLLEGE BOY, MR. IVY UNIVERSITY. YOU TELL ME.

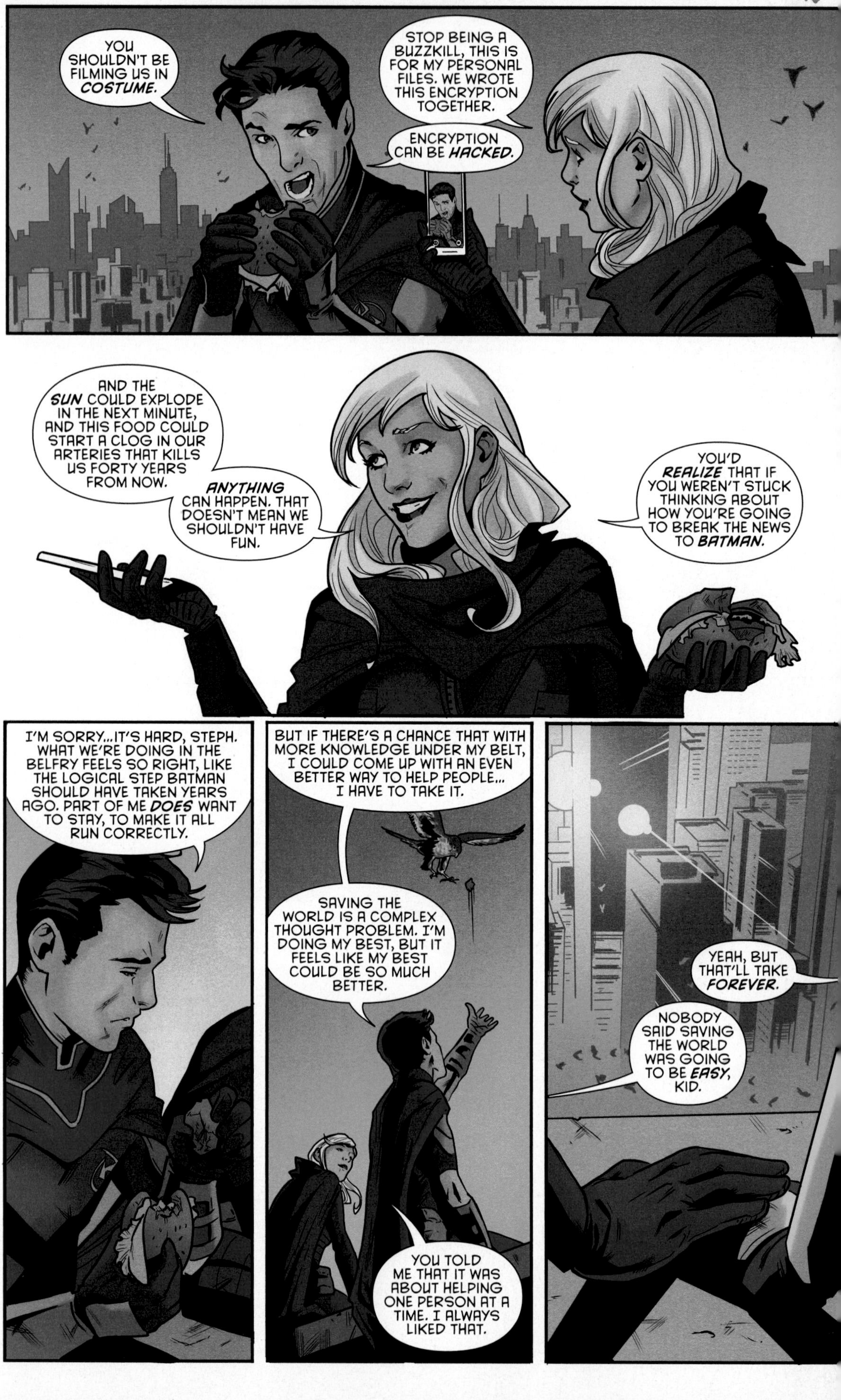
YOU SHOULDN'T BE FILMING US IN COSTUME.
STOP BEING A BUZZKILL, THIS IS FOR MY PERSONAL FILES. WE WROTE THIS ENCRYPTION TOGETHER.
ENCRYPTION CAN BE HACKED.
AND THE SUN COULD EXPLODE IN THE NEXT MINUTE, AND THIS FOOD COULD START A CLOG IN OUR ARTERIES THAT KILLS US FORTY YEARS FROM NOW.
ANYTHING CAN HAPPEN. THAT DOESN'T MEAN WE SHOULDN'T HAVE FUN.
YOU'D REALIZE THAT IF YOU WEREN'T STUCK THINKING ABOUT HOW YOU'RE GOING TO BREAK THE NEWS TO BATMAN.
I'M SORRY...IT'S HARD, STEPH. WHAT WE'RE DOING IN THE BELFRY FEELS SO RIGHT, LIKE THE LOGICAL STEP BATMAN SHOULD HAVE TAKEN YEARS AGO. PART OF ME DOES WANT TO STAY, TO MAKE IT ALL RUN CORRECTLY.
BUT IF THERE'S A CHANCE THAT WITH MORE KNOWLEDGE UNDER MY BELT, I COULD COME UP WITH AN EVEN BETTER WAY TO HELP PEOPLE... I HAVE TO TAKE IT.
SAVING THE WORLD IS A COMPLEX THOUGHT PROBLEM. I'M DOING MY BEST, BUT IT FEELS LIKE MY BEST COULD BE SO MUCH BETTER.
YOU TOLD ME THAT IT WAS ABOUT HELPING ONE PERSON AT A TIME. I ALWAYS LIKED THAT.
YEAH, BUT THAT'LL TAKE FOREVER.
NOBODY SAID SAVING THE WORLD WAS GOING TO BE EASY, KID.

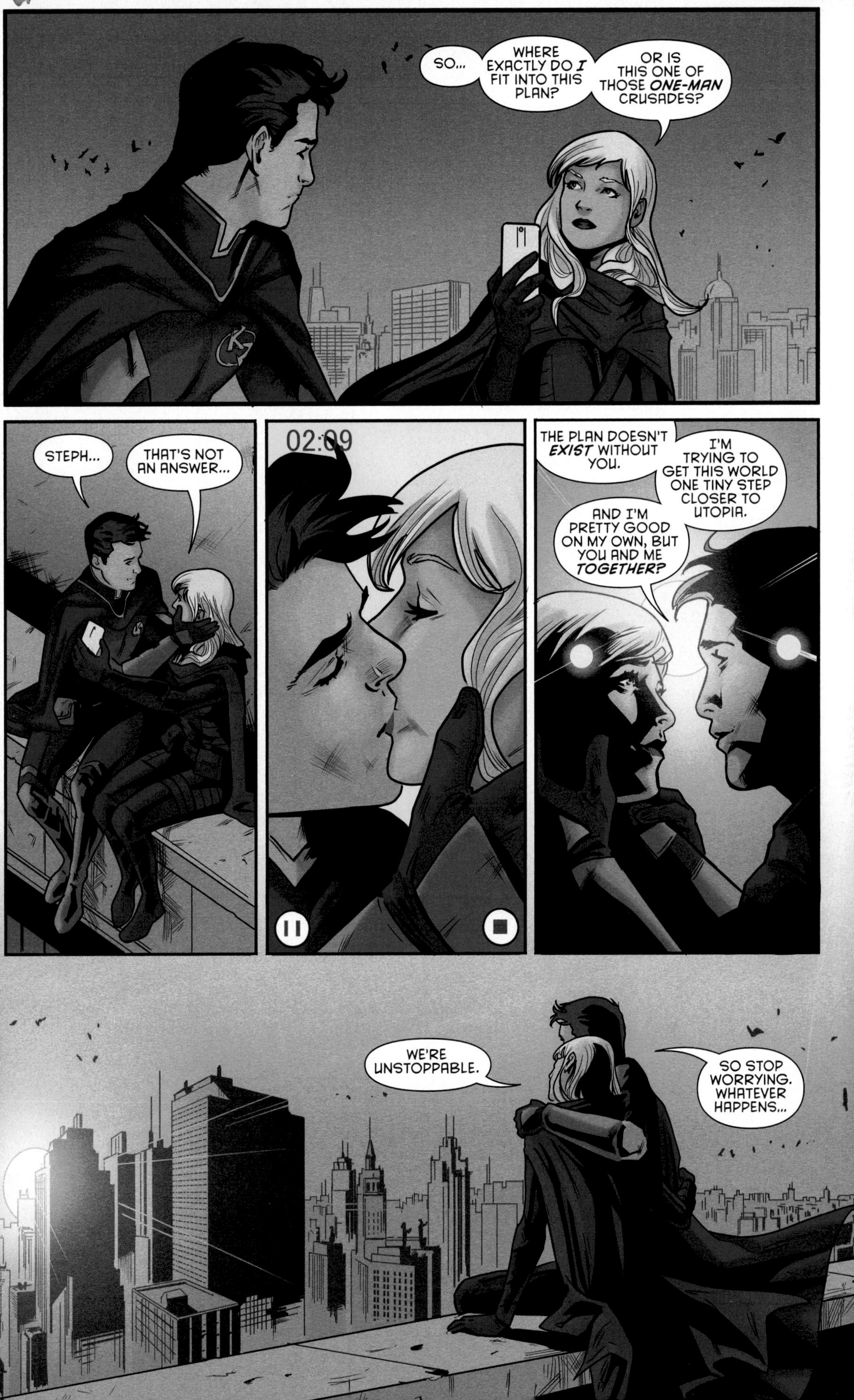
SO...
WHERE EXACTLY DO I FIT INTO THIS PLAN?
OR IS THIS ONE OF THOSE ONE-MAN CRUSADES?
STEPH...
THAT'S NOT AN ANSWER...
02:09
THE PLAN DOESN'T EXIST WITHOUT YOU.
I'M TRYING TO GET THIS WORLD ONE TINY STEP CLOSER TO UTOPIA.
AND I'M PRETTY GOOD ON MY OWN, BUT YOU AND ME TOGETHER?
WE'RE UNSTOPPABLE.
SO STOP WORRYING. WHATEVER HAPPENS...

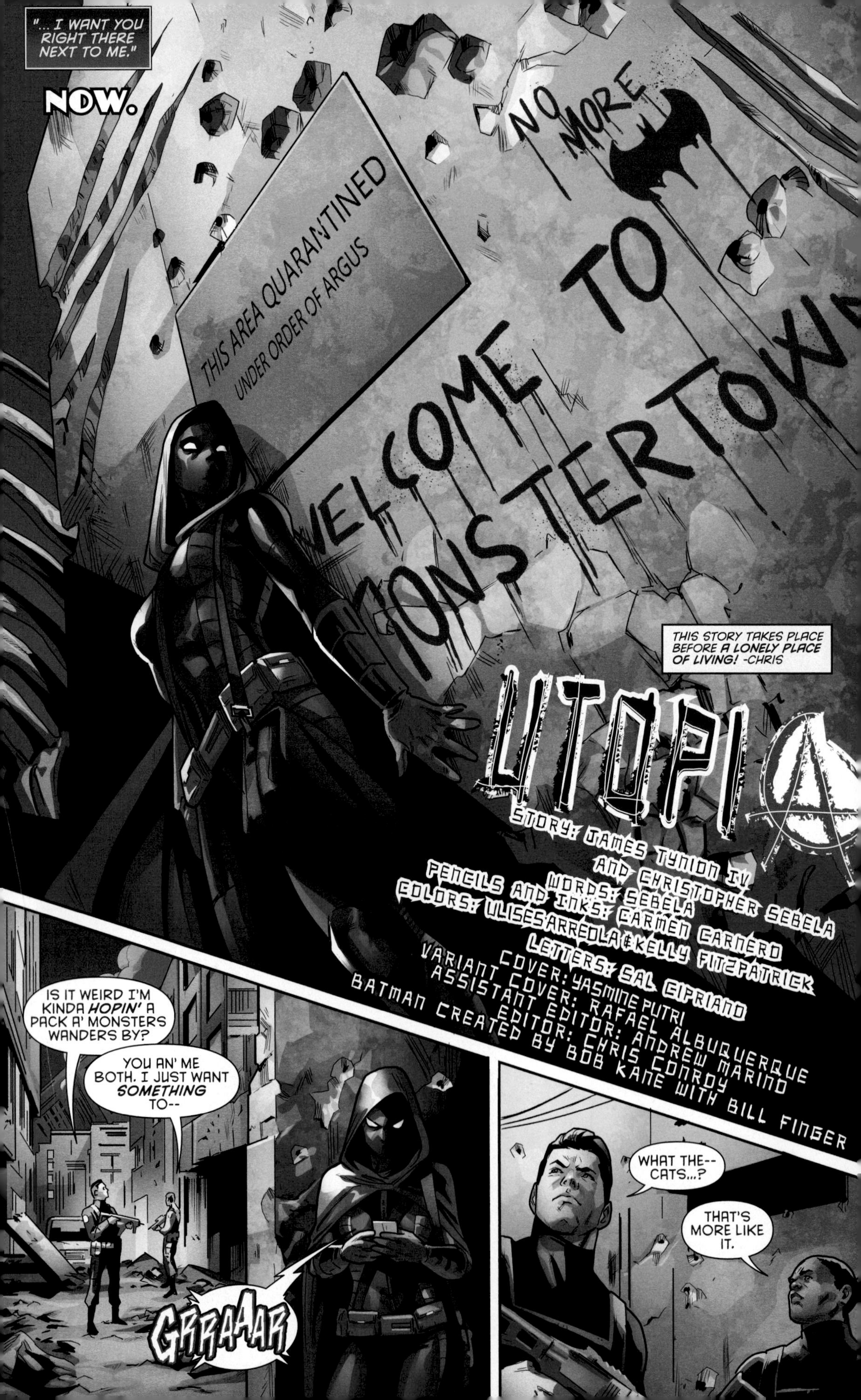
"... I WANT YOU RIGHT THERE NEXT TO ME."
NOW.
THIS AREA QUARANTINED
UNDER ORDER OF ARGUS
NO MORE
WELCOME TO MONSTERTOWN
THIS STORY TAKES PLACE BEFORE A LONELY PLACE OF LIVING! -CHRIS
UTOPIA
STORY: JAMES TYNION IV AND CHRISTOPHER SEBELA
WORDS: SEBELA
PENCILS AND INKS: CARMEN CARNERO
COLORS: ULISES ARREOLA & KELLY FITZPATRICK
LETTERS: SAL CIPRIANO
COVER: YASMINE PUTRI
VARIANT COVER: RAFAEL ALBUQUERQUE
ASSISTANT EDITOR: ANDREW MARINO
EDITOR: CHRIS CONROY
BATMAN CREATED BY BOB KANE WITH BILL FINGER
IS IT WEIRD I'M KINDA HOPIN' A PACK A' MONSTERS WANDERS BY?
YOU AN' ME BOTH. I JUST WANT SOMETHING TO--
GRRAAAR
WHAT THE--CATS...?
THAT'S MORE LIKE IT.

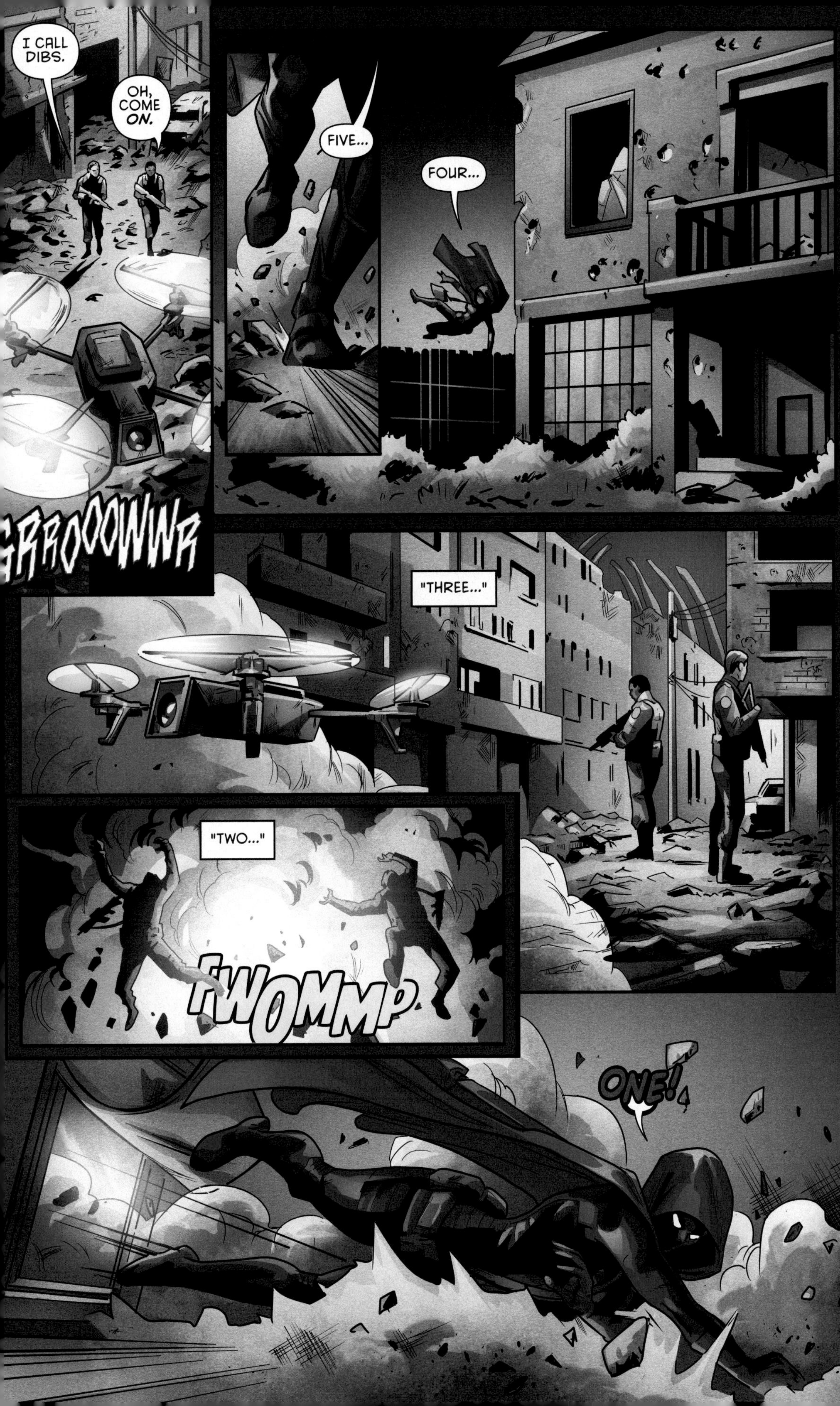
I CALL DIBS.
OH, COME ON.
GRROOOWWR
FIVE...
FOUR...
"THREE..."
"TWO..."
FWOMMP
ONE!

SPOILER. I WAS STARTING TO WORRY YOU WERE GOING TO MISS THE HAND-OFF.

PERHAPS I NEEDED TO SEE HOW FAR YOU WERE WILLING TO TAKE THIS.

YOU *DO* REALIZE THERE ARE LIKE, A HUNDRED PLACES IN GOTHAM WHERE WE COULD MEET THAT WOULDN'T HAVE COST ME ONE OF MY DRONES?

ARGUS AGENTS ARE STILL SWARMING ALL OVER MONSTERTOWN. I HAD TO KNOCK A FEW OUT JUST TO GET IN THE BUILDING.

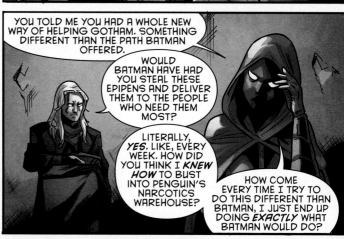

YOU TOLD ME YOU HAD A WHOLE NEW WAY OF HELPING GOTHAM. SOMETHING DIFFERENT THAN THE PATH BATMAN OFFERED.

WOULD BATMAN HAVE HAD YOU STEAL THESE EPIPENS AND DELIVER THEM TO THE PEOPLE WHO NEED THEM MOST?

LITERALLY, *YES.* LIKE, EVERY WEEK. HOW DID YOU THINK I *KNEW HOW* TO BUST INTO PENGUIN'S NARCOTICS WAREHOUSE?

HOW COME EVERY TIME I TRY TO DO THIS DIFFERENT THAN BATMAN, I JUST END UP DOING *EXACTLY* WHAT BATMAN WOULD DO?

I PROMISE YOU, STEPHANIE. I HAVE A BETTER WAY...WE'VE TALKED SO MUCH ABOUT HOW THE BAT'S METHODS FALL SHORT IN EVERY WAY...HOW THEY HURT MORE PEOPLE THAN THEY HELP.

AND THAT'S ALL IT IS, LONNIE. *TALK. I WANTED MORE* THAN THAT. IT'S JUST BEEN WEEKS OF VAGUE MENTIONS OF VAGUE PEOPLE YOU MAY OR MAY *NOT* BE HELPING.

I NEED MORE THAN *VAGUE.* I NEED MORE THAN *TALK.*

I DIDN'T REALIZE YOU FELT THIS WAY...I THOUGHT YOU WOULD UNDERSTAND THAT I NEEDED TO KNOW THAT I COULD TRUST YOU.

I'M NOT THE ONE WHO WON'T TAKE OFF THE *MASK,* LONNIE.

I'VE BEEN KEPT IN THE DARK BEFORE AND IT *SUCKS.*

THERE WAS A MOMENT THERE WHERE I THOUGHT THAT YOU AND I MIGHT BE ON THE SAME PAGE...

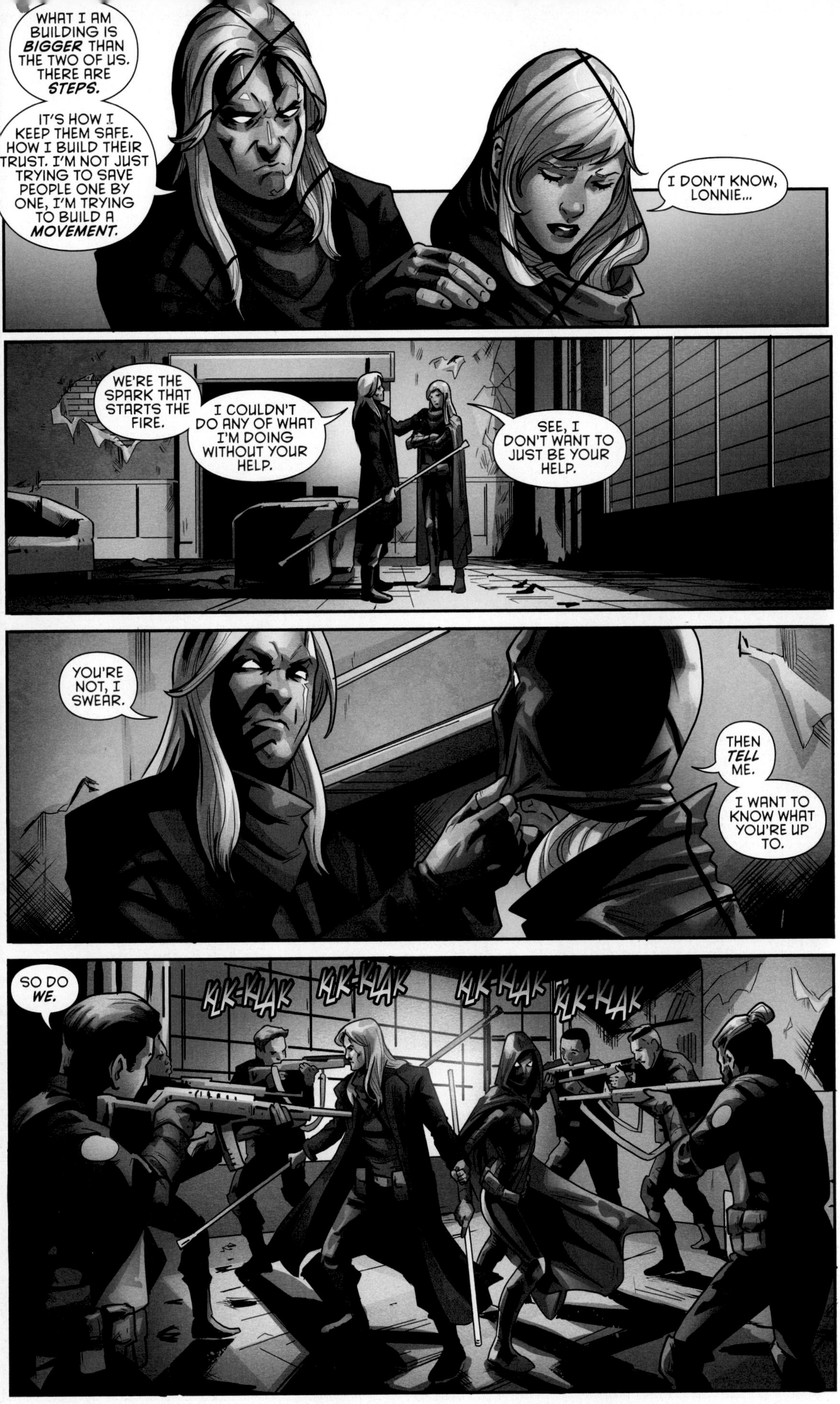
WHAT I AM BUILDING IS BIGGER THAN THE TWO OF US. THERE ARE STEPS.
IT'S HOW I KEEP THEM SAFE. HOW I BUILD THEIR TRUST. I'M NOT JUST TRYING TO SAVE PEOPLE ONE BY ONE, I'M TRYING TO BUILD A MOVEMENT.
I DON'T KNOW, LONNIE...
WE'RE THE SPARK THAT STARTS THE FIRE.
I COULDN'T DO ANY OF WHAT I'M DOING WITHOUT YOUR HELP.
SEE, I DON'T WANT TO JUST BE YOUR HELP.
YOU'RE NOT, I SWEAR.
THEN TELL ME.
I WANT TO KNOW WHAT YOU'RE UP TO.
SO DO WE.
KLIK-KLAK
KLIK-KLAK
KLIK-KLAK
KLIK-KLAK

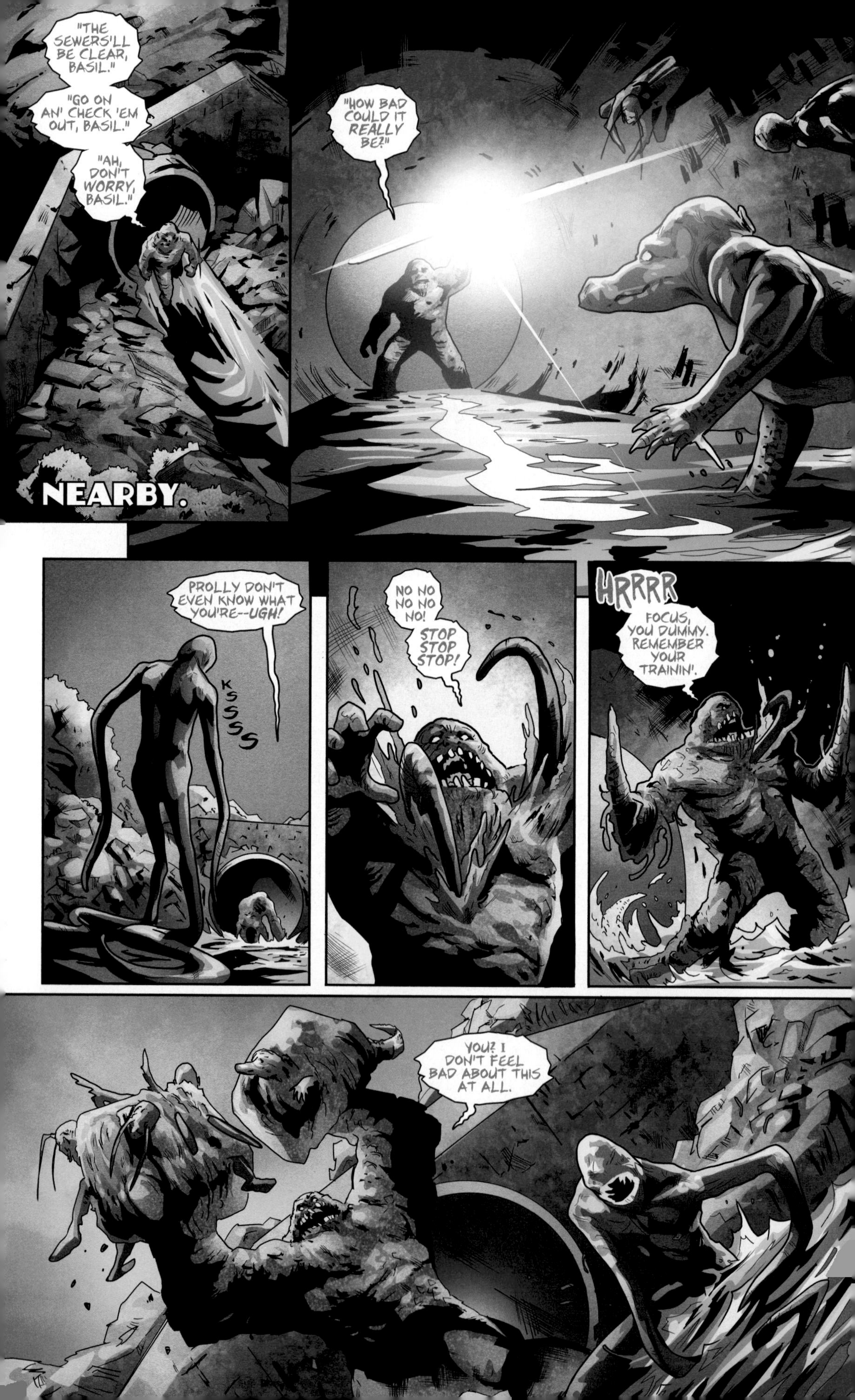
"THE SEWERS'LL BE CLEAR, BASIL."
"GO ON AN' CHECK 'EM OUT, BASIL."
"AH, DON'T WORRY, BASIL."
NEARBY.
"HOW BAD COULD IT REALLY BE?"
PROLLY DON'T EVEN KNOW WHAT YOU'RE--UGH!
KSSSS
NO NO NO NO NO!
STOP STOP STOP!
HRRRR
FOCUS, YOU DUMMY. REMEMBER YOUR TRAININ'.
YOU? I DON'T FEEL BAD ABOUT THIS AT ALL.

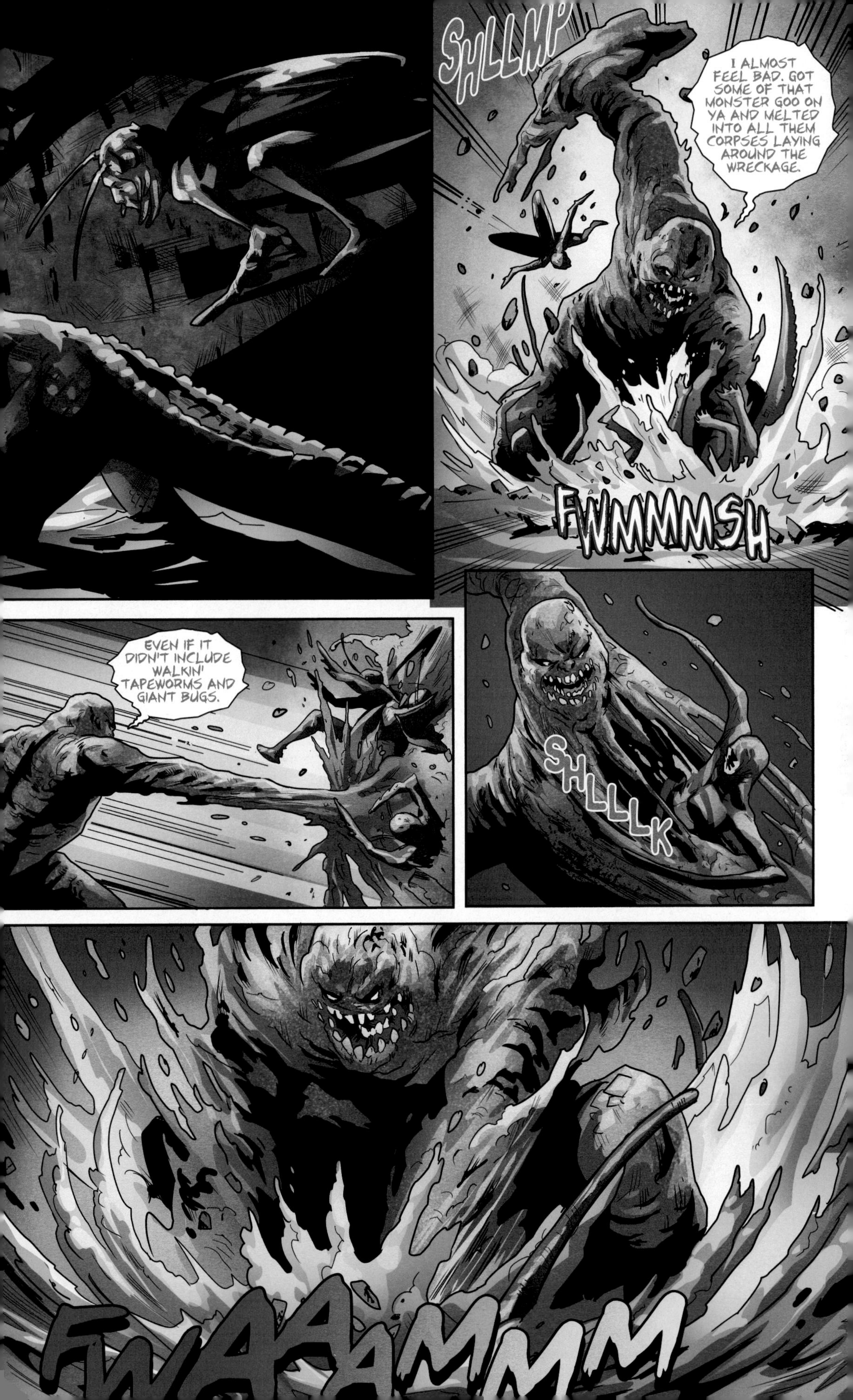
SHLLMP
I ALMOST FEEL BAD. GOT SOME OF THAT MONSTER GOO ON YA AND MELTED INTO ALL THEM CORPSES LAYING AROUND THE WRECKAGE.
FWMMMSH
EVEN IF IT DIDN'T INCLUDE WALKIN' TAPEWORMS AND GIANT BUGS.
SHLLLK
FWAAAMMM

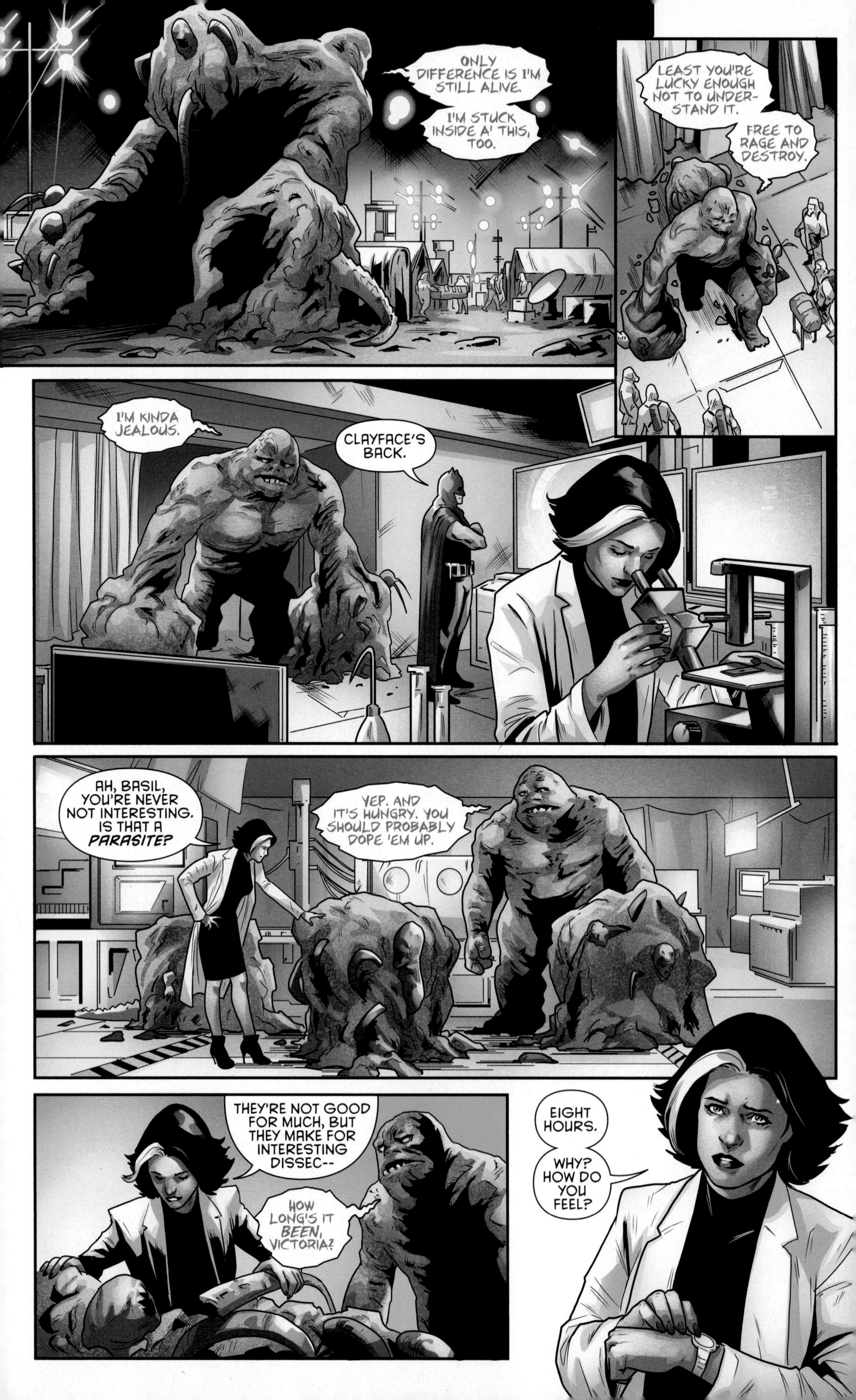
ONLY DIFFERENCE IS I'M STILL ALIVE.
I'M STUCK INSIDE A' THIS, TOO.
LEAST YOU'RE LUCKY ENOUGH NOT TO UNDER-STAND IT.
FREE TO RAGE AND DESTROY.
I'M KINDA JEALOUS.
CLAYFACE'S BACK.
AH, BASIL, YOU'RE NEVER NOT INTERESTING. IS THAT A *PARASITE?*
YEP. AND IT'S HUNGRY. YOU SHOULD PROBABLY DOPE 'EM UP.
THEY'RE NOT GOOD FOR MUCH, BUT THEY MAKE FOR INTERESTING DISSEC--
HOW LONG'S IT *BEEN,* VICTORIA?
EIGHT HOURS.
WHY? HOW DO YOU FEEL?

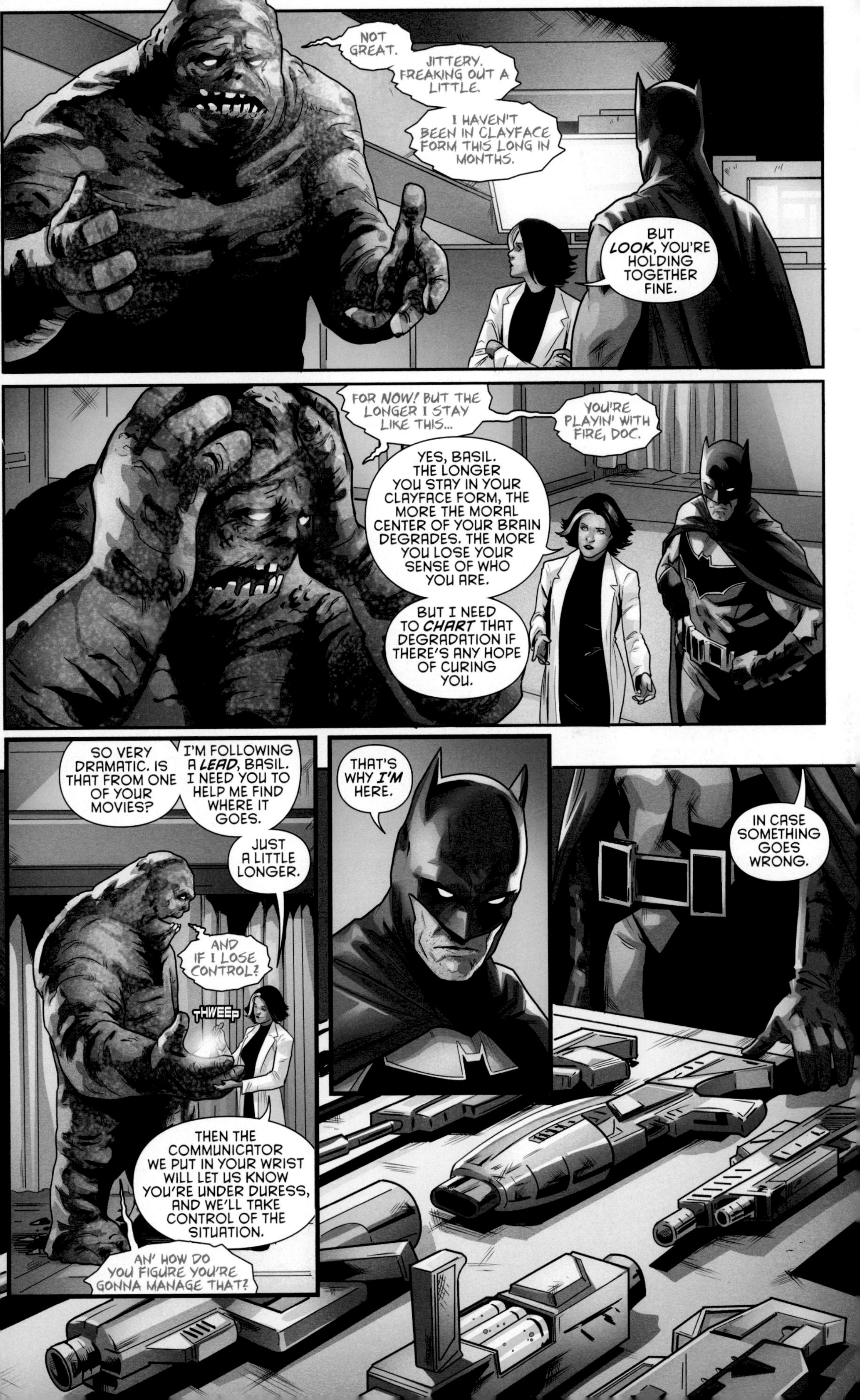
NOT GREAT.
JITTERY. FREAKING OUT A LITTLE.
I HAVEN'T BEEN IN CLAYFACE FORM THIS LONG IN MONTHS.
BUT LOOK, YOU'RE HOLDING TOGETHER FINE.
FOR NOW! BUT THE LONGER I STAY LIKE THIS...
YOU'RE PLAYIN' WITH FIRE, DOC.
YES, BASIL. THE LONGER YOU STAY IN YOUR CLAYFACE FORM, THE MORE THE MORAL CENTER OF YOUR BRAIN DEGRADES. THE MORE YOU LOSE YOUR SENSE OF WHO YOU ARE.
BUT I NEED TO CHART THAT DEGRADATION IF THERE'S ANY HOPE OF CURING YOU.
SO VERY DRAMATIC. IS THAT FROM ONE OF YOUR MOVIES?
I'M FOLLOWING A LEAD, BASIL. I NEED YOU TO HELP ME FIND WHERE IT GOES.
JUST A LITTLE LONGER.
AND IF I LOSE CONTROL?
THWEEP
THEN THE COMMUNICATOR WE PUT IN YOUR WRIST WILL LET US KNOW YOU'RE UNDER DURESS, AND WE'LL TAKE CONTROL OF THE SITUATION.
AN' HOW DO YOU FIGURE YOU'RE GONNA MANAGE THAT?
THAT'S WHY I'M HERE.
IN CASE SOMETHING GOES WRONG.

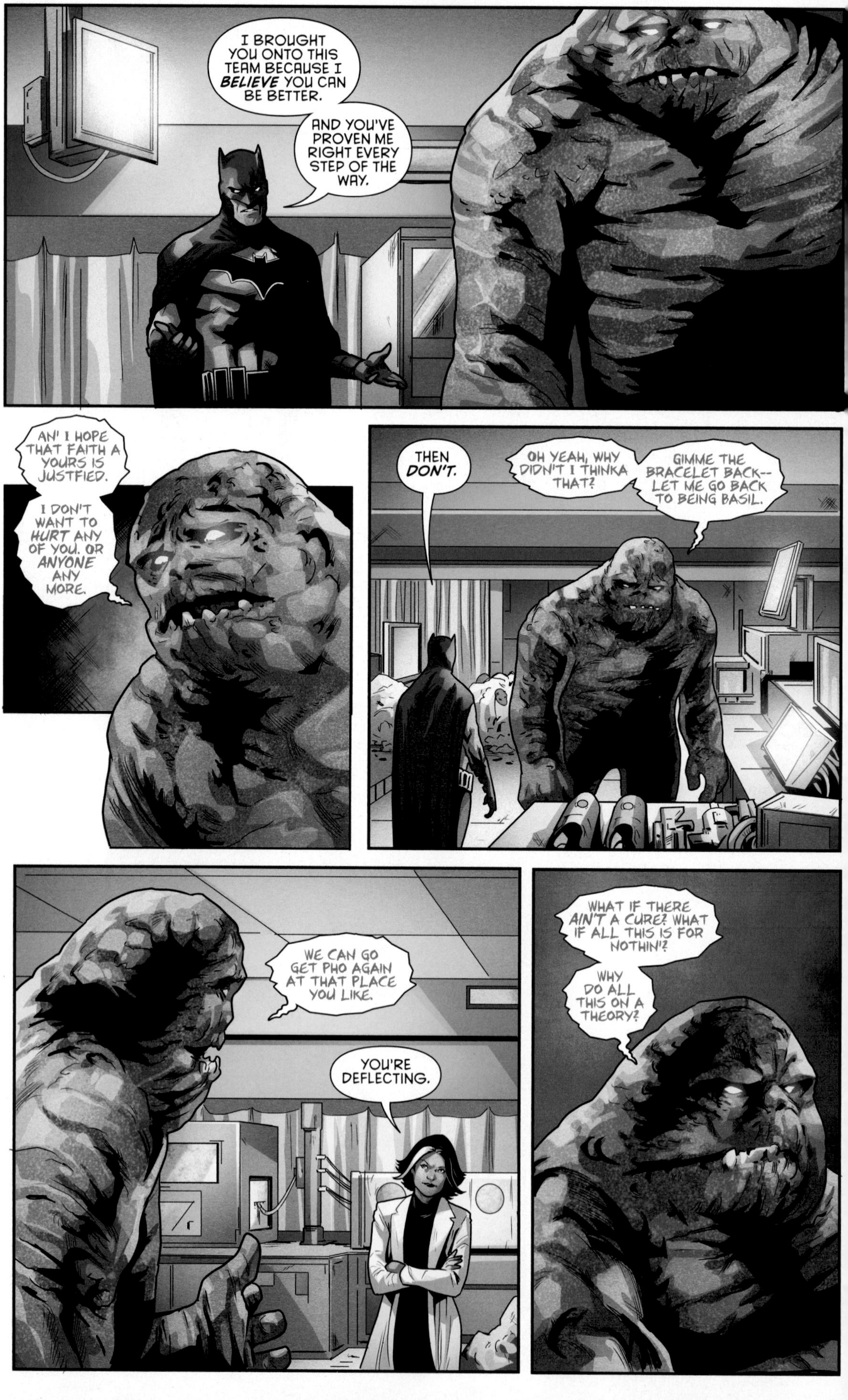
I BROUGHT YOU ONTO THIS TEAM BECAUSE I *BELIEVE* YOU CAN BE BETTER.
AND YOU'VE PROVEN ME RIGHT EVERY STEP OF THE WAY.
AN' I HOPE THAT FAITH A YOURS IS JUSTFIED.
I DON'T WANT TO *HURT* ANY OF YOU. OR *ANYONE* ANY MORE.
THEN *DON'T.*
OH YEAH, WHY DIDN'T I THINKA THAT?
GIMME THE BRACELET BACK-- LET ME GO BACK TO BEING BASIL.
WE CAN GO GET PHO AGAIN AT THAT PLACE YOU LIKE.
YOU'RE DEFLECTING.
WHAT IF THERE *AIN'T* A CURE? WHAT IF ALL THIS IS FOR NOTHIN'?
WHY DO ALL THIS ON A THEORY?

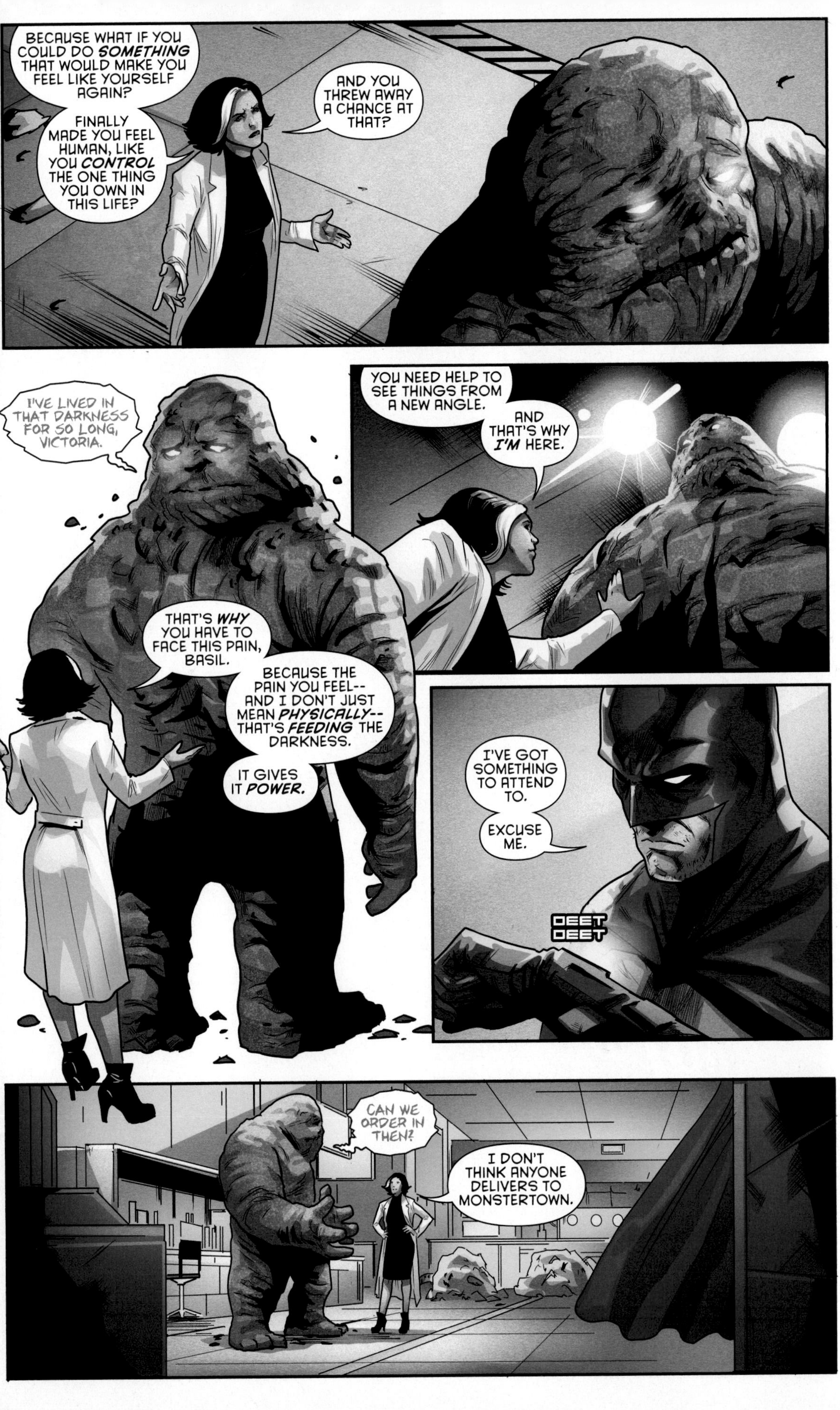

BECAUSE WHAT IF YOU COULD DO SOMETHING THAT WOULD MAKE YOU FEEL LIKE YOURSELF AGAIN?
FINALLY MADE YOU FEEL HUMAN, LIKE YOU CONTROL THE ONE THING YOU OWN IN THIS LIFE?
AND YOU THREW AWAY A CHANCE AT THAT?
I'VE LIVED IN THAT DARKNESS FOR SO LONG, VICTORIA.
THAT'S WHY YOU HAVE TO FACE THIS PAIN, BASIL.
BECAUSE THE PAIN YOU FEEL--AND I DON'T JUST MEAN PHYSICALLY--THAT'S FEEDING THE DARKNESS.
IT GIVES IT POWER.
YOU NEED HELP TO SEE THINGS FROM A NEW ANGLE.
AND THAT'S WHY I'M HERE.
I'VE GOT SOMETHING TO ATTEND TO.
EXCUSE ME.
DEET DEET
CAN WE ORDER IN THEN?
I DON'T THINK ANYONE DELIVERS TO MONSTERTOWN.

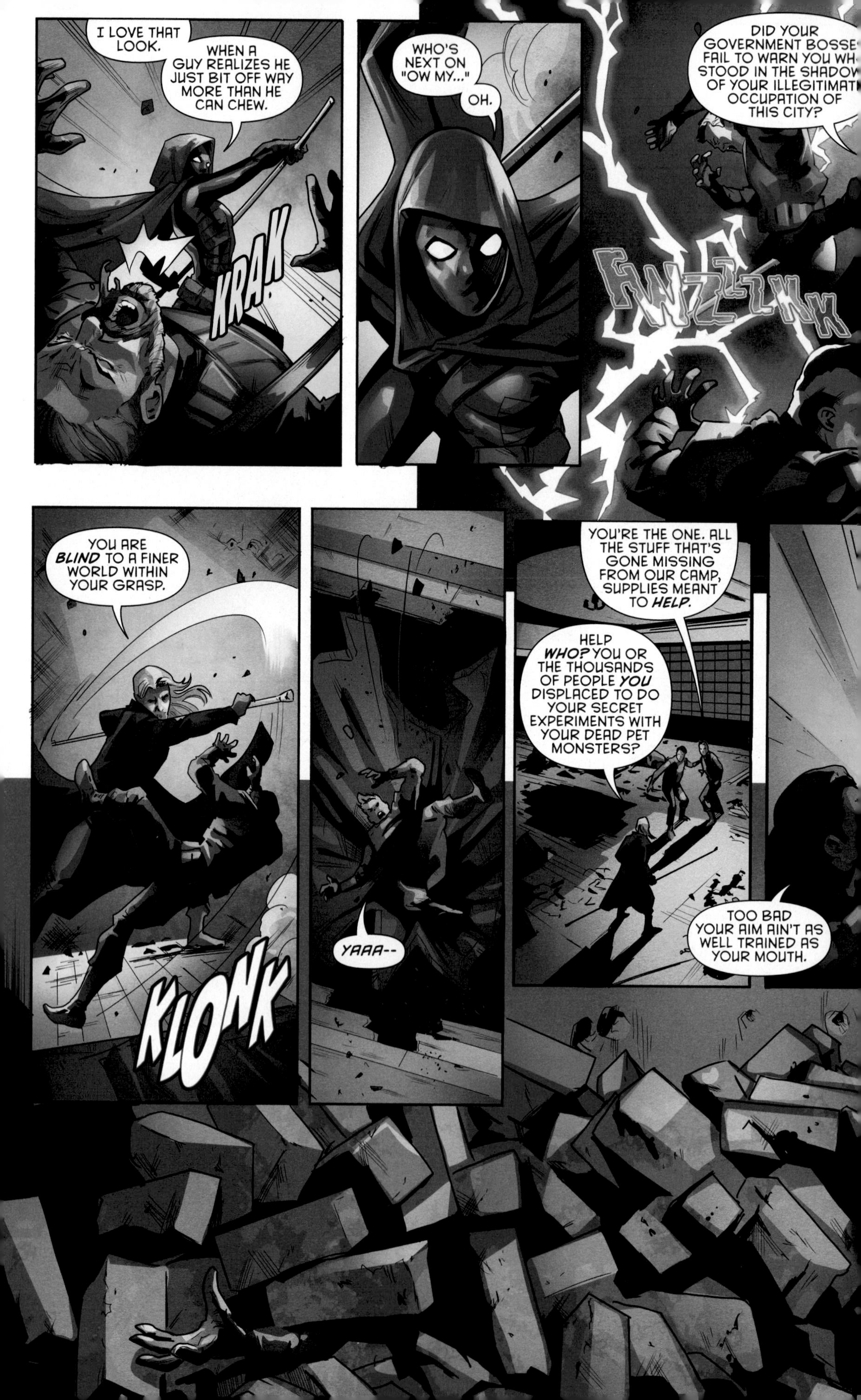

I LOVE THAT LOOK.
WHEN A GUY REALIZES HE JUST BIT OFF WAY MORE THAN HE CAN CHEW.
KRAK
WHO'S NEXT ON "OW MY..."
OH.
DID YOUR GOVERNMENT BOSSE FAIL TO WARN YOU WH STOOD IN THE SHADOW OF YOUR ILLEGITIMAT OCCUPATION OF THIS CITY?
FWZZZZKK
YOU ARE BLIND TO A FINER WORLD WITHIN YOUR GRASP.
KLONK
YAAA--
YOU'RE THE ONE. ALL THE STUFF THAT'S GONE MISSING FROM OUR CAMP, SUPPLIES MEANT TO HELP.
HELP WHO? YOU OR THE THOUSANDS OF PEOPLE YOU DISPLACED TO DO YOUR SECRET EXPERIMENTS WITH YOUR DEAD PET MONSTERS?
TOO BAD YOUR AIM AIN'T AS WELL TRAINED AS YOUR MOUTH.

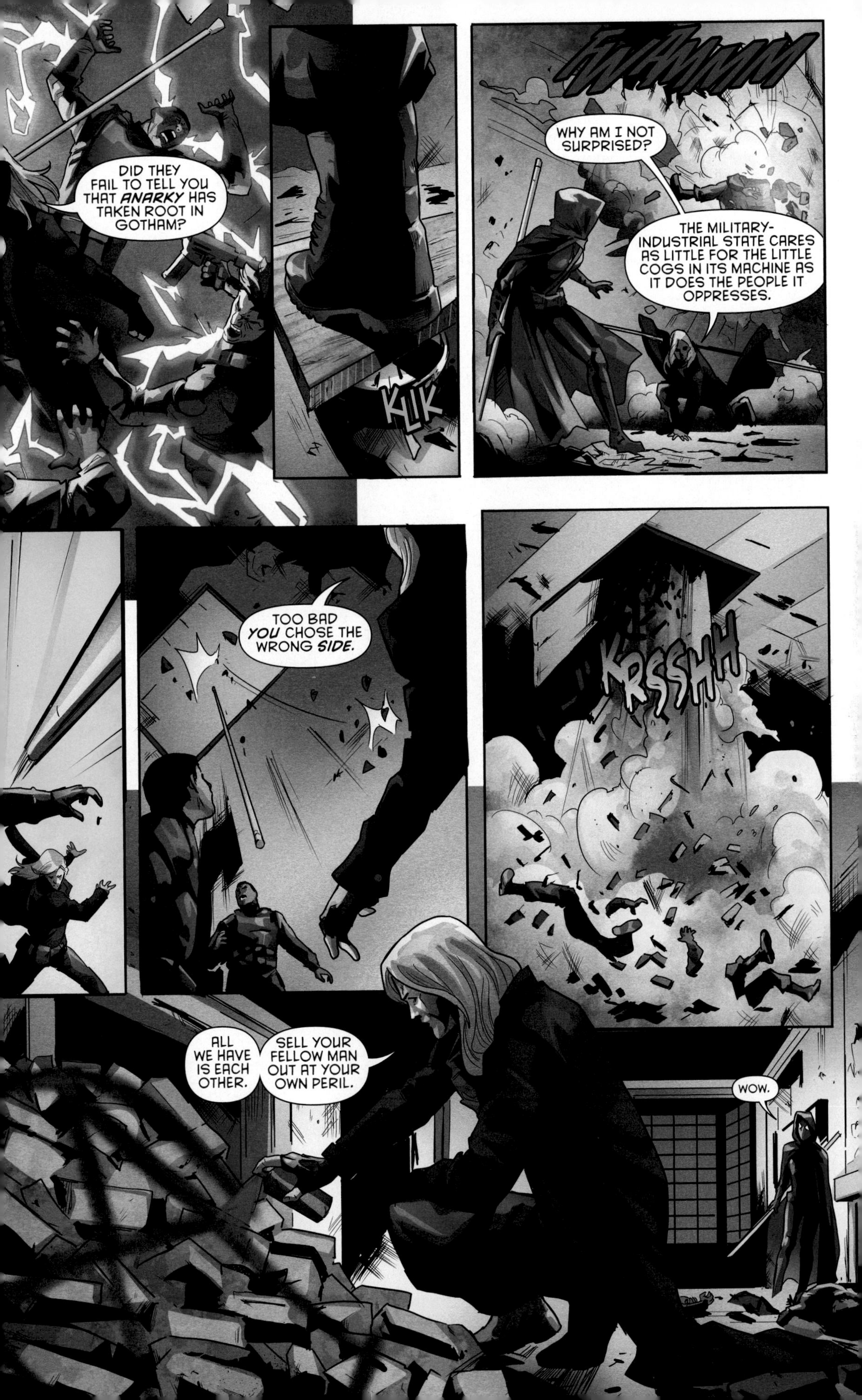
DID THEY FAIL TO TELL YOU THAT ANARKY HAS TAKEN ROOT IN GOTHAM?
KLIK
WHY AM I NOT SURPRISED?
THE MILITARY-INDUSTRIAL STATE CARES AS LITTLE FOR THE LITTLE COGS IN ITS MACHINE AS IT DOES THE PEOPLE IT OPPRESSES.
TOO BAD YOU CHOSE THE WRONG SIDE.
KRSSHH
ALL WE HAVE IS EACH OTHER.
SELL YOUR FELLOW MAN OUT AT YOUR OWN PERIL.
WOW.

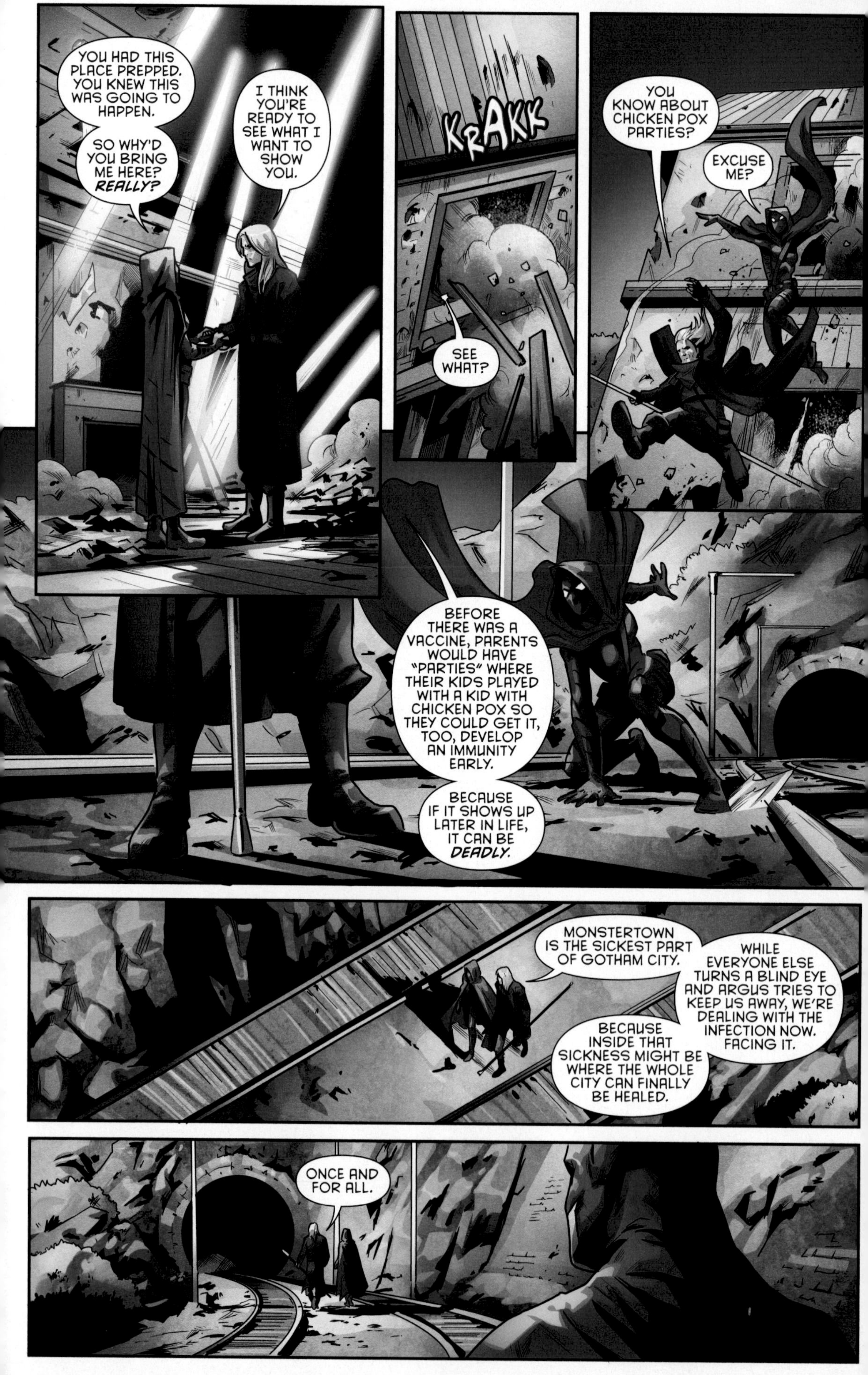

YOU HAD THIS PLACE PREPPED. YOU KNEW THIS WAS GOING TO HAPPEN.
SO WHY'D YOU BRING ME HERE? *REALLY?*
I THINK YOU'RE READY TO SEE WHAT I WANT TO SHOW YOU.
KRAKK
SEE WHAT?
YOU KNOW ABOUT CHICKEN POX PARTIES?
EXCUSE ME?
BEFORE THERE WAS A VACCINE, PARENTS WOULD HAVE "PARTIES" WHERE THEIR KIDS PLAYED WITH A KID WITH CHICKEN POX SO THEY COULD GET IT, TOO, DEVELOP AN IMMUNITY EARLY.
BECAUSE IF IT SHOWS UP LATER IN LIFE, IT CAN BE *DEADLY.*
MONSTERTOWN IS THE SICKEST PART OF GOTHAM CITY.
WHILE EVERYONE ELSE TURNS A BLIND EYE AND ARGUS TRIES TO KEEP US AWAY, WE'RE DEALING WITH THE INFECTION NOW. FACING IT.
BECAUSE INSIDE THAT SICKNESS MIGHT BE WHERE THE WHOLE CITY CAN FINALLY BE HEALED.
ONCE AND FOR ALL.

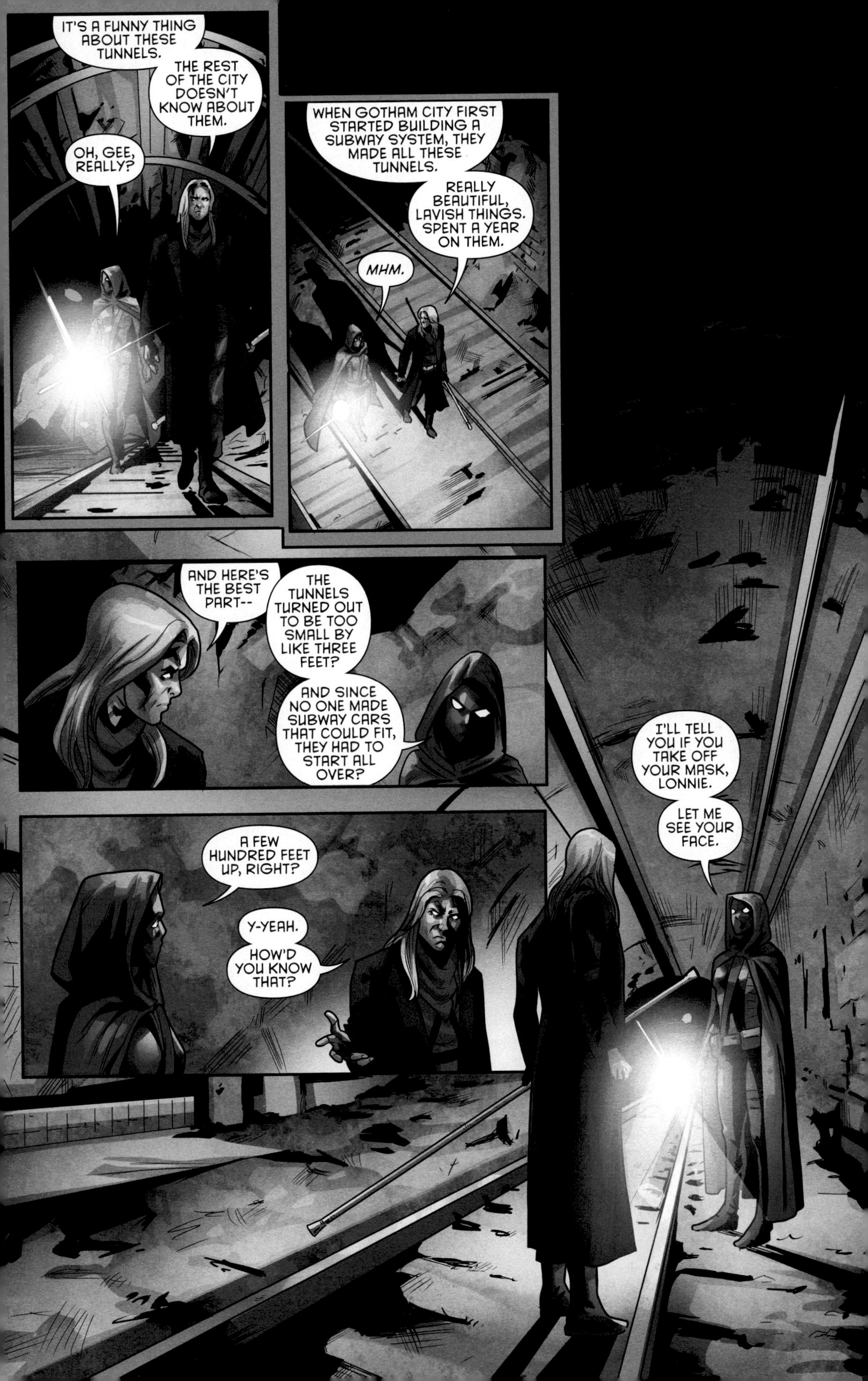
IT'S A FUNNY THING ABOUT THESE TUNNELS.
THE REST OF THE CITY DOESN'T KNOW ABOUT THEM.
OH, GEE, REALLY?
WHEN GOTHAM CITY FIRST STARTED BUILDING A SUBWAY SYSTEM, THEY MADE ALL THESE TUNNELS.
REALLY BEAUTIFUL, LAVISH THINGS. SPENT A YEAR ON THEM.
MHM.
AND HERE'S THE BEST PART--
THE TUNNELS TURNED OUT TO BE TOO SMALL BY LIKE THREE FEET?
AND SINCE NO ONE MADE SUBWAY CARS THAT COULD FIT, THEY HAD TO START ALL OVER?
A FEW HUNDRED FEET UP, RIGHT?
Y-YEAH.
HOW'D YOU KNOW THAT?
I'LL TELL YOU IF YOU TAKE OFF YOUR MASK, LONNIE.
LET ME SEE YOUR FACE.

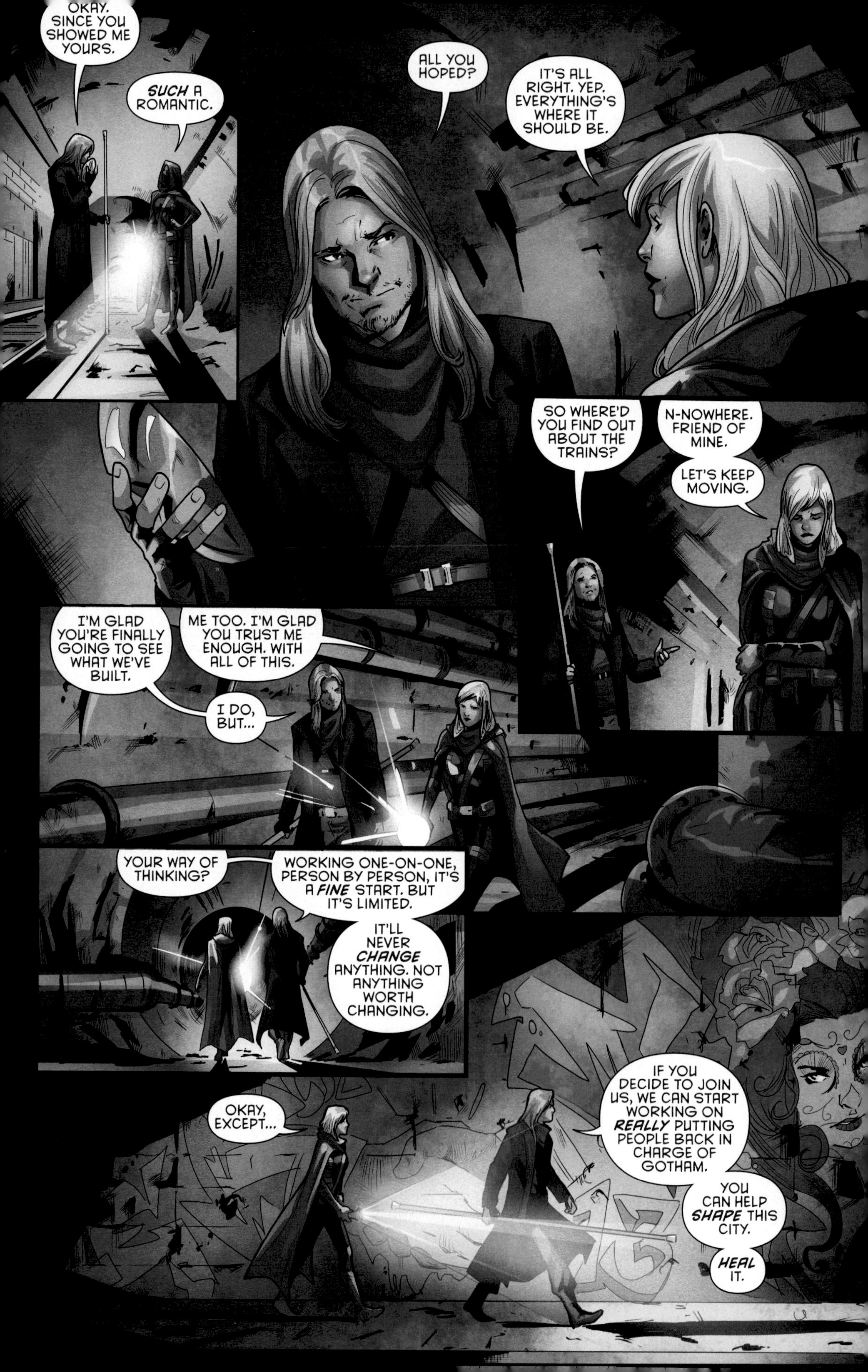
OKAY. SINCE YOU SHOWED ME YOURS.
SUCH A ROMANTIC.
ALL YOU HOPED?
IT'S ALL RIGHT. YEP. EVERYTHING'S WHERE IT SHOULD BE.
SO WHERE'D YOU FIND OUT ABOUT THE TRAINS?
N-NOWHERE. FRIEND OF MINE.
LET'S KEEP MOVING.
I'M GLAD YOU'RE FINALLY GOING TO SEE WHAT WE'VE BUILT.
ME TOO. I'M GLAD YOU TRUST ME ENOUGH. WITH ALL OF THIS.
I DO, BUT...
YOUR WAY OF THINKING?
WORKING ONE-ON-ONE, PERSON BY PERSON, IT'S A FINE START. BUT IT'S LIMITED.
IT'LL NEVER CHANGE ANYTHING. NOT ANYTHING WORTH CHANGING.
OKAY, EXCEPT...
IF YOU DECIDE TO JOIN US, WE CAN START WORKING ON REALLY PUTTING PEOPLE BACK IN CHARGE OF GOTHAM.
YOU CAN HELP SHAPE THIS CITY.
HEAL IT.

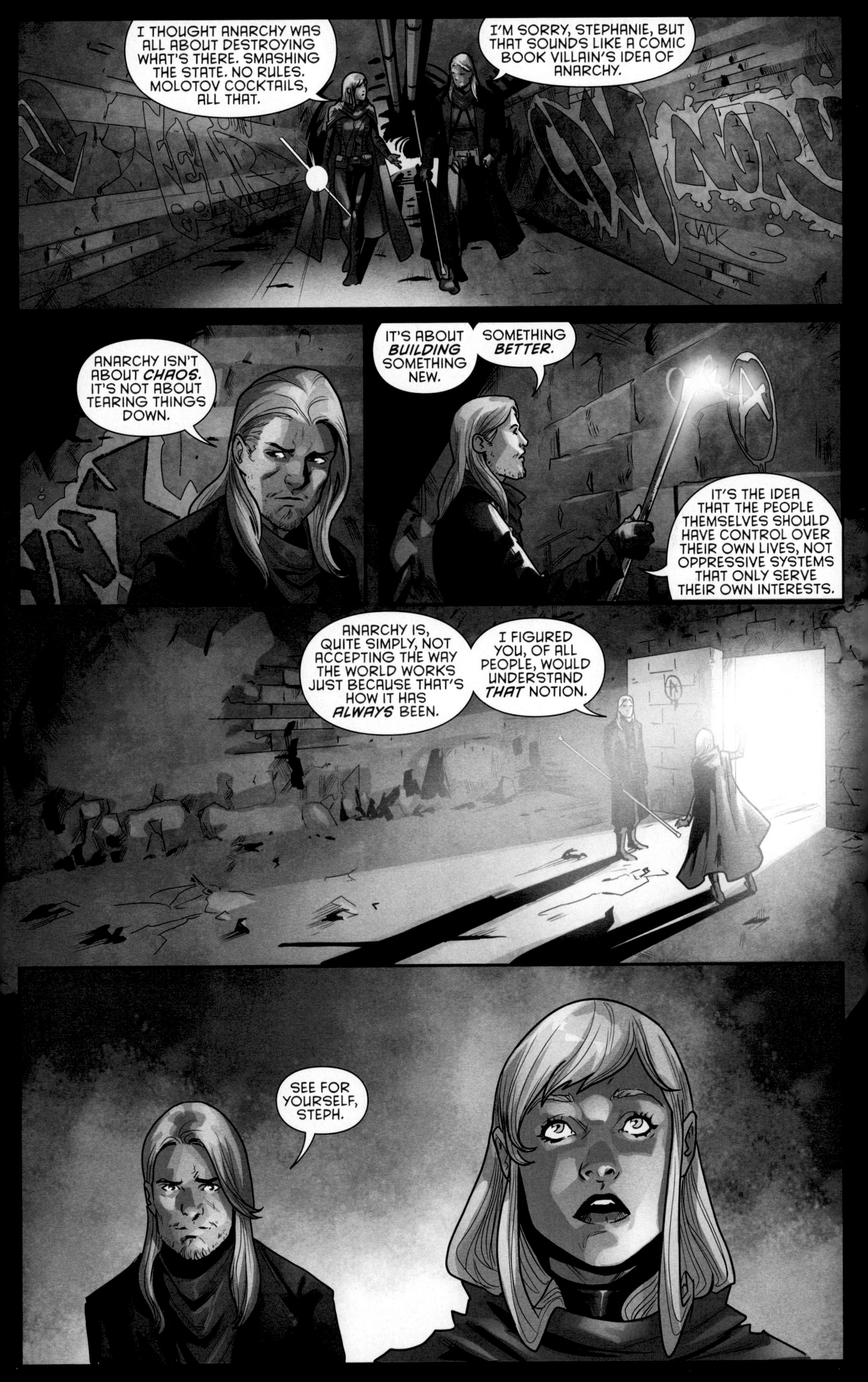
I THOUGHT ANARCHY WAS ALL ABOUT DESTROYING WHAT'S THERE. SMASHING THE STATE. NO RULES. MOLOTOV COCKTAILS, ALL THAT.
I'M SORRY, STEPHANIE, BUT THAT SOUNDS LIKE A COMIC BOOK VILLAIN'S IDEA OF ANARCHY.
JACK
ANARCHY ISN'T ABOUT CHAOS. IT'S NOT ABOUT TEARING THINGS DOWN.
IT'S ABOUT BUILDING SOMETHING NEW.
SOMETHING BETTER.
IT'S THE IDEA THAT THE PEOPLE THEMSELVES SHOULD HAVE CONTROL OVER THEIR OWN LIVES, NOT OPPRESSIVE SYSTEMS THAT ONLY SERVE THEIR OWN INTERESTS.
ANARCHY IS, QUITE SIMPLY, NOT ACCEPTING THE WAY THE WORLD WORKS JUST BECAUSE THAT'S HOW IT HAS ALWAYS BEEN.
I FIGURED YOU, OF ALL PEOPLE, WOULD UNDERSTAND THAT NOTION.
SEE FOR YOURSELF, STEPH.

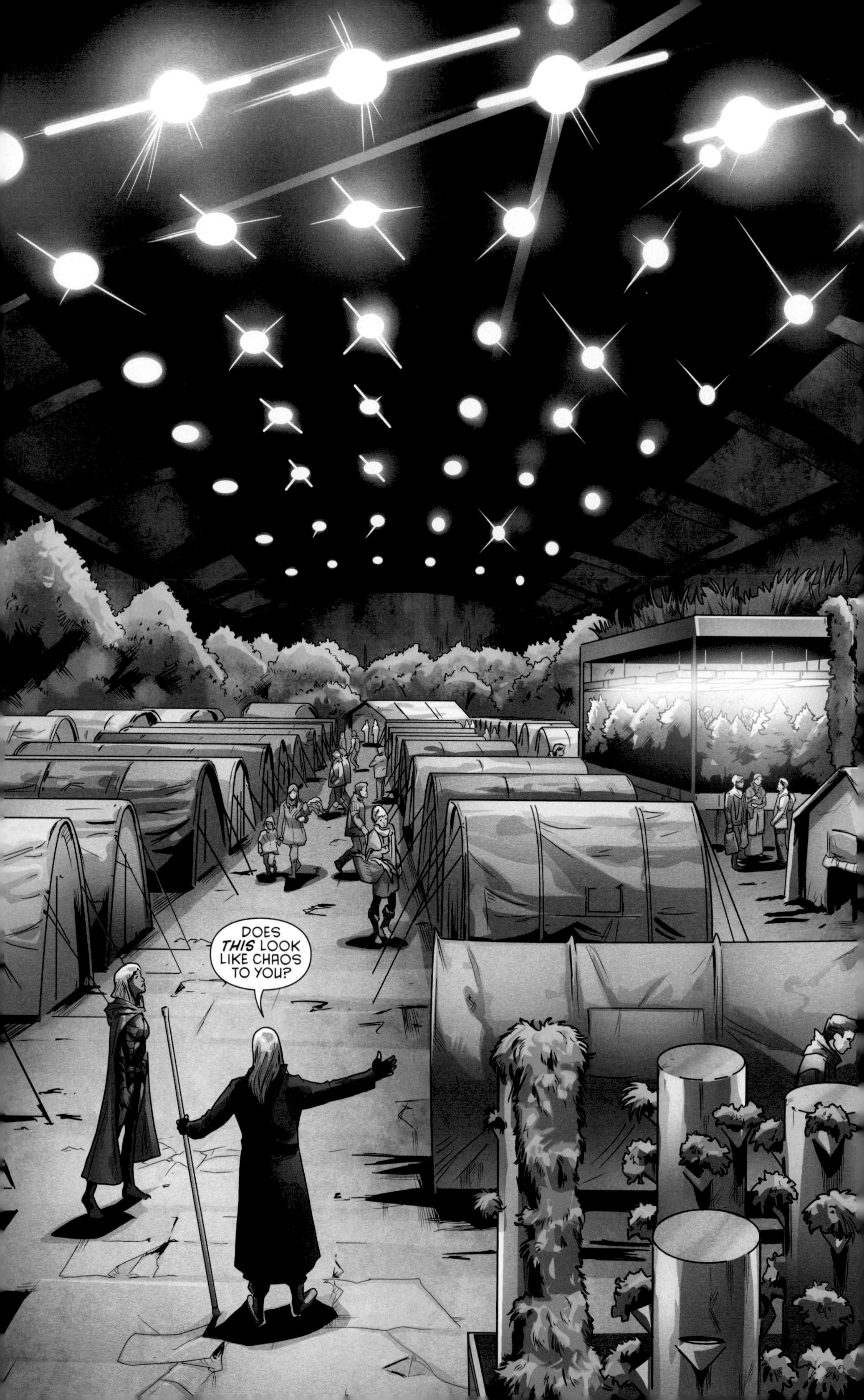
DOES *THIS* LOOK LIKE CHAOS TO YOU?

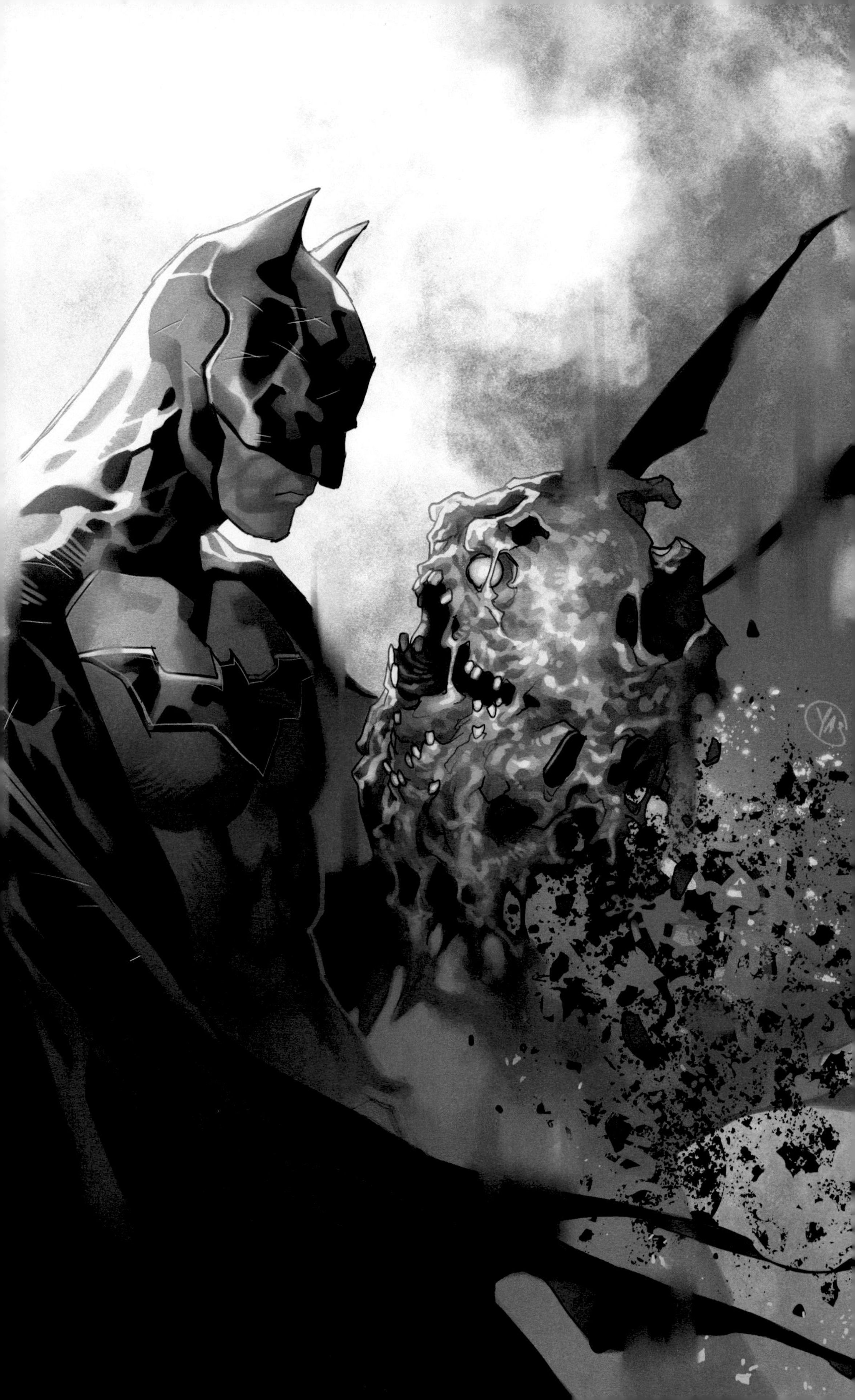

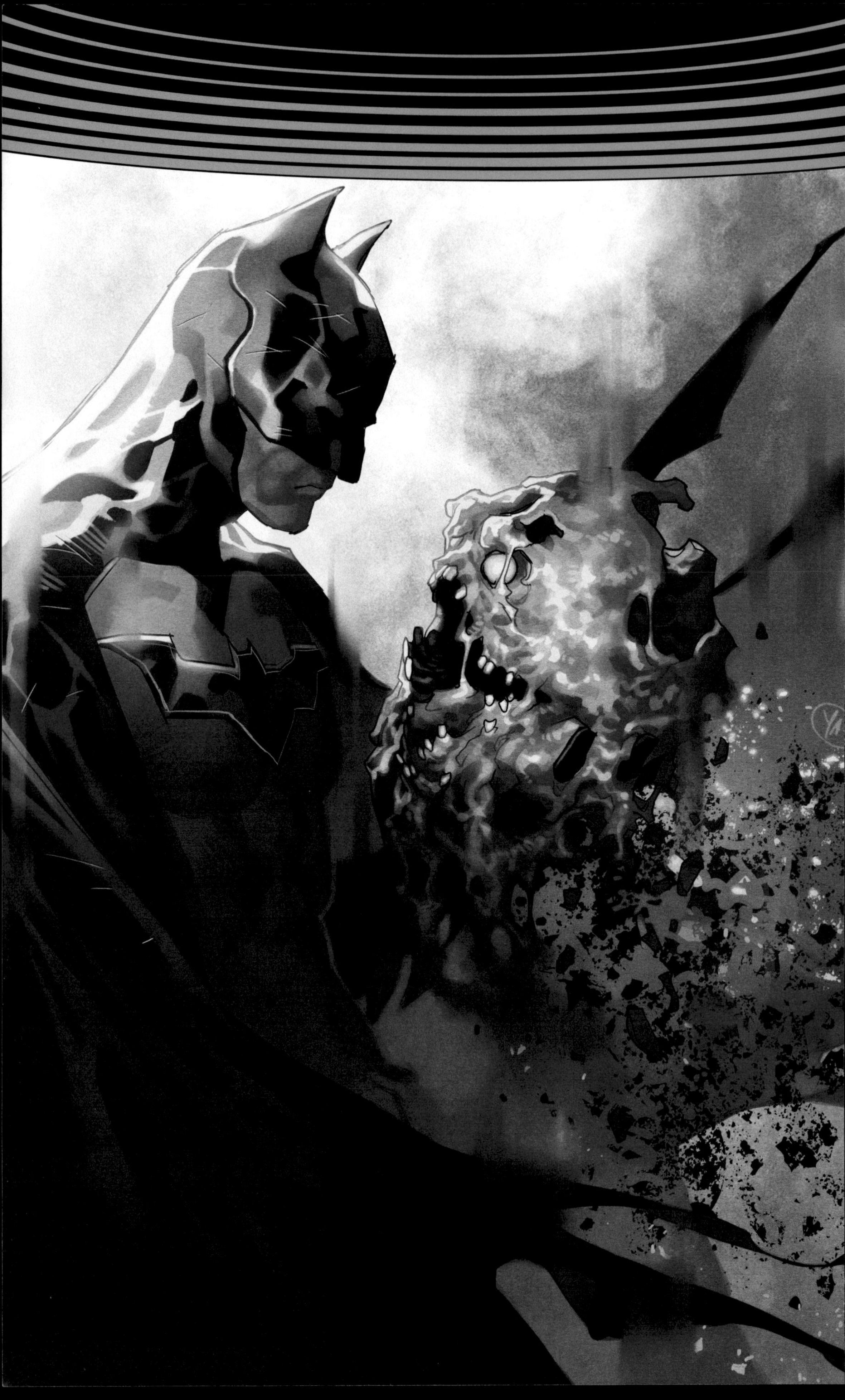

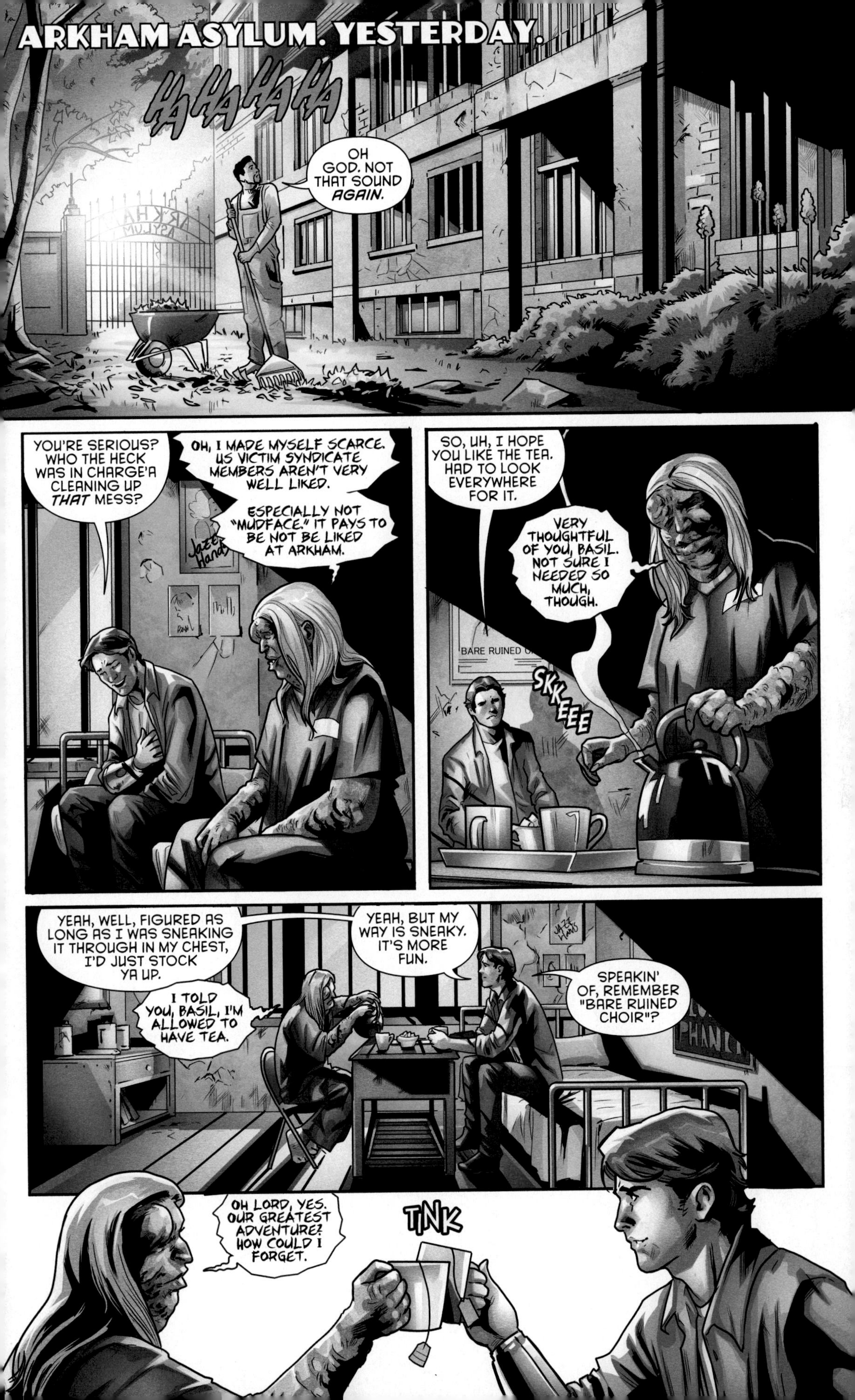
ARKHAM ASYLUM. YESTERDAY.
HA HA HA HA
ARKHAM ASYLUM
OH GOD. NOT THAT SOUND AGAIN.
YOU'RE SERIOUS? WHO THE HECK WAS IN CHARGE'A CLEANING UP THAT MESS?
OH, I MADE MYSELF SCARCE. US VICTIM SYNDICATE MEMBERS AREN'T VERY WELL LIKED.
ESPECIALLY NOT "MUDFACE." IT PAYS TO BE NOT BE LIKED AT ARKHAM.
Jazz Hands
SO, UH, I HOPE YOU LIKE THE TEA. HAD TO LOOK EVERYWHERE FOR IT.
VERY THOUGHTFUL OF YOU, BASIL. NOT SURE I NEEDED SO MUCH, THOUGH.
BARE RUINED C
SKKEEE
YEAH, WELL, FIGURED AS LONG AS I WAS SNEAKING IT THROUGH IN MY CHEST, I'D JUST STOCK YA UP.
I TOLD YOU, BASIL, I'M ALLOWED TO HAVE TEA.
YEAH, BUT MY WAY IS SNEAKY. IT'S MORE FUN.
SPEAKIN' OF, REMEMBER "BARE RUINED CHOIR"?
OH LORD, YES. OUR GREATEST ADVENTURE? HOW COULD I FORGET.
TINK

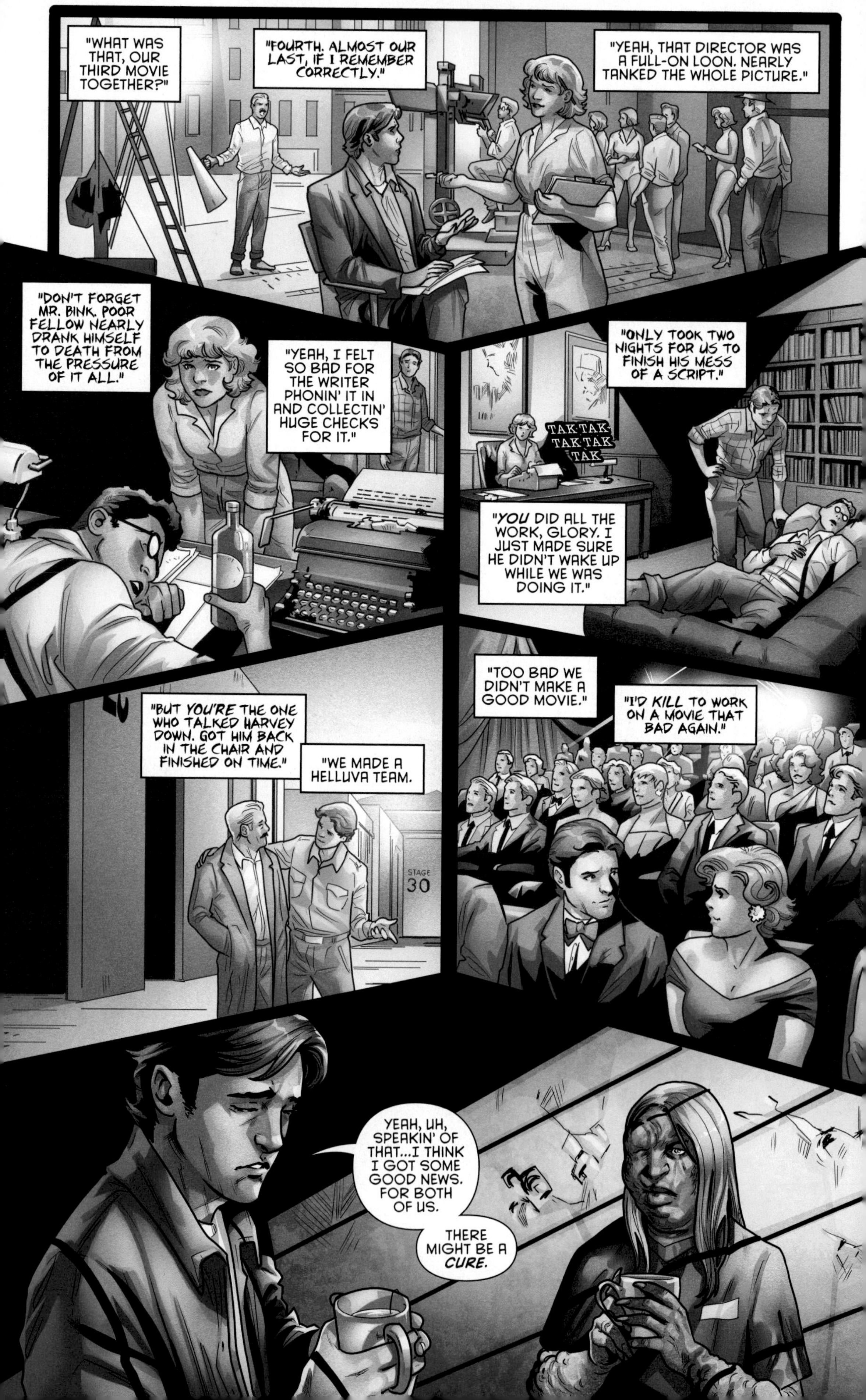
"WHAT WAS THAT, OUR THIRD MOVIE TOGETHER?"
"FOURTH. ALMOST OUR LAST, IF I REMEMBER CORRECTLY."
"YEAH, THAT DIRECTOR WAS A FULL-ON LOON. NEARLY TANKED THE WHOLE PICTURE."
"DON'T FORGET MR. BINK. POOR FELLOW NEARLY DRANK HIMSELF TO DEATH FROM THE PRESSURE OF IT ALL."
"YEAH, I FELT SO BAD FOR THE WRITER PHONIN' IT IN AND COLLECTIN' HUGE CHECKS FOR IT."
"ONLY TOOK TWO NIGHTS FOR US TO FINISH HIS MESS OF A SCRIPT."
TAK TAK TAK TAK TAK
"YOU DID ALL THE WORK, GLORY. I JUST MADE SURE HE DIDN'T WAKE UP WHILE WE WAS DOING IT."
"BUT YOU'RE THE ONE WHO TALKED HARVEY DOWN. GOT HIM BACK IN THE CHAIR AND FINISHED ON TIME."
"WE MADE A HELLUVA TEAM.
STAGE 30
"TOO BAD WE DIDN'T MAKE A GOOD MOVIE."
"I'D KILL TO WORK ON A MOVIE THAT BAD AGAIN."
YEAH, UH, SPEAKIN' OF THAT...I THINK I GOT SOME GOOD NEWS. FOR BOTH OF US.
THERE MIGHT BE A CURE.

I SEE.

Y-YEAH. IT'S PROMISIN'.

THIS DOCTOR I MET, OCTOBER, SHE'S REAL SMART, HAS SOME IDEAS ABOUT HOW TO FIX THIS...

...THIS *THING* YOU AN' ME GOT.

NOW, IT'S NOT A HUNDRED PERCENT, BUT SHE THINKS SHE FOUND A WAY. I'M GONNA MEET WITH HER LATER TO START THE TESTS.

AND A'COURSE, YOU WERE THE FIRST ONE I THOUGHT OF.

WE CAN BE FREE.

FINALLY PUT ALL OF THIS BEHIND US.

...

BEHIND US?

DID YOU *REALLY* JUST SAY YOU THINK WE CAN PUT THIS BEHIND US?

WELL, YEAH... I WANT TO PUT THINGS RIGHT. MAKE IT UP TO YOU. GET BACK TO HOW THINGS WERE.

BASIL... THERE'S NO GOING BACK.

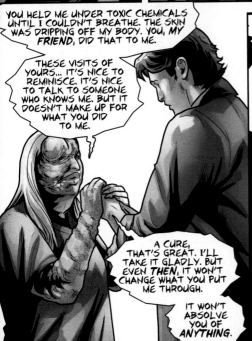

YOU HELD ME UNDER TOXIC CHEMICALS UNTIL I COULDN'T BREATHE. THE SKIN WAS DRIPPING OFF MY BODY. YOU, *MY FRIEND*, DID THAT TO ME.

THESE VISITS OF YOURS... IT'S NICE TO REMINISCE. IT'S NICE TO TALK TO SOMEONE WHO KNOWS ME. BUT IT DOESN'T MAKE UP FOR WHAT YOU DID TO ME.

A CURE, THAT'S GREAT. I'LL TAKE IT GLADLY. BUT EVEN *THEN*, IT WON'T CHANGE WHAT YOU PUT ME THROUGH.

IT WON'T ABSOLVE YOU OF *ANYTHING*.

I KNOW YOU WANT AN EASY WAY OUT, BUT IT'S CRUEL OF YOU TO ASK THAT OF ME. EVERYTHING YOU DID TO ME IS *STILL* ON YOUR HEAD.

YOU THINK THAT IF YOU TAKE AWAY CLAYFACE, YOUR SLATE WILL BE CLEAN? IT DOESN'T CHANGE THE MEMORY OF MY FRIEND TRANSFORMING INTO SOMETHING MONSTROUS AND DESTROYING MY LIFE.

NO MATTER *WHAT* YOU LOOK LIKE, BASIL...

27 3

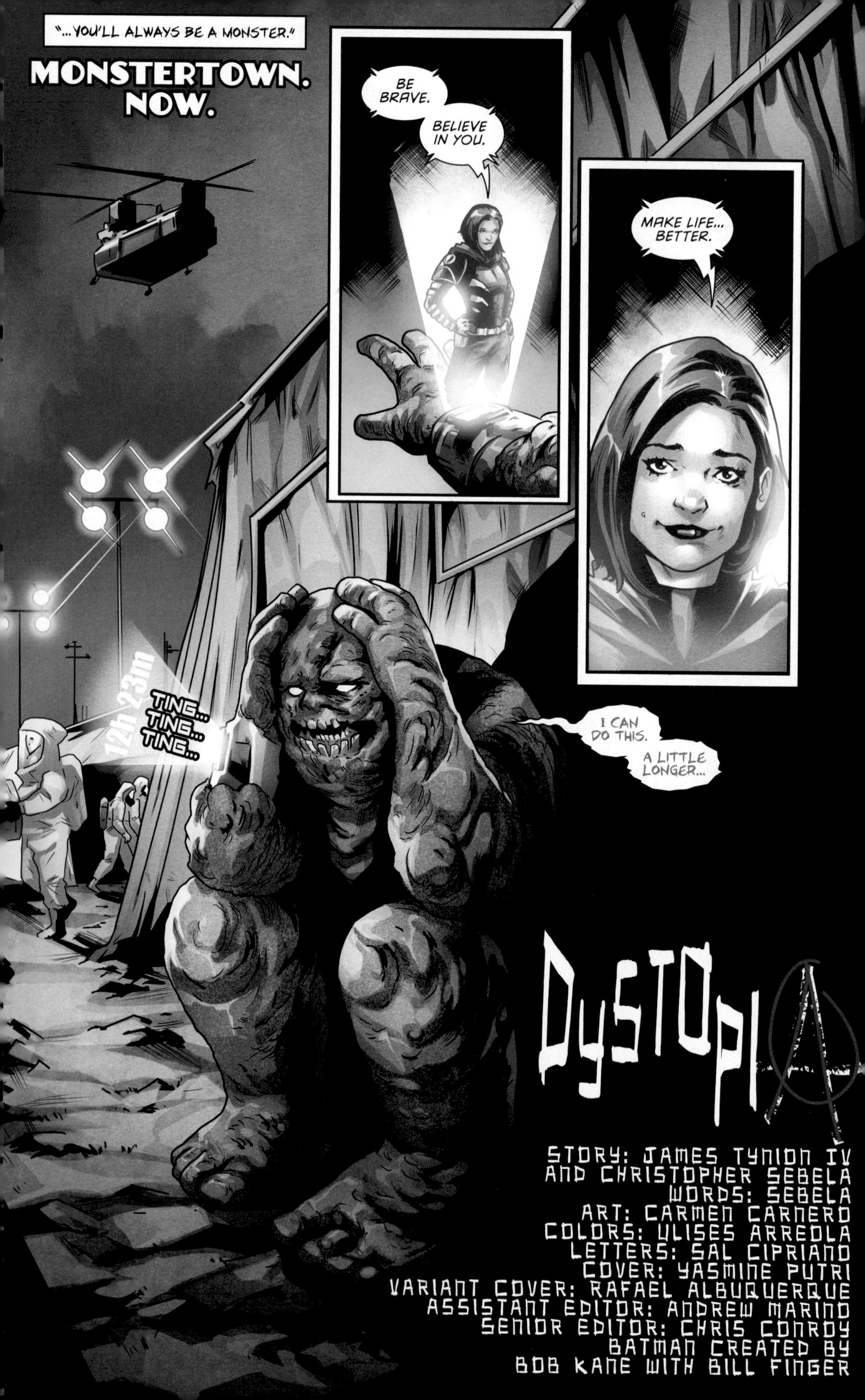
"...YOU'LL ALWAYS BE A MONSTER."
MONSTERTOWN. NOW.
BE BRAVE.
BELIEVE IN YOU.
MAKE LIFE... BETTER.
12h 23m
TING... TING... TING...
I CAN DO THIS.
A LITTLE LONGER...
DYSTOPIA
STORY: JAMES TYNION IV AND CHRISTOPHER SEBELA
WORDS: SEBELA
ART: CARMEN CARNERO
COLORS: ULISES ARREOLA
LETTERS: SAL CIPRIANO
COVER: YASMINE PUTRI
VARIANT COVER: RAFAEL ALBUQUERQUE
ASSISTANT EDITOR: ANDREW MARINO
SENIOR EDITOR: CHRIS CONROY
BATMAN CREATED BY BOB KANE WITH BILL FINGER

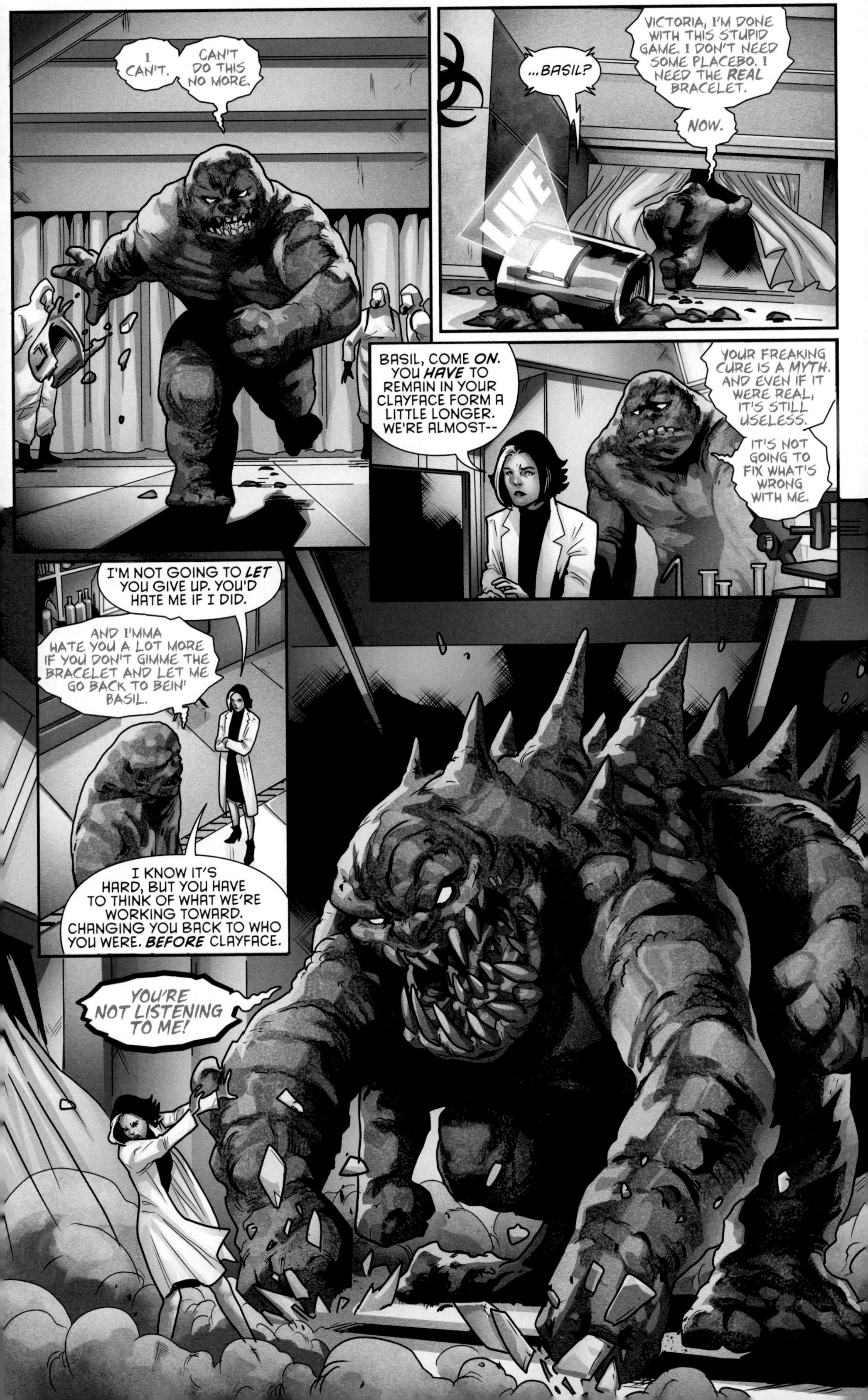
I CAN'T.
CAN'T DO THIS NO MORE.
...BASIL?
VICTORIA, I'M DONE WITH THIS STUPID GAME. I DON'T NEED SOME PLACEBO. I NEED THE *REAL* BRACELET.
NOW.
LIVE
BASIL, COME *ON.* YOU *HAVE* TO REMAIN IN YOUR CLAYFACE FORM A LITTLE LONGER. WE'RE ALMOST--
YOUR FREAKING CURE IS A *MYTH.* AND EVEN IF IT WERE REAL, IT'S STILL USELESS.
IT'S NOT GOING TO FIX WHAT'S WRONG WITH ME.
I'M NOT GOING TO *LET* YOU GIVE UP. YOU'D HATE ME IF I DID.
AND I'MMA HATE YOU A LOT MORE IF YOU DON'T GIMME THE BRACELET AND LET ME GO BACK TO BEIN' BASIL.
I KNOW IT'S HARD, BUT YOU HAVE TO THINK OF WHAT WE'RE WORKING TOWARD. CHANGING YOU BACK TO WHO YOU WERE. *BEFORE* CLAYFACE.
YOU'RE NOT LISTENING TO ME!

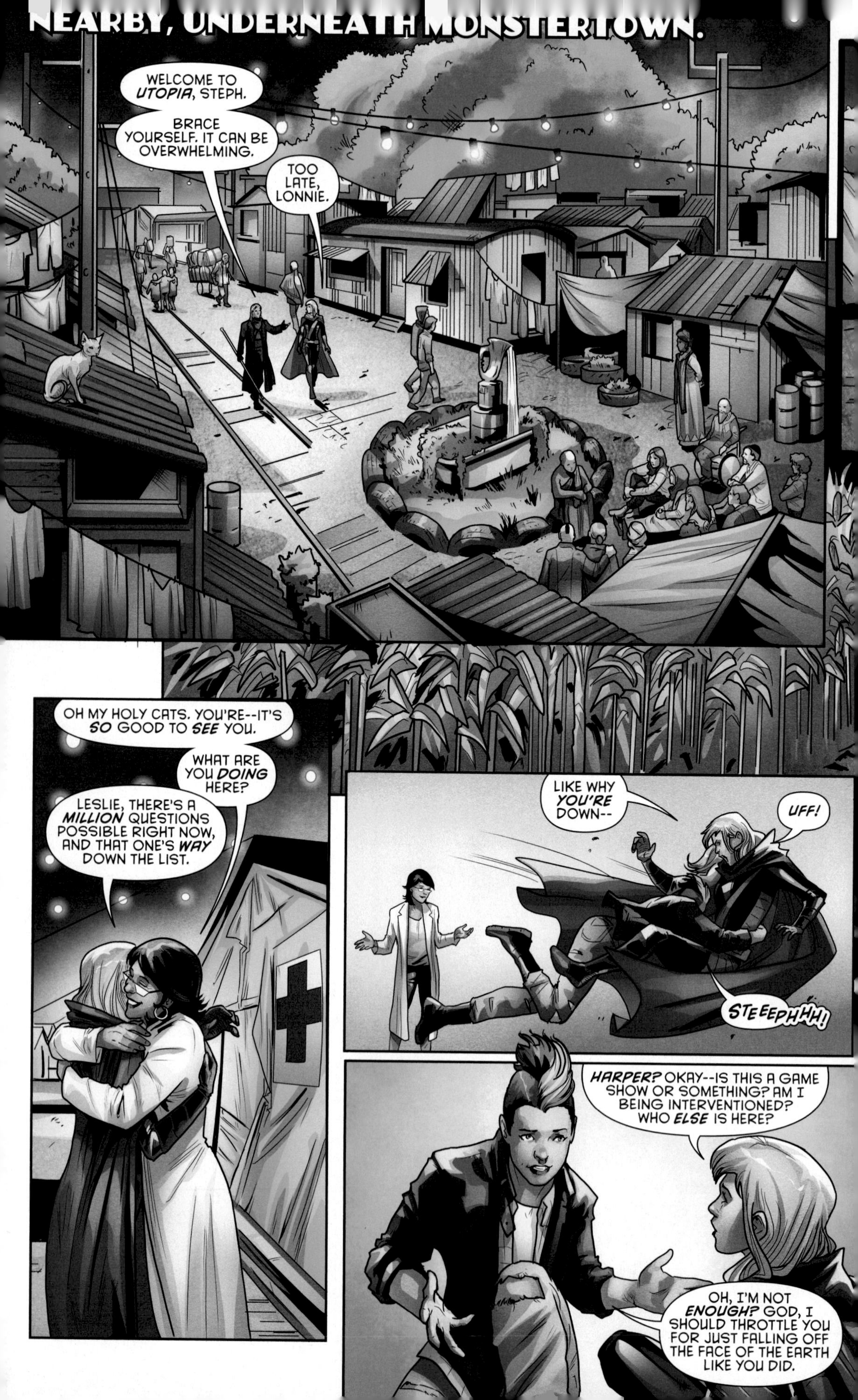

NEARBY, UNDERNEATH MONSTERTOWN.
WELCOME TO UTOPIA, STEPH.
BRACE YOURSELF. IT CAN BE OVERWHELMING.
TOO LATE, LONNIE.
OH MY HOLY CATS. YOU'RE--IT'S SO GOOD TO SEE YOU.
WHAT ARE YOU DOING HERE?
LESLIE, THERE'S A MILLION QUESTIONS POSSIBLE RIGHT NOW, AND THAT ONE'S WAY DOWN THE LIST.
LIKE WHY YOU'RE DOWN--
UFF!
STEEEPHHH!
HARPER? OKAY--IS THIS A GAME SHOW OR SOMETHING? AM I BEING INTERVENTIONED? WHO ELSE IS HERE?
OH, I'M NOT ENOUGH? GOD, I SHOULD THROTTLE YOU FOR JUST FALLING OFF THE FACE OF THE EARTH LIKE YOU DID.

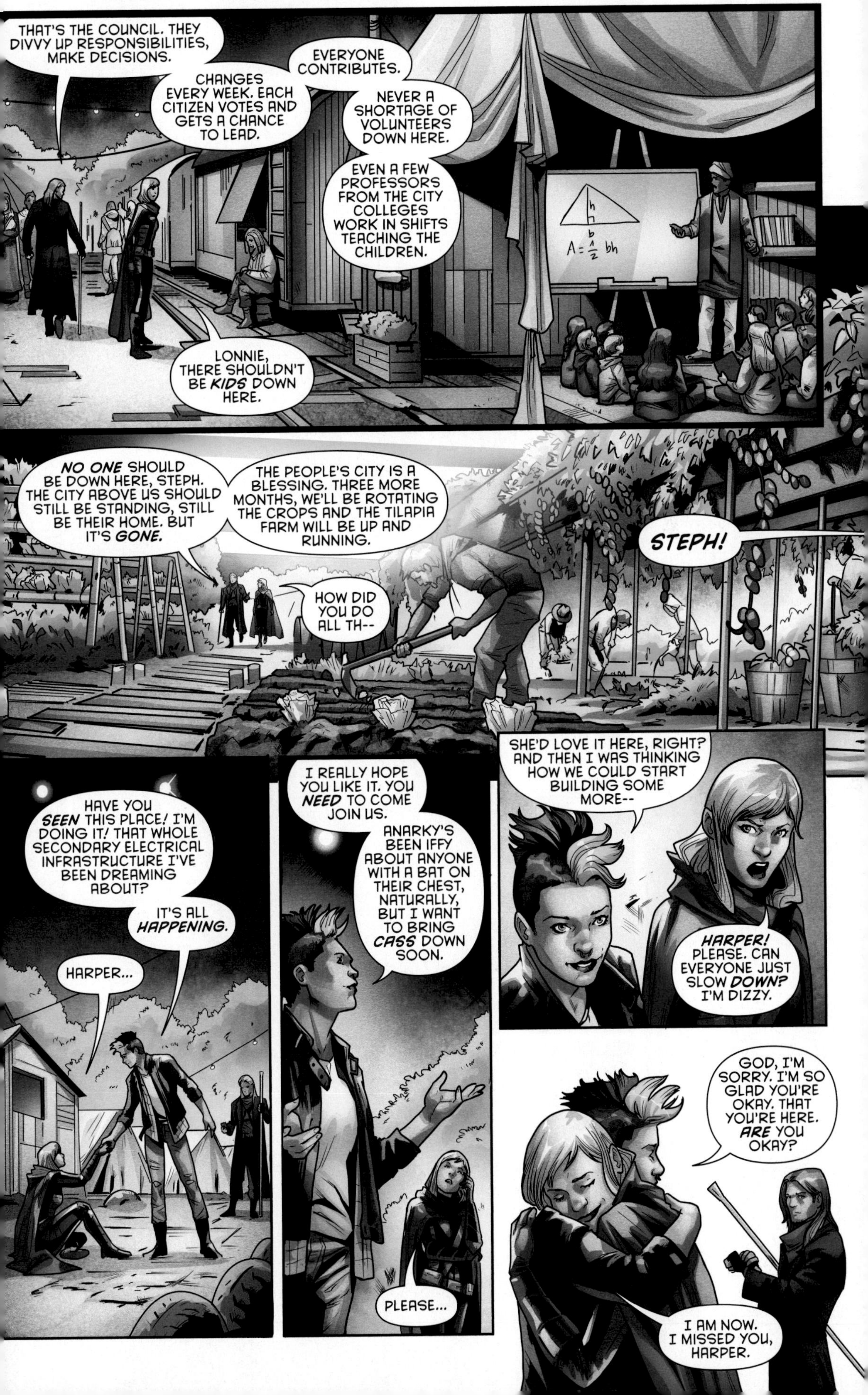
THAT'S THE COUNCIL. THEY DIVVY UP RESPONSIBILITIES, MAKE DECISIONS.
CHANGES EVERY WEEK. EACH CITIZEN VOTES AND GETS A CHANCE TO LEAD.
EVERYONE CONTRIBUTES.
NEVER A SHORTAGE OF VOLUNTEERS DOWN HERE.
EVEN A FEW PROFESSORS FROM THE CITY COLLEGES WORK IN SHIFTS TEACHING THE CHILDREN.
A = 1/2 bh
LONNIE, THERE SHOULDN'T BE KIDS DOWN HERE.
NO ONE SHOULD BE DOWN HERE, STEPH. THE CITY ABOVE US SHOULD STILL BE STANDING, STILL BE THEIR HOME. BUT IT'S GONE.
THE PEOPLE'S CITY IS A BLESSING. THREE MORE MONTHS, WE'LL BE ROTATING THE CROPS AND THE TILAPIA FARM WILL BE UP AND RUNNING.
HOW DID YOU DO ALL TH--
STEPH!
HAVE YOU SEEN THIS PLACE! I'M DOING IT! THAT WHOLE SECONDARY ELECTRICAL INFRASTRUCTURE I'VE BEEN DREAMING ABOUT?
IT'S ALL HAPPENING.
HARPER...
I REALLY HOPE YOU LIKE IT. YOU NEED TO COME JOIN US.
ANARKY'S BEEN IFFY ABOUT ANYONE WITH A BAT ON THEIR CHEST, NATURALLY, BUT I WANT TO BRING CASS DOWN SOON.
PLEASE...
SHE'D LOVE IT HERE, RIGHT? AND THEN I WAS THINKING HOW WE COULD START BUILDING SOME MORE--
HARPER! PLEASE. CAN EVERYONE JUST SLOW DOWN? I'M DIZZY.
GOD, I'M SORRY. I'M SO GLAD YOU'RE OKAY. THAT YOU'RE HERE. ARE YOU OKAY?
I AM NOW. I MISSED YOU, HARPER.

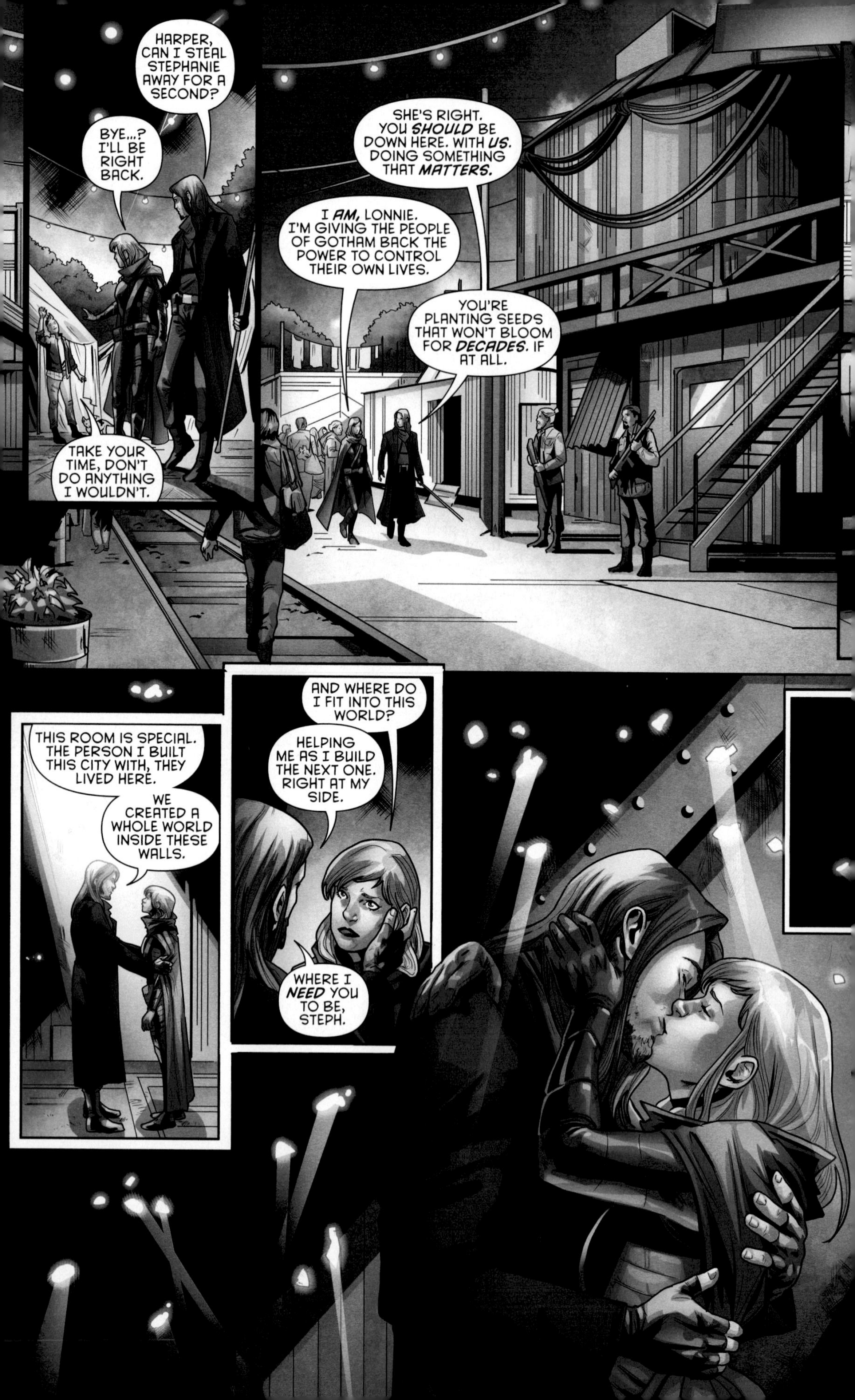
HARPER, CAN I STEAL STEPHANIE AWAY FOR A SECOND?
BYE...? I'LL BE RIGHT BACK.
TAKE YOUR TIME, DON'T DO ANYTHING I WOULDN'T.
SHE'S RIGHT. YOU SHOULD BE DOWN HERE. WITH US. DOING SOMETHING THAT MATTERS.
I AM, LONNIE. I'M GIVING THE PEOPLE OF GOTHAM BACK THE POWER TO CONTROL THEIR OWN LIVES.
YOU'RE PLANTING SEEDS THAT WON'T BLOOM FOR DECADES. IF AT ALL.
THIS ROOM IS SPECIAL. THE PERSON I BUILT THIS CITY WITH, THEY LIVED HERE.
WE CREATED A WHOLE WORLD INSIDE THESE WALLS.
AND WHERE DO I FIT INTO THIS WORLD?
HELPING ME AS I BUILD THE NEXT ONE. RIGHT AT MY SIDE.
WHERE I NEED YOU TO BE, STEPH.

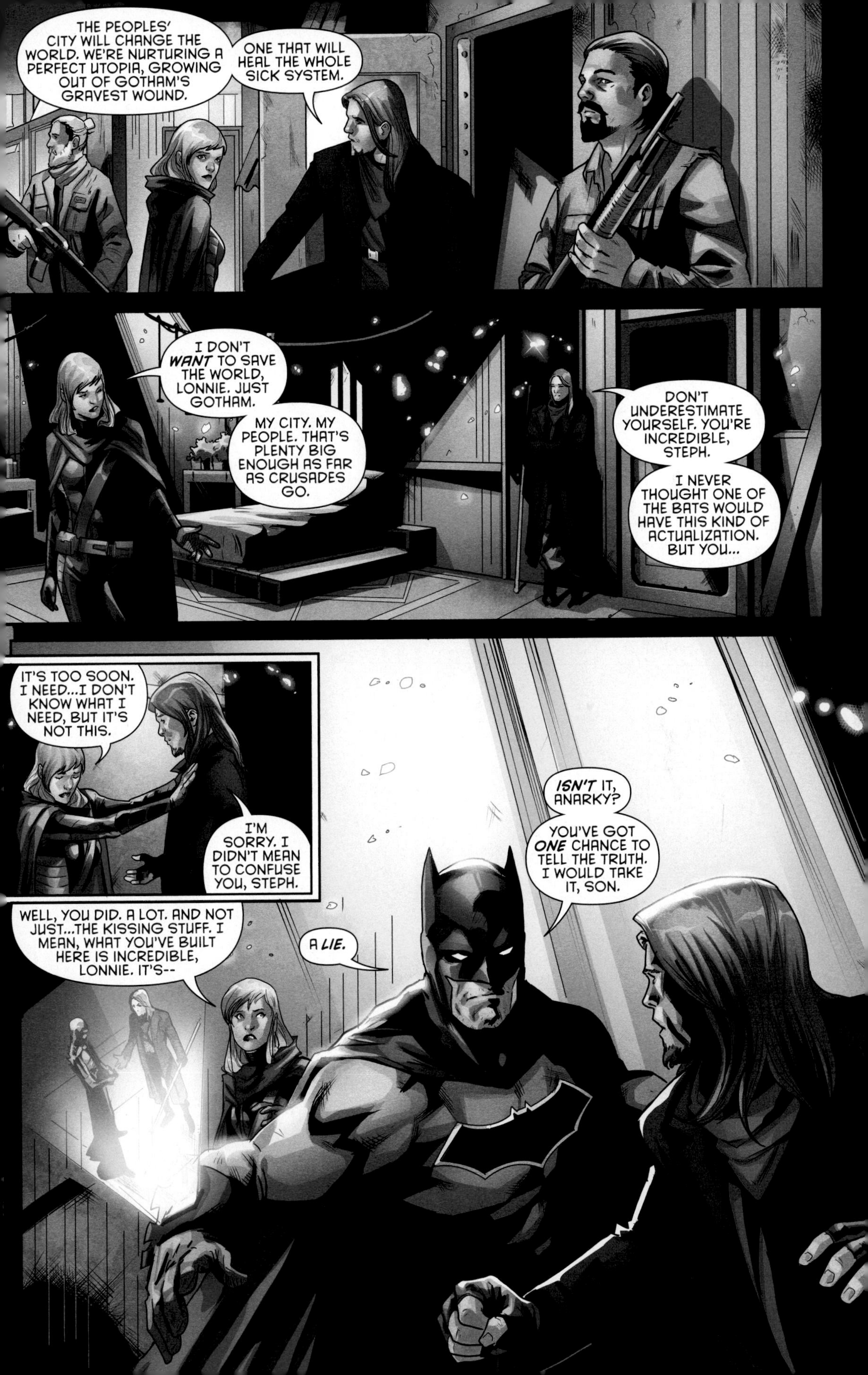
THE PEOPLES' CITY WILL CHANGE THE WORLD. WE'RE NURTURING A PERFECT UTOPIA, GROWING OUT OF GOTHAM'S GRAVEST WOUND.
ONE THAT WILL HEAL THE WHOLE SICK SYSTEM.
I DON'T *WANT* TO SAVE THE WORLD, LONNIE. JUST GOTHAM.
MY CITY. MY PEOPLE. THAT'S PLENTY BIG ENOUGH AS FAR AS CRUSADES GO.
DON'T UNDERESTIMATE YOURSELF. YOU'RE INCREDIBLE, STEPH.
I NEVER THOUGHT ONE OF THE BATS WOULD HAVE THIS KIND OF ACTUALIZATION. BUT YOU...
IT'S TOO SOON. I NEED...I DON'T KNOW WHAT I NEED, BUT IT'S NOT THIS.
I'M SORRY. I DIDN'T MEAN TO CONFUSE YOU, STEPH.
WELL, YOU DID. A LOT. AND NOT JUST...THE KISSING STUFF. I MEAN, WHAT YOU'VE BUILT HERE IS INCREDIBLE, LONNIE. IT'S--
A *LIE.*
ISN'T IT, ANARKY?
YOU'VE GOT *ONE* CHANCE TO TELL THE TRUTH. I WOULD TAKE IT, SON.

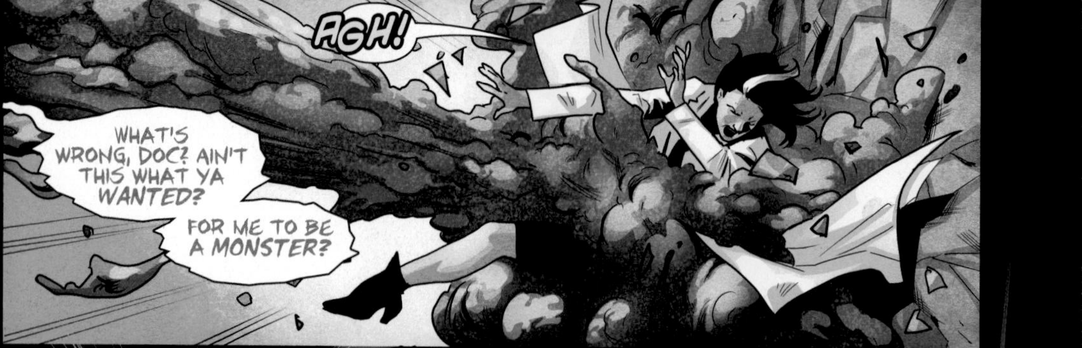
AGH!
WHAT'S WRONG, DOC? AIN'T THIS WHAT YA WANTED?
FOR ME TO BE A MONSTER?

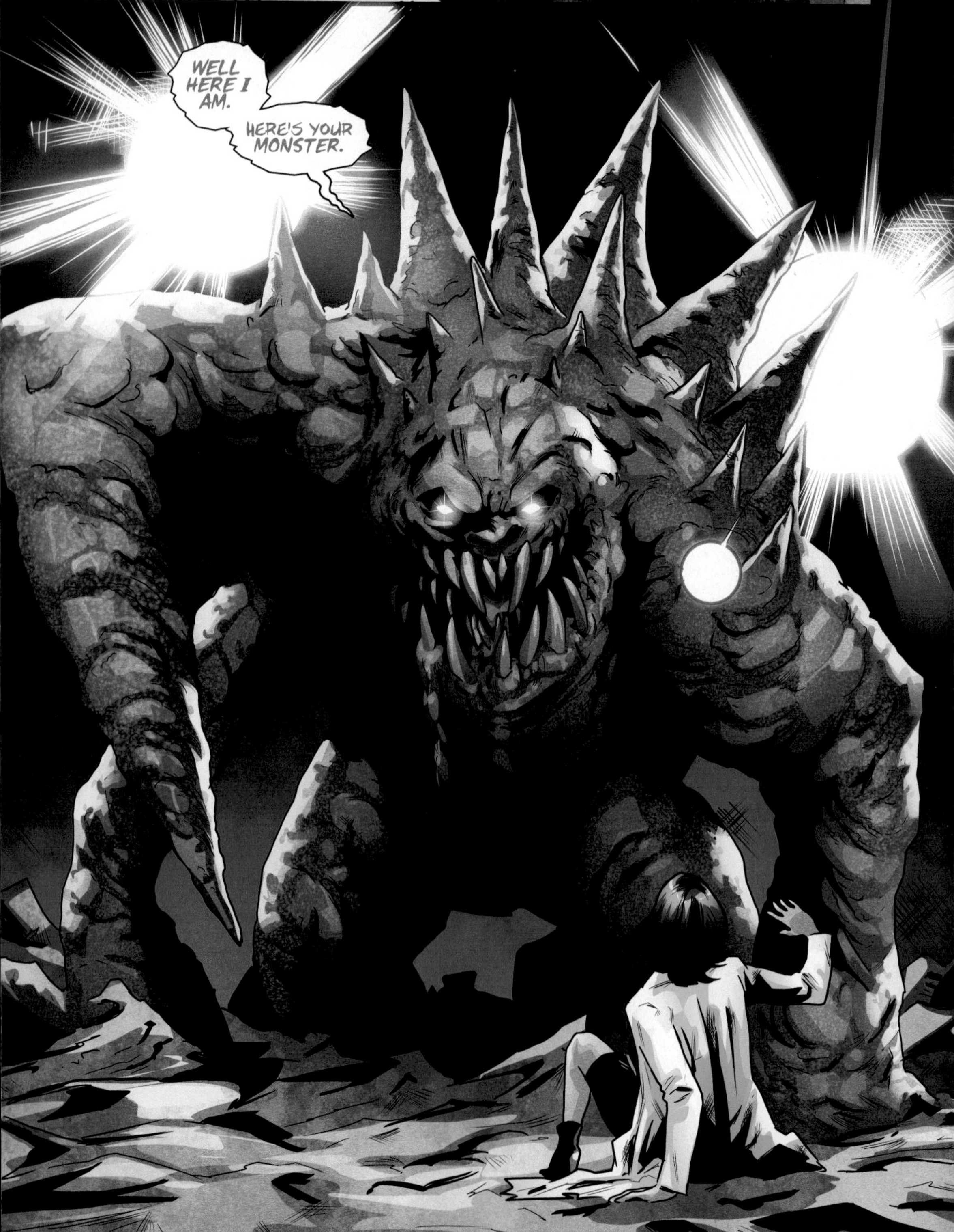
WELL HERE I AM.
HERE'S YOUR MONSTER.

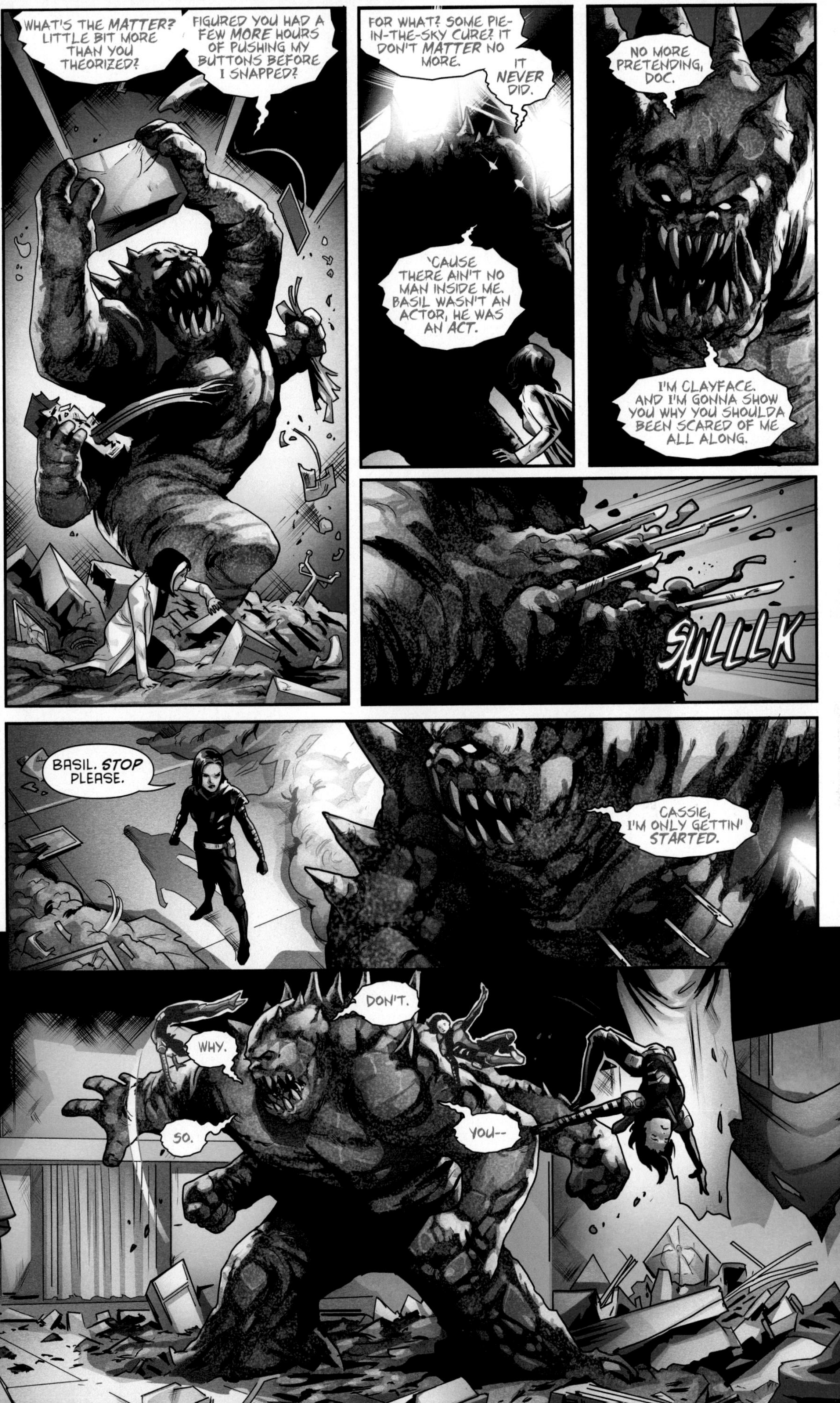
WHAT'S THE MATTER? LITTLE BIT MORE THAN YOU THEORIZED?
FIGURED YOU HAD A FEW MORE HOURS OF PUSHING MY BUTTONS BEFORE I SNAPPED?
FOR WHAT? SOME PIE-IN-THE-SKY CURE? IT DON'T MATTER NO MORE.
IT NEVER DID.
'CAUSE THERE AIN'T NO MAN INSIDE ME. BASIL WASN'T AN ACTOR, HE WAS AN ACT.
NO MORE PRETENDING, DOC.
I'M CLAYFACE. AND I'M GONNA SHOW YOU WHY YOU SHOULDA BEEN SCARED OF ME ALL ALONG.
SHLLLK
BASIL. STOP PLEASE.
CASSIE, I'M ONLY GETTIN' STARTED.
WHY.
DON'T.
SO.
YOU--

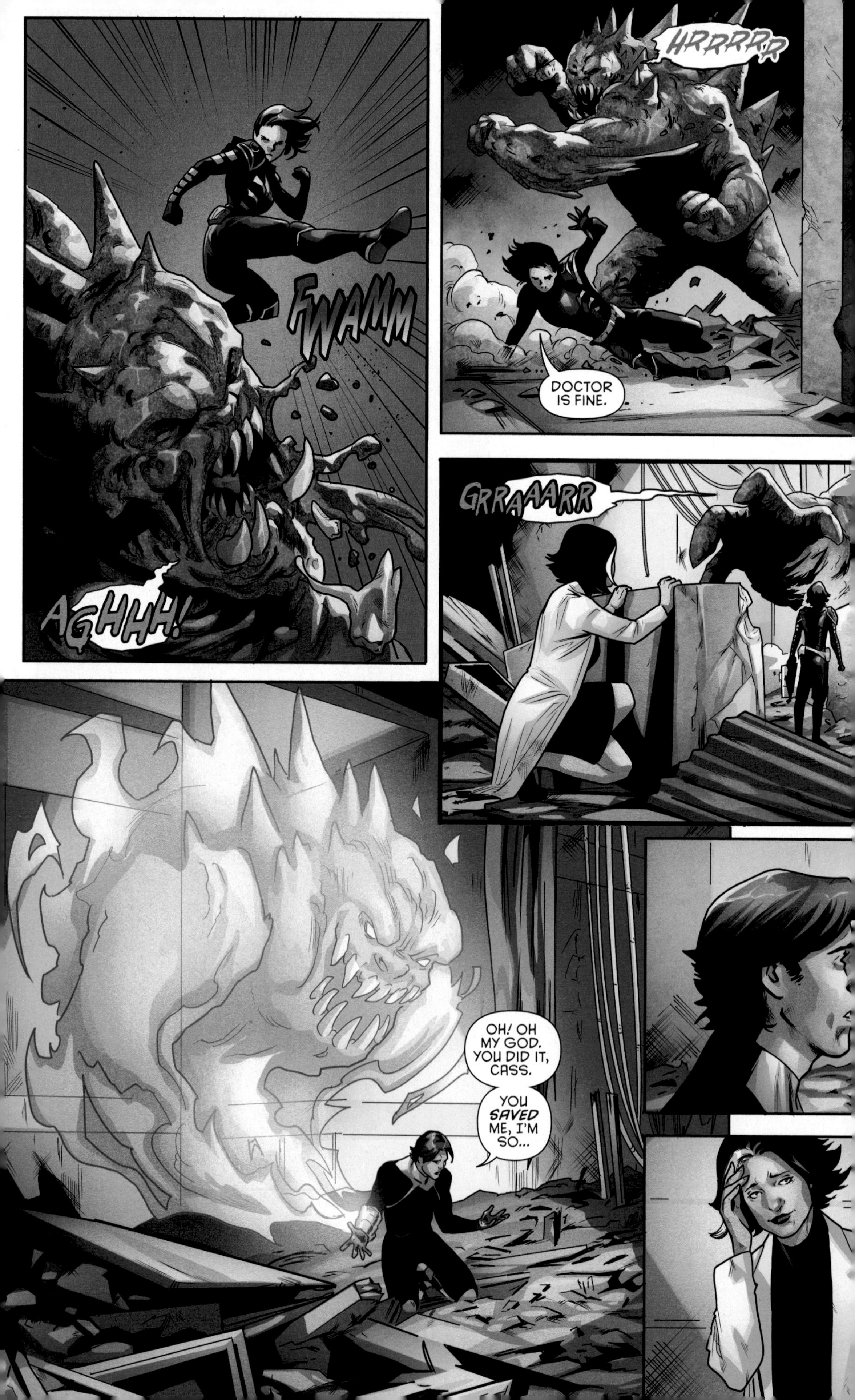
FWAMM
AGHHH!
HRRRRR
DOCTOR IS FINE.
GRRAAARR
OH! OH MY GOD. YOU DID IT, CASS.
YOU *SAVED* ME, I'M SO...

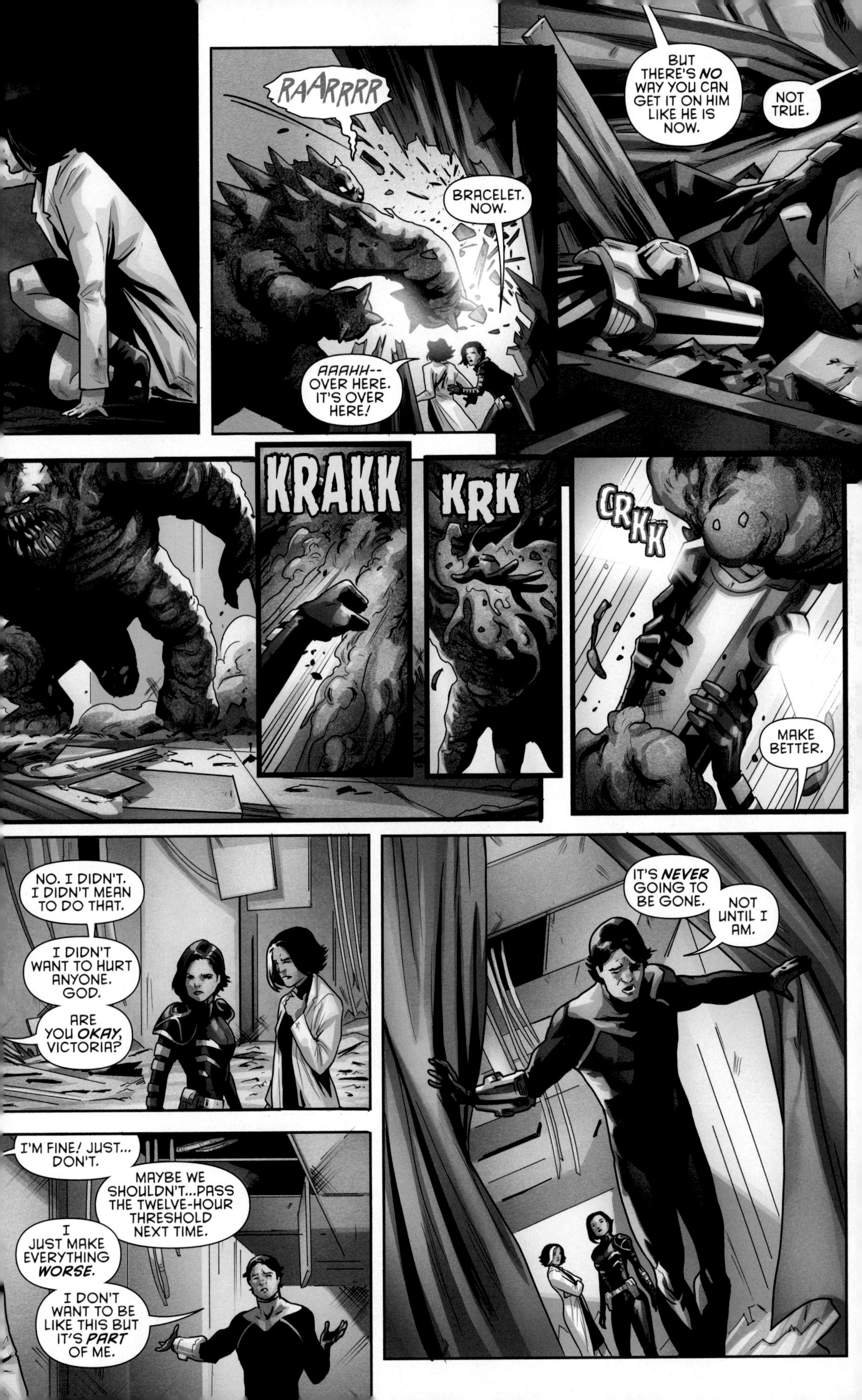
RAARRRR
BRACELET. NOW.
AAAHH-- OVER HERE. IT'S OVER HERE!
BUT THERE'S NO WAY YOU CAN GET IT ON HIM LIKE HE IS NOW.
NOT TRUE.
KRAKK
KRK
CRKK
MAKE BETTER.
NO. I DIDN'T. I DIDN'T MEAN TO DO THAT.
I DIDN'T WANT TO HURT ANYONE. GOD.
ARE YOU OKAY, VICTORIA?
I'M FINE! JUST... DON'T.
MAYBE WE SHOULDN'T...PASS THE TWELVE-HOUR THRESHOLD NEXT TIME.
I JUST MAKE EVERYTHING WORSE.
I DON'T WANT TO BE LIKE THIS BUT IT'S PART OF ME.
IT'S NEVER GOING TO BE GONE.
NOT UNTIL I AM.

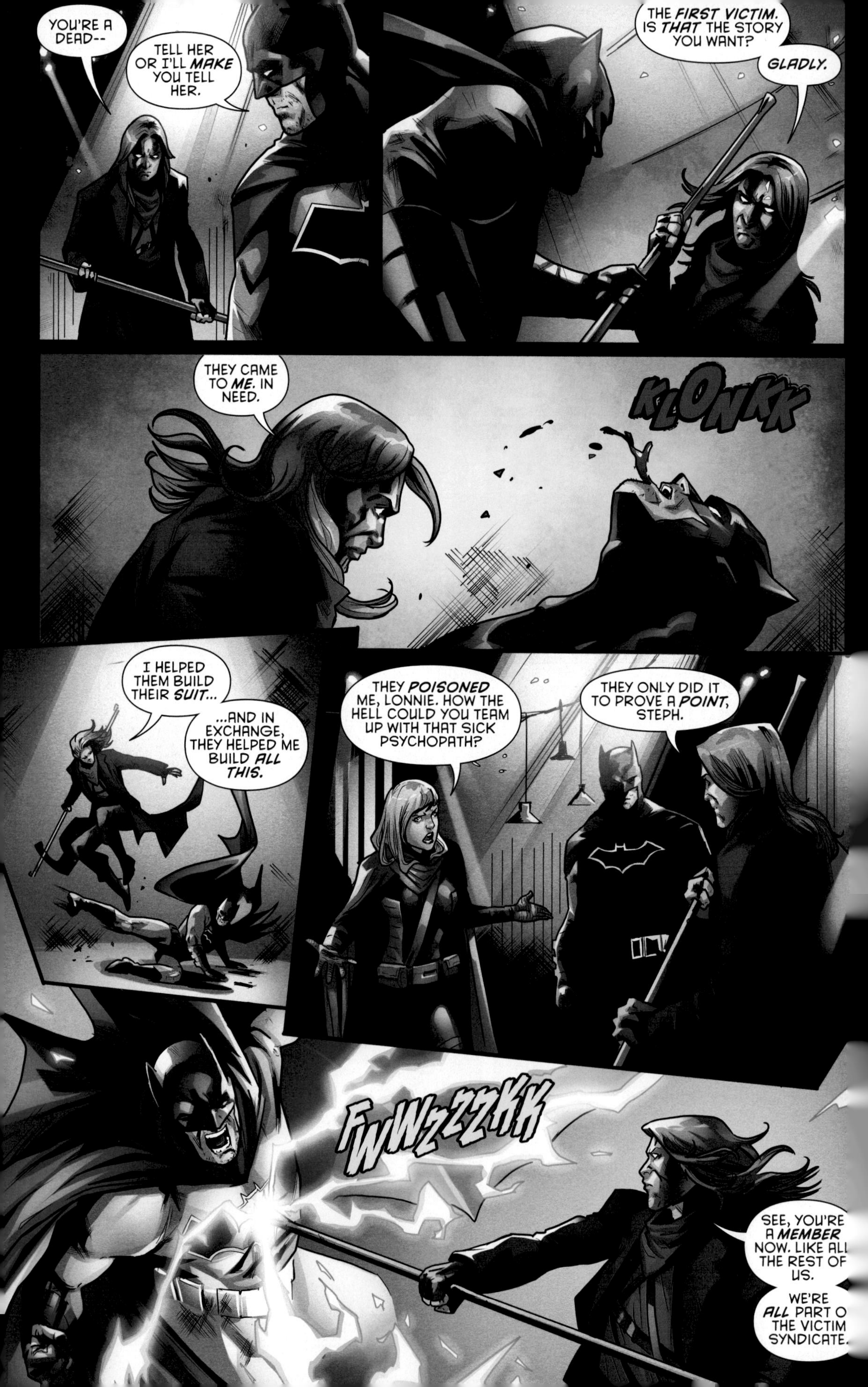
YOU'RE A DEAD--
TELL HER OR I'LL MAKE YOU TELL HER.
THE FIRST VICTIM. IS THAT THE STORY YOU WANT?
GLADLY.
THEY CAME TO ME. IN NEED.
KLONKK
I HELPED THEM BUILD THEIR SUIT...
...AND IN EXCHANGE, THEY HELPED ME BUILD ALL THIS.
THEY POISONED ME, LONNIE. HOW THE HELL COULD YOU TEAM UP WITH THAT SICK PSYCHOPATH?
THEY ONLY DID IT TO PROVE A POINT, STEPH.
FWWZZZKK
SEE, YOU'RE A MEMBER NOW. LIKE ALL THE REST OF US.
WE'RE ALL PART OF THE VICTIM SYNDICATE.

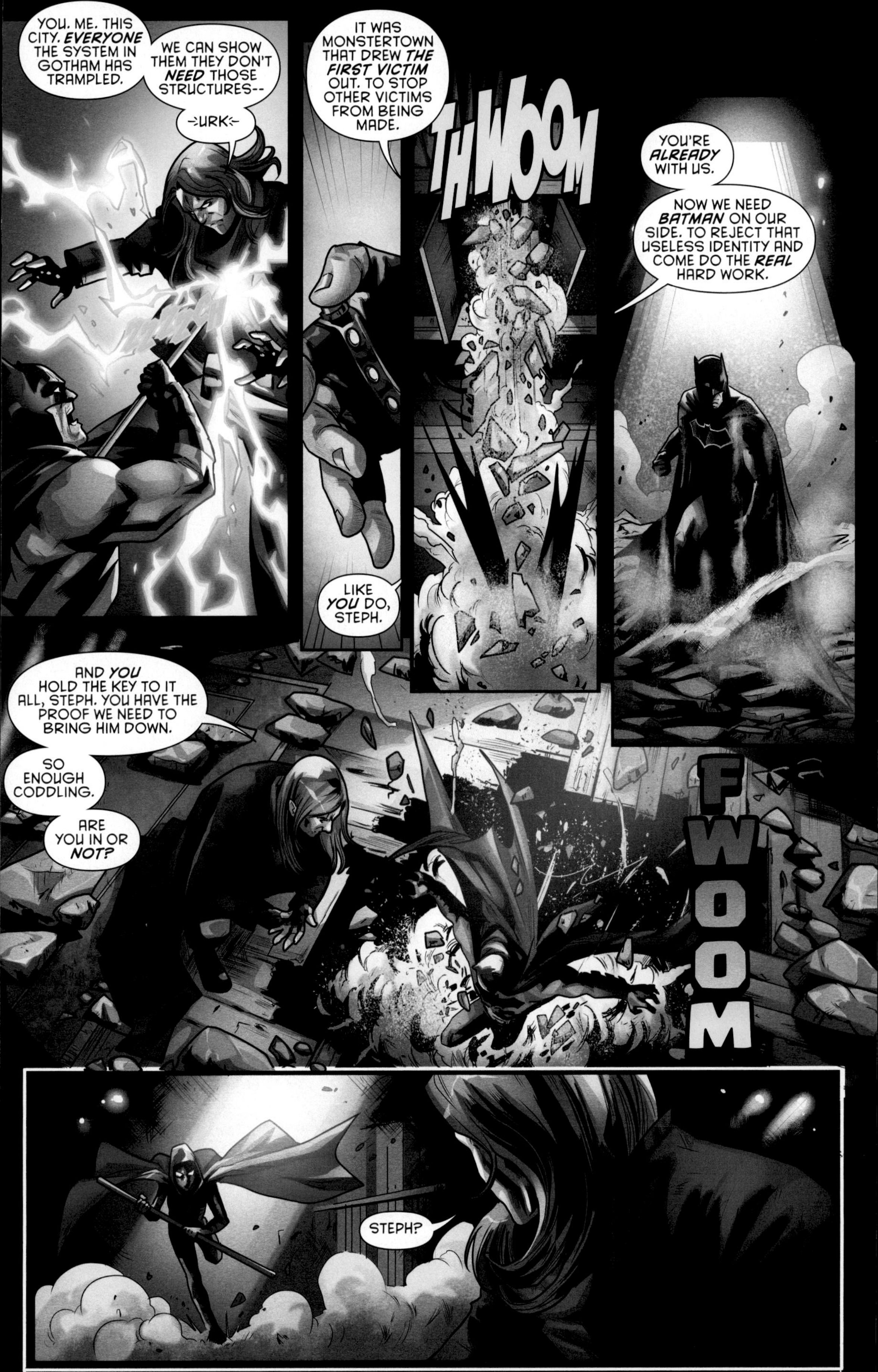
YOU. ME. THIS CITY. EVERYONE THE SYSTEM IN GOTHAM HAS TRAMPLED.
WE CAN SHOW THEM THEY DON'T NEED THOSE STRUCTURES--
URK
IT WAS MONSTERTOWN THAT DREW THE FIRST VICTIM OUT. TO STOP OTHER VICTIMS FROM BEING MADE.
LIKE YOU DO, STEPH.
THWOOM
YOU'RE ALREADY WITH US.
NOW WE NEED BATMAN ON OUR SIDE. TO REJECT THAT USELESS IDENTITY AND COME DO THE REAL HARD WORK.
AND YOU HOLD THE KEY TO IT ALL, STEPH. YOU HAVE THE PROOF WE NEED TO BRING HIM DOWN.
SO ENOUGH CODDLING.
ARE YOU IN OR NOT?
FWOOM
STEPH?

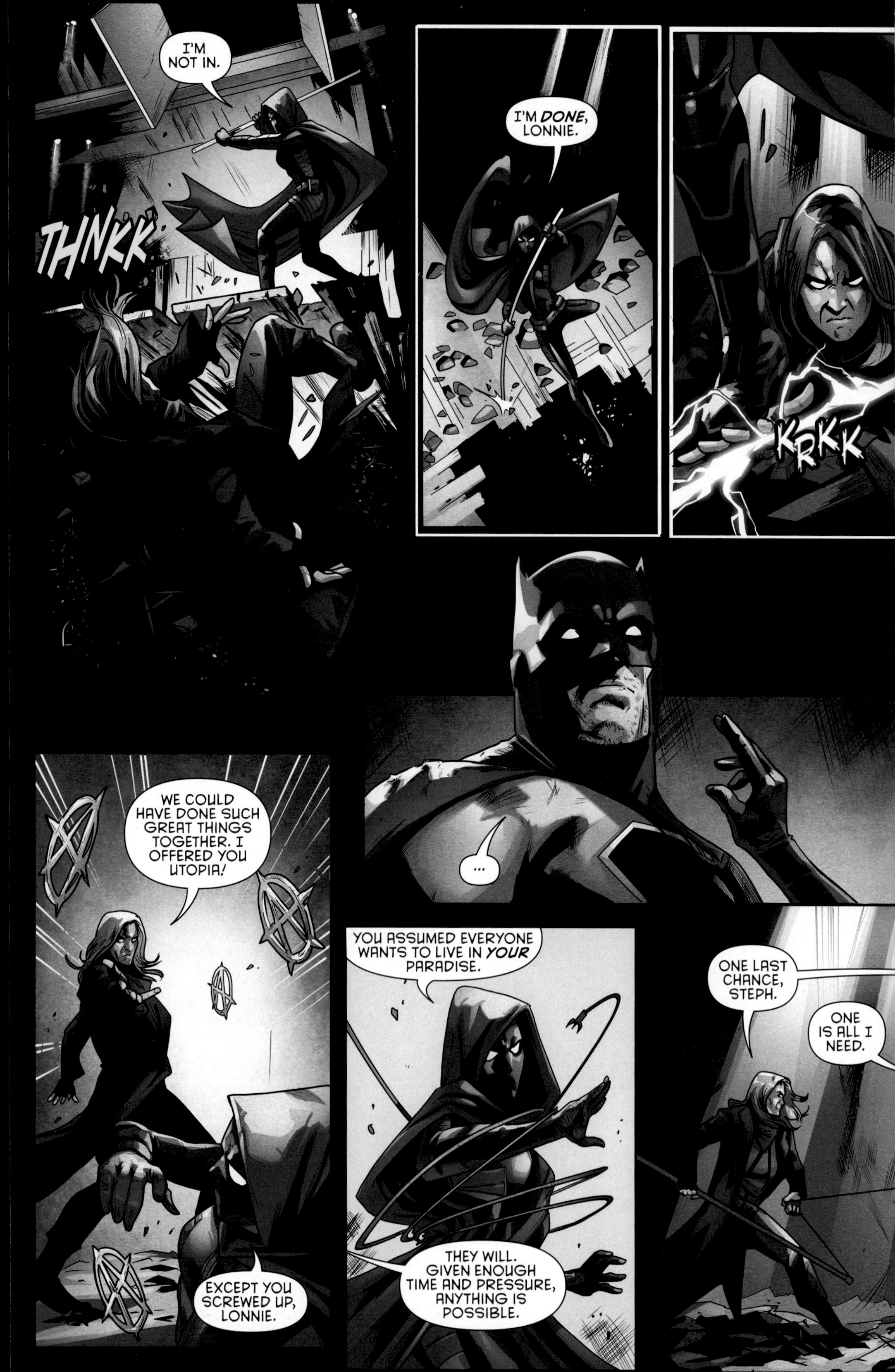
I'M NOT IN.
THNKK
I'M *DONE*, LONNIE.
KRKK
...
WE COULD HAVE DONE SUCH GREAT THINGS TOGETHER. I OFFERED YOU UTOPIA!
EXCEPT YOU SCREWED UP, LONNIE.
YOU ASSUMED EVERYONE WANTS TO LIVE IN *YOUR* PARADISE.
THEY WILL. GIVEN ENOUGH TIME AND PRESSURE, ANYTHING IS POSSIBLE.
ONE LAST CHANCE, STEPH.
ONE IS ALL I NEED.

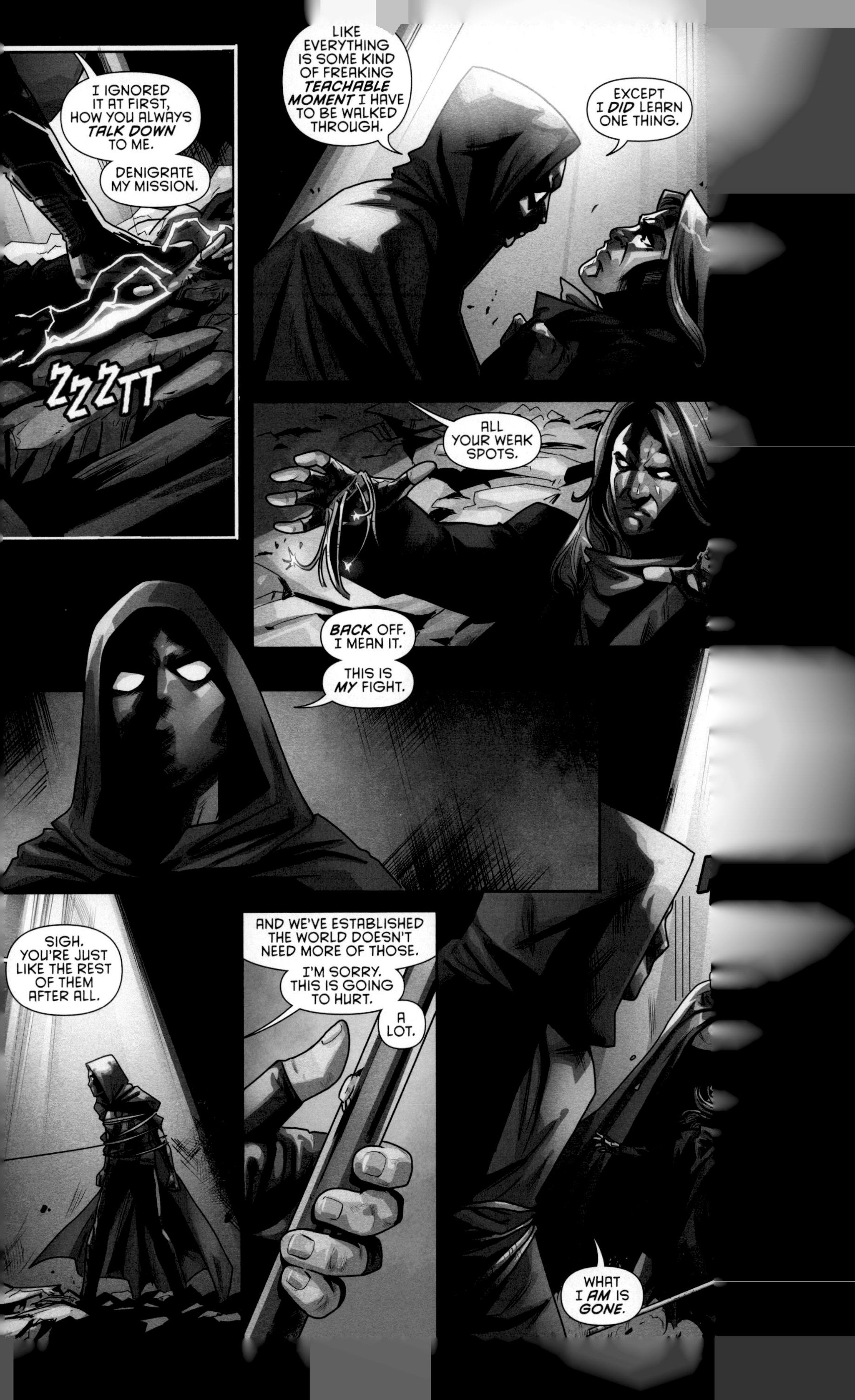
I IGNORED IT AT FIRST, HOW YOU ALWAYS TALK DOWN TO ME.
DENIGRATE MY MISSION.
ZZZTT
LIKE EVERYTHING IS SOME KIND OF FREAKING TEACHABLE MOMENT I HAVE TO BE WALKED THROUGH.
EXCEPT I DID LEARN ONE THING.
ALL YOUR WEAK SPOTS.
BACK OFF. I MEAN IT.
THIS IS MY FIGHT.
SIGH. YOU'RE JUST LIKE THE REST OF THEM AFTER ALL.
AND WE'VE ESTABLISHED THE WORLD DOESN'T NEED MORE OF THOSE.
I'M SORRY. THIS IS GOING TO HURT.
A LOT.
WHAT I AM IS GONE.

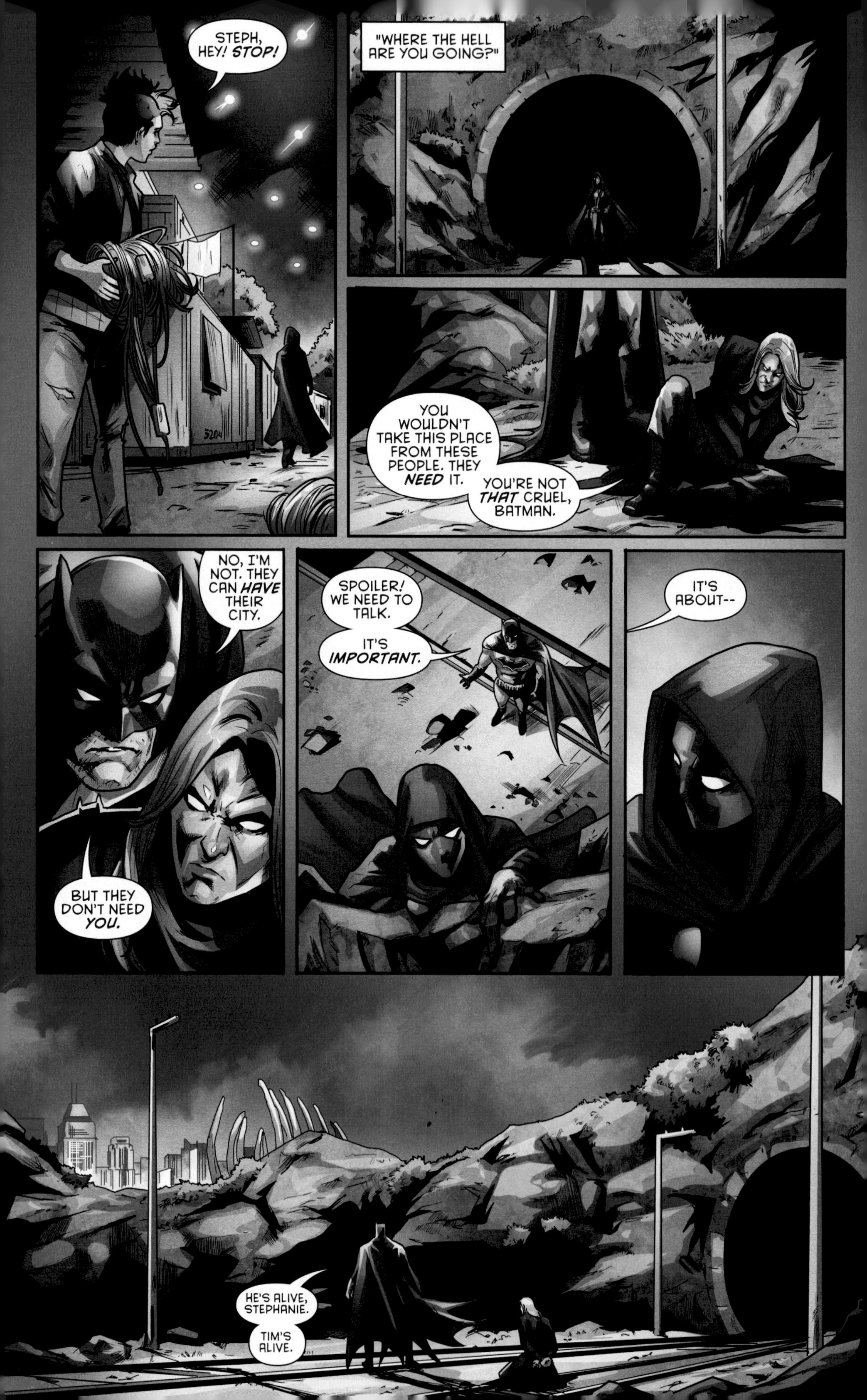
STEPH, HEY! STOP!
"WHERE THE HELL ARE YOU GOING?"
YOU WOULDN'T TAKE THIS PLACE FROM THESE PEOPLE. THEY NEED IT.
YOU'RE NOT THAT CRUEL, BATMAN.
NO, I'M NOT. THEY CAN HAVE THEIR CITY.
BUT THEY DON'T NEED YOU.
SPOILER! WE NEED TO TALK.
IT'S IMPORTANT.
IT'S ABOUT--
HE'S ALIVE, STEPHANIE.
TIM'S ALIVE.

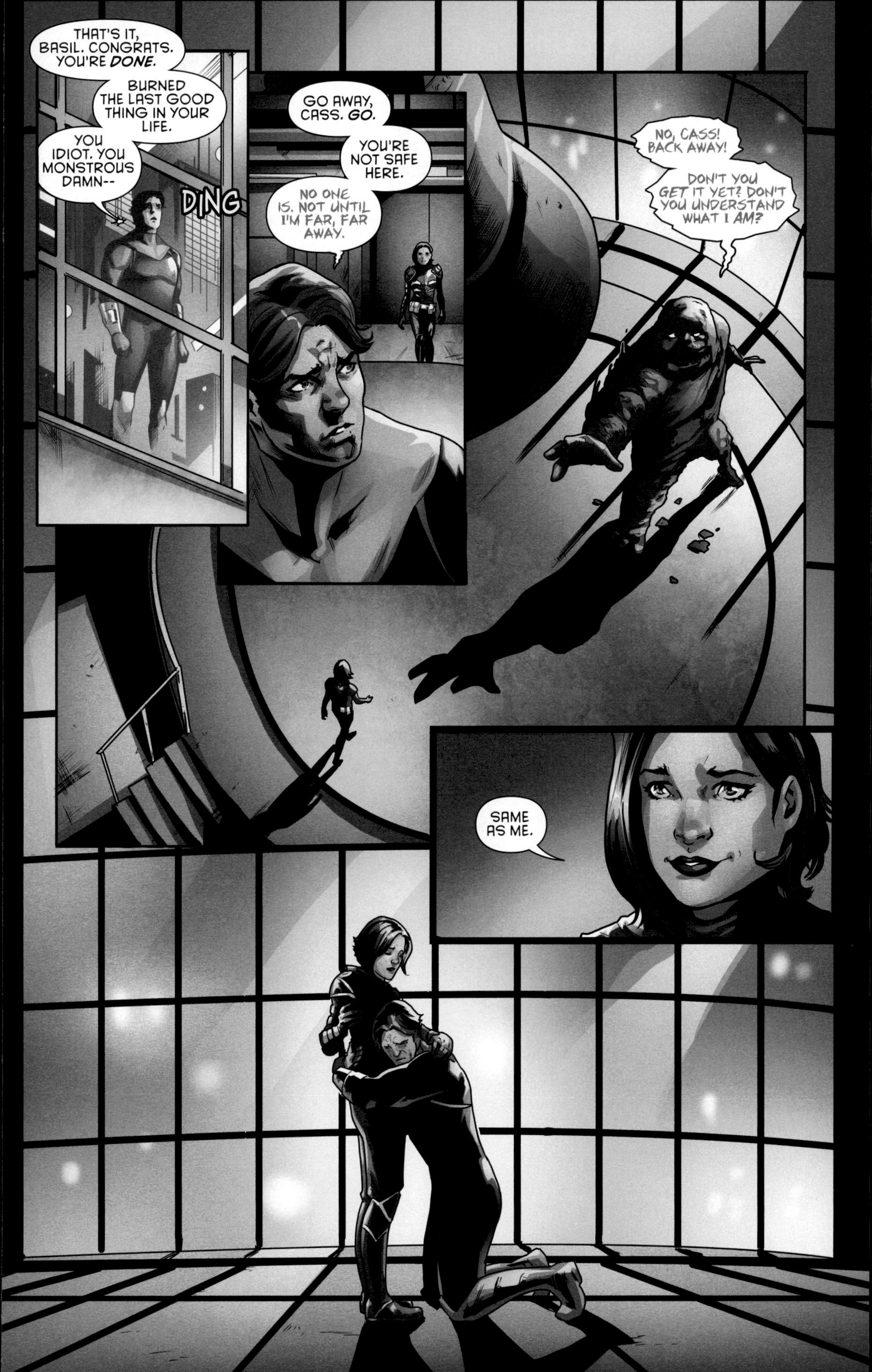
THAT'S IT, BASIL. CONGRATS. YOU'RE DONE.
BURNED THE LAST GOOD THING IN YOUR LIFE.
YOU IDIOT. YOU MONSTROUS DAMN--
DING
GO AWAY, CASS. GO.
YOU'RE NOT SAFE HERE.
NO ONE IS. NOT UNTIL I'M FAR, FAR AWAY.
NO, CASS! BACK AWAY!
DON'T YOU GET IT YET? DON'T YOU UNDERSTAND WHAT I AM?
SAME AS ME.

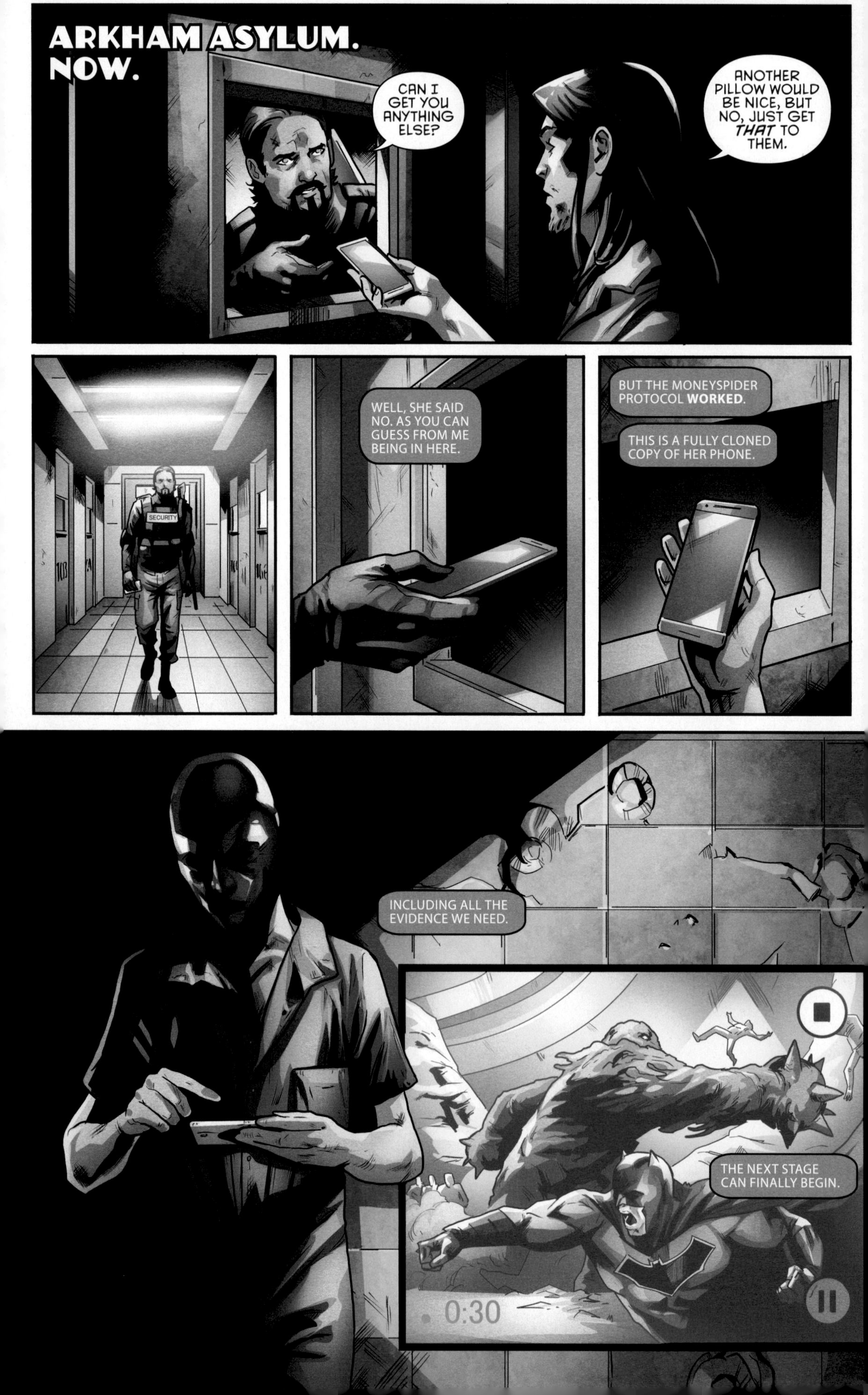
ARKHAM ASYLUM. NOW.
CAN I GET YOU ANYTHING ELSE?
ANOTHER PILLOW WOULD BE NICE, BUT NO, JUST GET *THAT* TO THEM.
SECURITY
WELL, SHE SAID NO. AS YOU CAN GUESS FROM ME BEING IN HERE.
BUT THE MONEYSPIDER PROTOCOL **WORKED**.
THIS IS A FULLY CLONED COPY OF HER PHONE.
INCLUDING ALL THE EVIDENCE WE NEED.
THE NEXT STAGE CAN FINALLY BEGIN.
0:30

BATMAN DETECTIVE COMICS

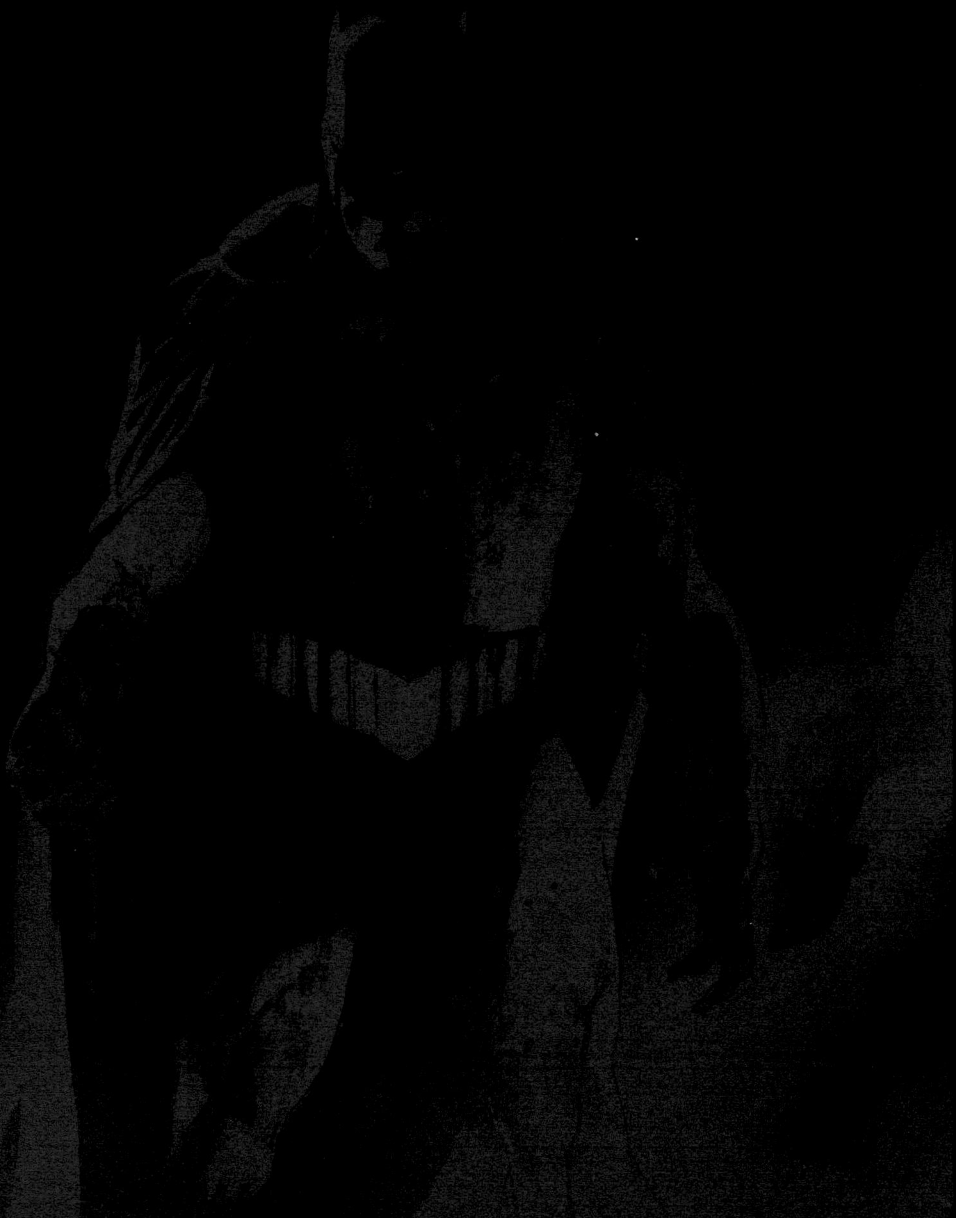

VARIANT COVER GALLERY

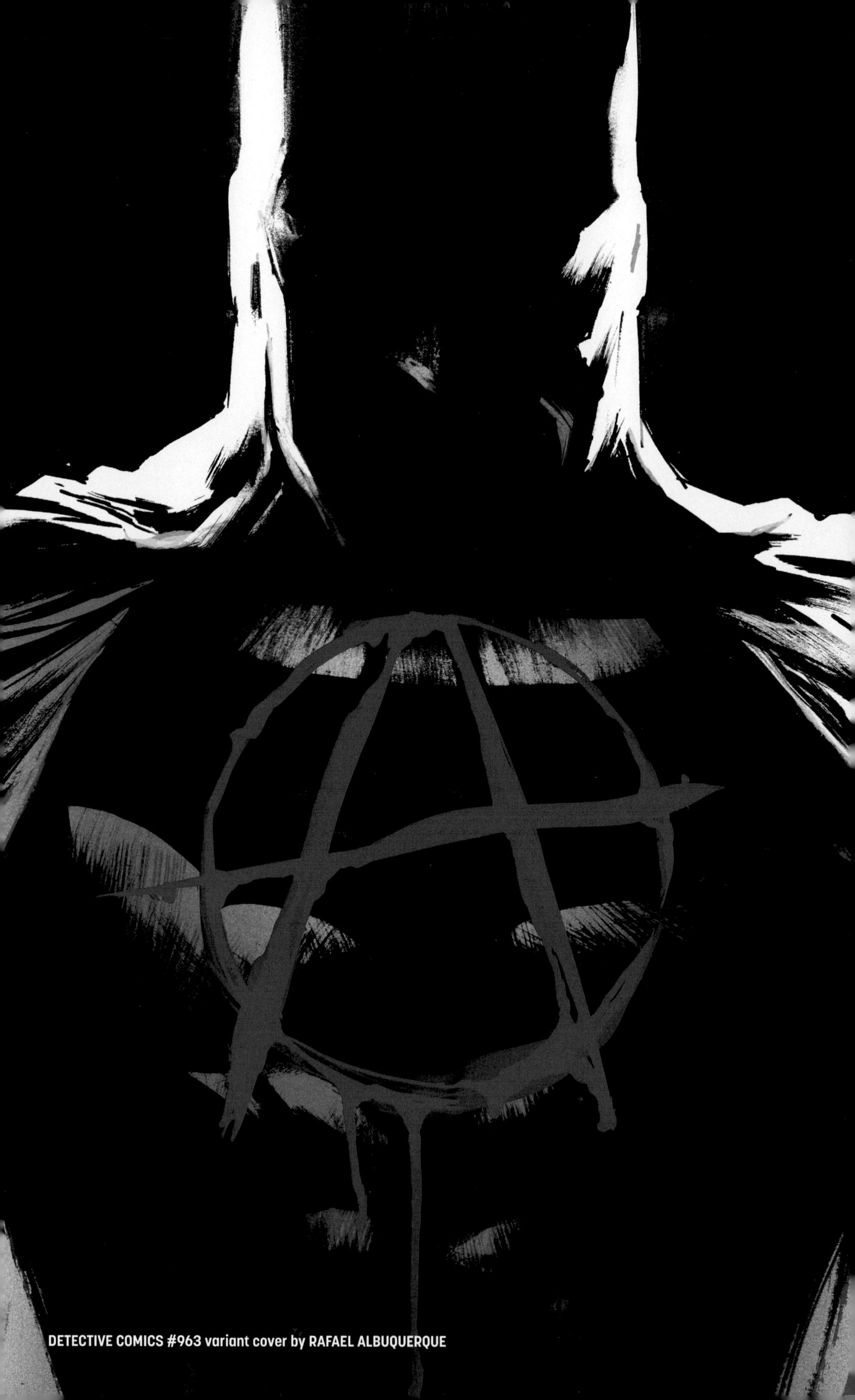

DETECTIVE COMICS #963 variant cover by RAFAEL ALBUQUERQUE

DETECTIVE COMICS #964 variant cover by RAFAEL ALBUQUERQUE

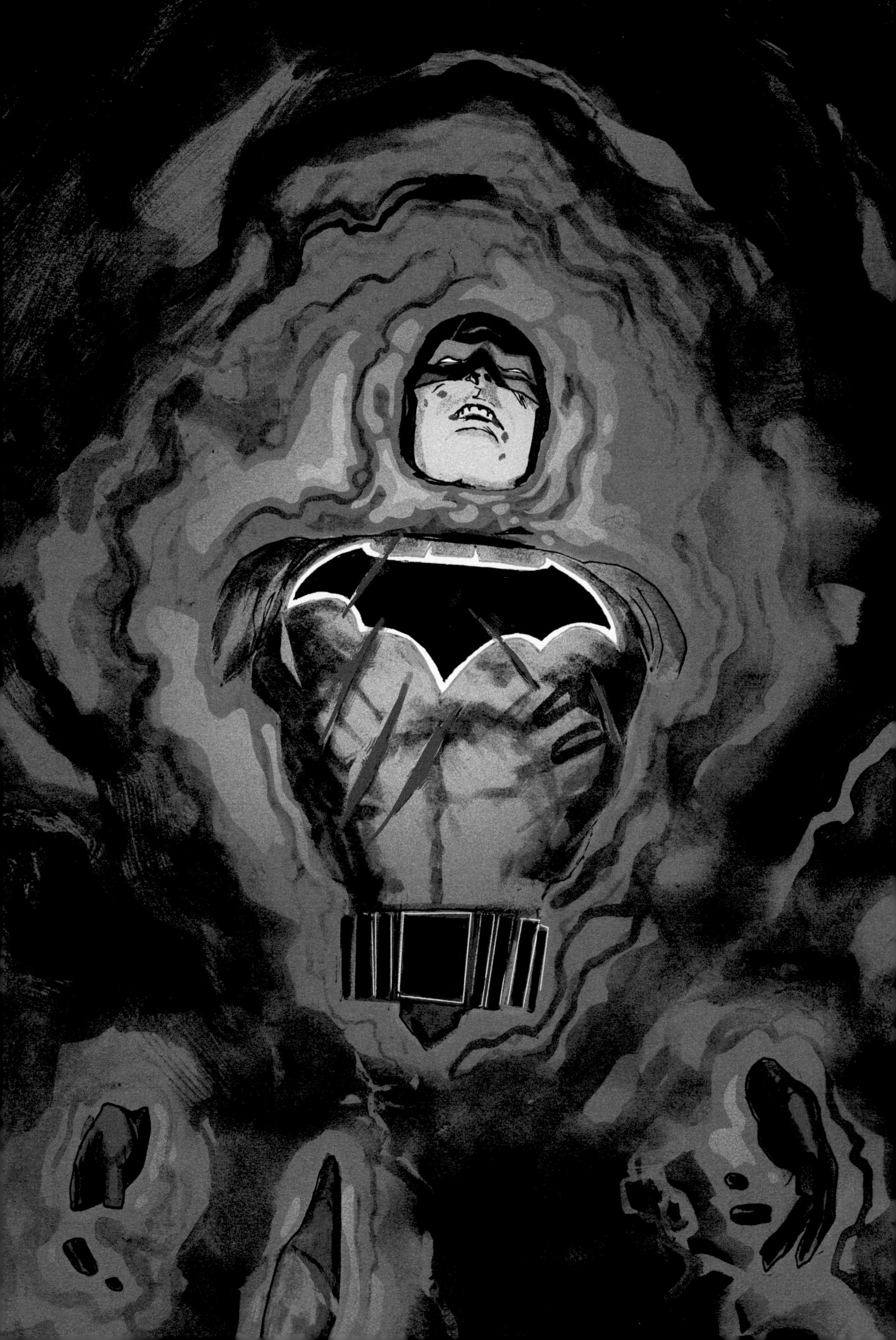

DETECTIVE COMICS #965 variant cover by RAFAEL ALBUQUERQUE

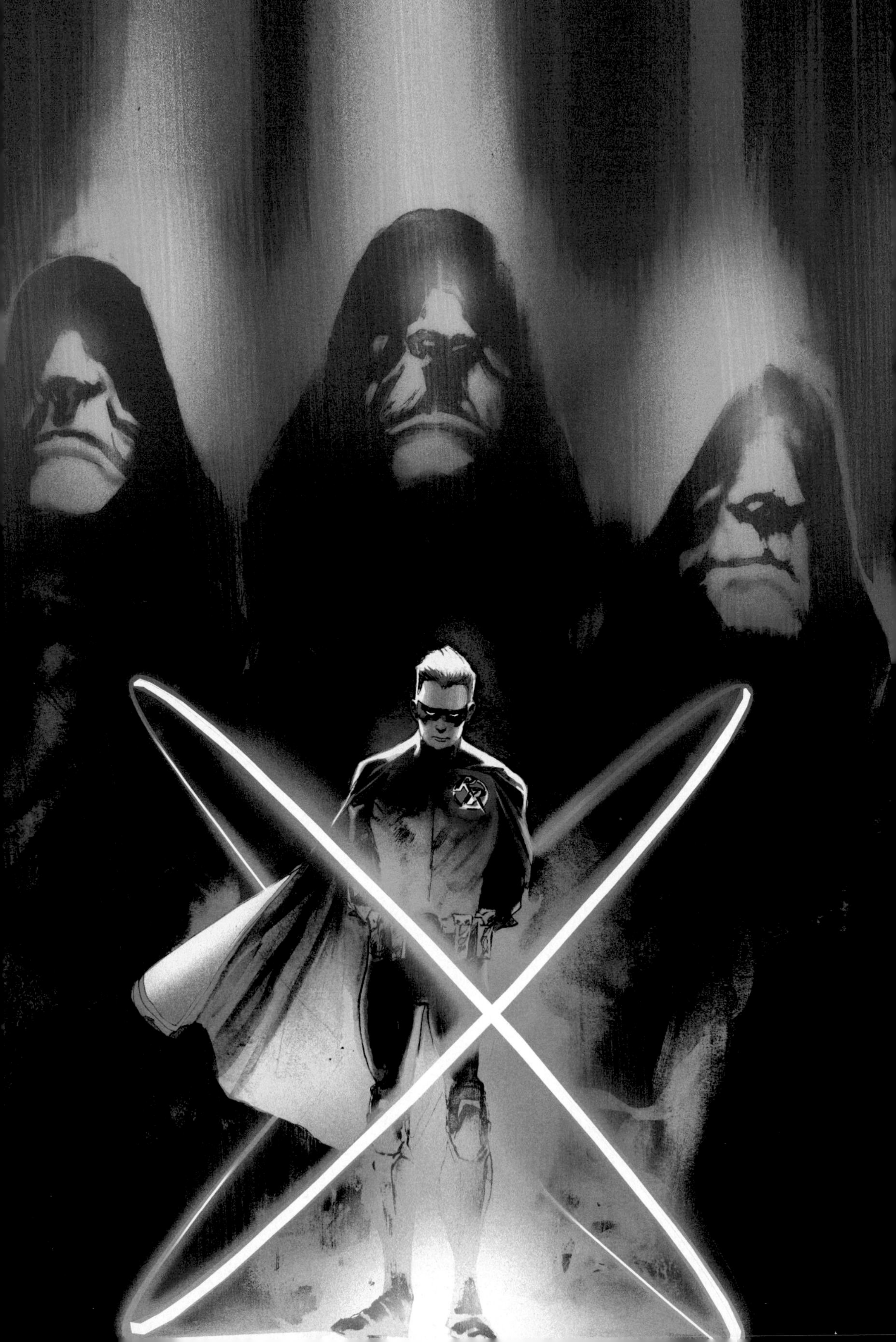

DETECTIVE COMICS #966 variant cover by RAFAEL ALBUQUERQUE

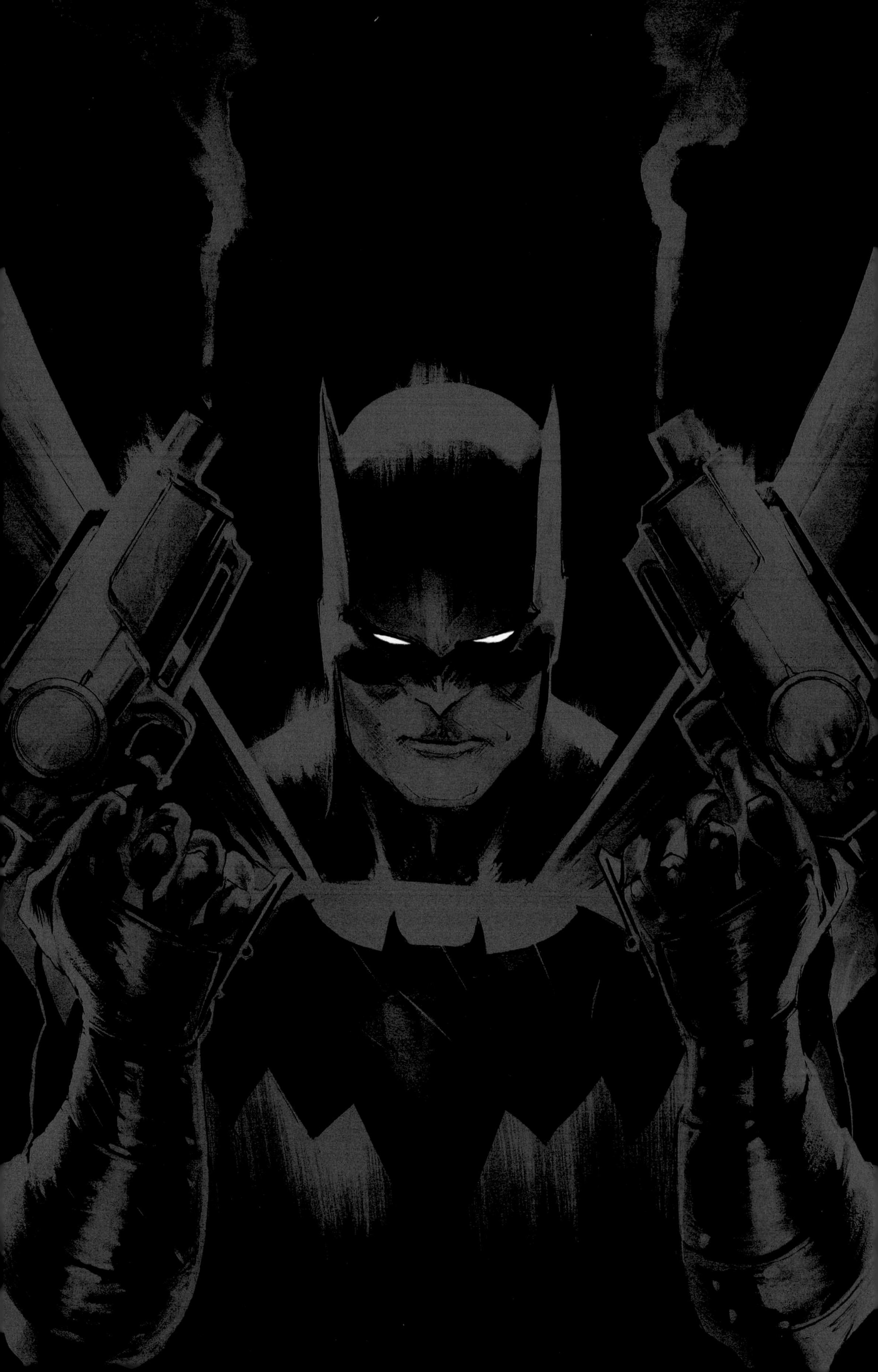

DETECTIVE COMICS #967 variant cover by RAFAEL ALBUQUERQUE

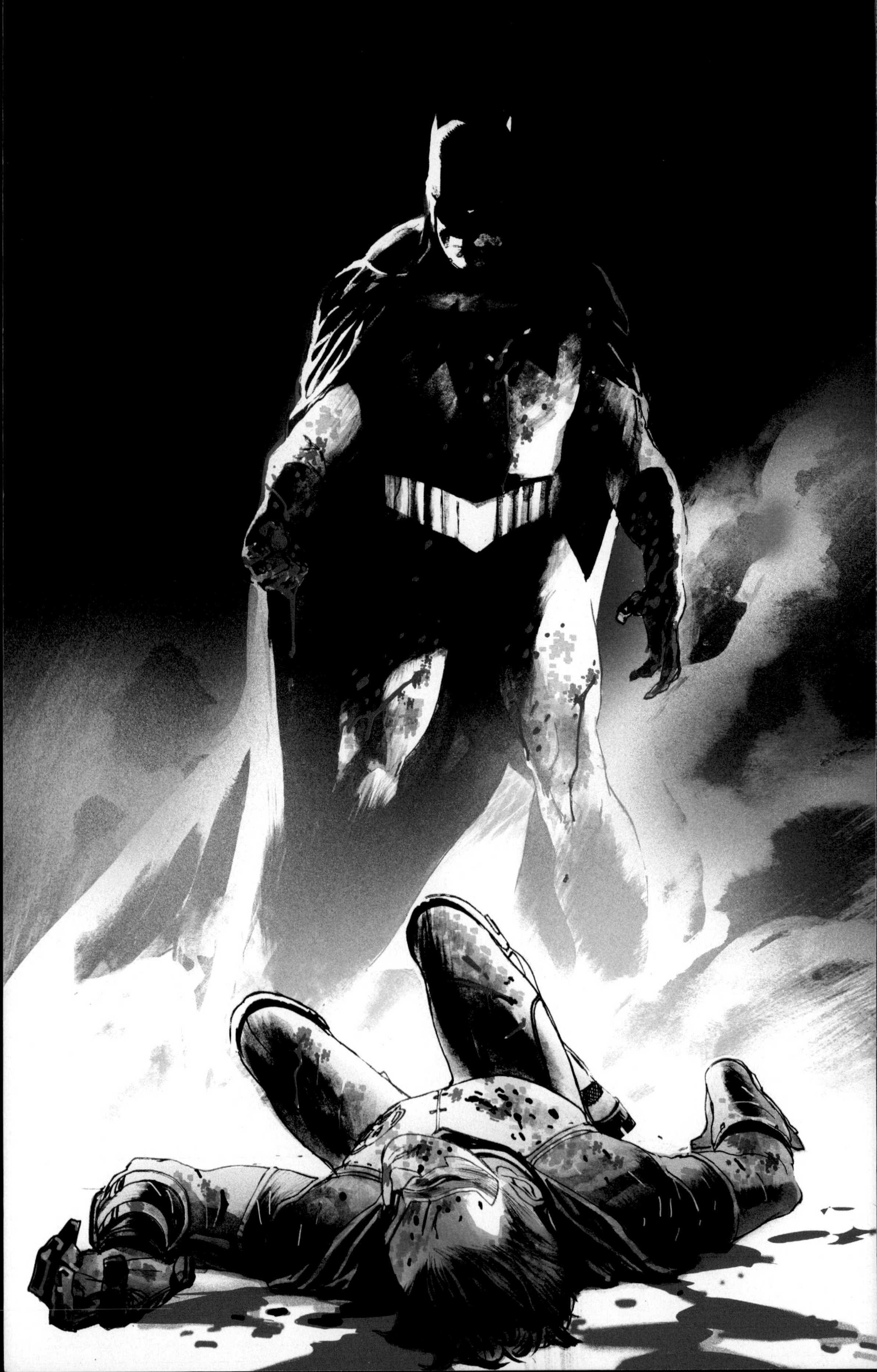

DETECTIVE COMICS #968 variant cover by CULLY HAMNER

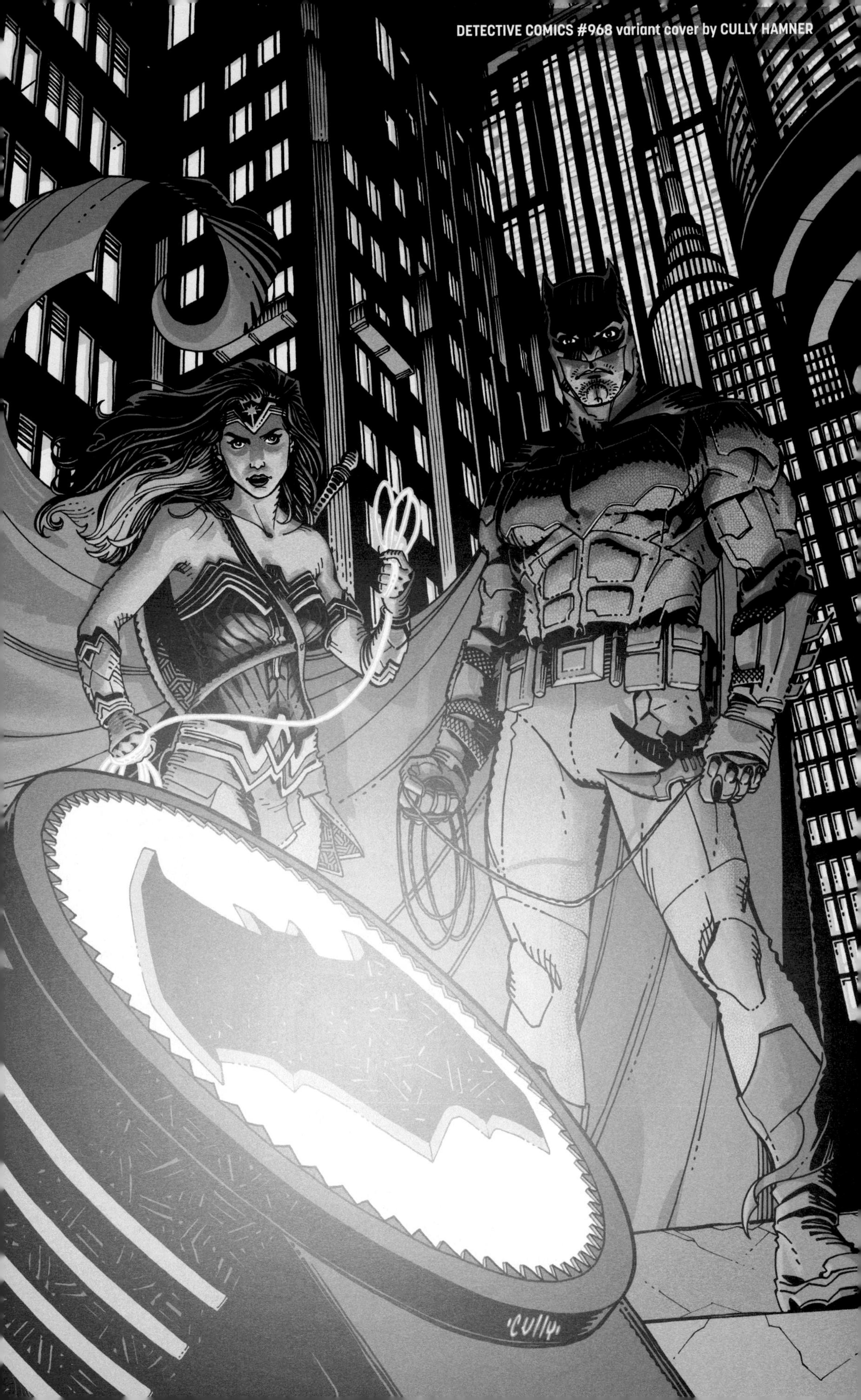
CULLY

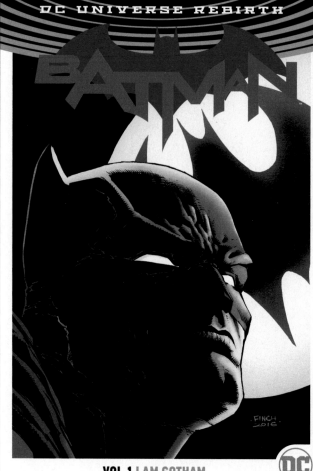

VOL.1 I AM GOTHAM
TOM KING ★ DAVID FINCH

DC UNIVERSE REBIRTH
BATMAN

VOL. 1: I AM GOTHAM
TOM KING
with DAVID FINCH

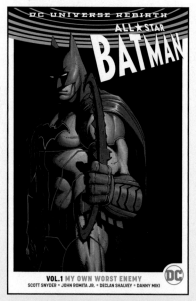

**ALL-STAR BATMAN VOL. 1:
MY OWN WORST ENEMY**

**NIGHTWING VOL. 1:
BETTER THAN BATMAN**

**DETECTIVE COMICS VOL. 1:
RISE OF THE BATMEN**

els wherever comics and books are sold!